The Old Faith in a New Nation

The Old Faith in a New Nation

American Protestants and the Christian Past

PAUL J. GUTACKER

OXFORD
UNIVERSITY PRESS

OXFORD
UNIVERSITY PRESS

Oxford University Press is a department of the University of Oxford. It furthers
the University's objective of excellence in research, scholarship, and education
by publishing worldwide. Oxford is a registered trade mark of Oxford University
Press in the UK and certain other countries.

Published in the United States of America by Oxford University Press
198 Madison Avenue, New York, NY 10016, United States of America.

Library of Congress Cataloging-in-Publication Data
Names: Gutacker, Paul J., author.
Title: The old faith in a new nation : American Protestants and the Christian past / Paul J. Gutacker.
Description: New York, NY, United States of America : Oxford University Press, [2023] |
Includes bibliographical references and index.
Identifiers: LCCN 2022027331 (print) | LCCN 2022027332 (ebook) |
ISBN 9780197639146 (hb) | ISBN 9780197639153 (pb) | ISBN 9780197639177 (epub) |
ISBN 9780197639184
Subjects: LCSH: Protestantism—United States—History—19th century. |
Evangelicalism—United States—History—19th century.
Classification: LCC BR515 .G88 2023 (print) | LCC BR515 (ebook) |
DDC 241/.0404—dc23/eng/20220725
LC record available at https://lccn.loc.gov/2022027331
LC ebook record available at https://lccn.loc.gov/2022027332

DOI: 10.1093/oso/9780197639146.001.0001

1 3 5 7 9 8 6 4 2

Paperback printed by Marquis, Canada
Hardback printed by Bridgeport National Bindery, Inc., United States of America

To my first teachers,
Jim and Sue Ellen Gutacker

Contents

Acknowledgments

This research was made possible through generous funding from the Religious Freedom Project at Georgetown University, the Southern Baptist Historical Library and Archives, Drew University, and Baylor's Graduate School and Department of History. I received invaluable help from a number of librarians and archivists: Taffey Hall at SBHLA, Charlene Peacock at the Presbyterian Historical Society, Patricia Goodall at Princeton Theological Seminary, Betty Bolden at the Burke Library at Union Theological Seminary, Leon Miller at Tulane's Louisiana Research Collection, Mary Klein at the Episcopalian Diocese of Maryland, Brian Shetler at Drew University's Archives, Baylor Central Library's Eileen Bentsen, and Jennifer Borderud and Cynthia Burgess at Baylor's Armstrong Browning Library.

I'm grateful for the feedback received from commenters at the Society for US Intellectual History, the American Society of Church History, the Conference on Faith and History, the Baylor Symposium on Faith and Culture, and the Baylor History Colloquium, as well as readers and editors at the *Journal of Ecclesiastical History*, the *Journal of Southern History*, and *Church History*. Thank you to the Torrey Honors Institute at Biola University and the Honors Program at John Brown University, who invited me to present my research.

This book owes much to those who shaped my thinking and writing over the years. First and foremost, hearty thanks to my dissertation committee—Tommy Kidd, Andrea Turpin, Joe Stubenrauch, Bob Elder, and Josh King—for your thoughtful engagement. My argument is immeasurably stronger because of your insights and questions. It was an honor to learn the craft of the historian first at Regent College and then in the Baylor Department of History, which offered scholarly community and support of all kinds. Special thanks to the writing group: Ryan Butler, Lynneth Miller, and Elise Leal. I cannot adequately express my gratitude to those who shaped my vocation over the years: especially Bruce Hindmarsh, Hans Boersma, Sarah Williams, Tommy Kidd, Andrea Turpin, Joe Stubenrauch, Barry Hankins, and Beth Allison Barr. For the late Don Lewis, whose teaching and friendship changed my life, I am especially thankful—light perpetual.

I am also indebted to those who generously read and offered both criticism and encouragement: Mark Noll, David Bebbington, Elise Leal, Tim Grundmeier, Joel Iliff, and Sam Young all helped sharpen my argument. Paul Putz and Nick Pruitt offered invaluable advice at the proposal stage. Great thanks to Theo Calderara and the editorial staff at Oxford University Press who believed in this project and worked to make it stronger. My warmest appreciation to Elise Leal and Tim Grundmeier for reading through the manuscript in its final stages, to Paige Gutacker, Brittany McComb, and Jonathan Kanary for joining in the arduous work of proofing, and to Emma Sloan and Chris Norton for helping with bibliographic matters. As always, I am solely to blame for any remaining errors.

For eight years, Waco has proved a rich intellectual and spiritual community, and I cannot imagine what this book would be without our friends. I'm deeply grateful for Christ Church Waco, Fr. Lee Nelson, Graduate Anglicans, the Brazos Fellows, and, especially, our Friday dinner group. Alex Fogleman, Fr. Nicholas Norman-Krause, Fr. Jonathan Kanary, Christina Lambert, Matthew Lee Anderson, Skylar Ray, Sam Young, and Cody Strecker have been intellectual companions of the highest degree. My cheering section has been (quite literally) loud: my wonderful family, Jim and Sue Ellen, Gail, Esther and Luis, Hannah and Steve, Matt and Ali, Lydia and Josh, Laura and Whit, and the extended Gutacker clan; also my dear friends, Paul "Tacky" Middlekauff, Joel and Jessi Trigger, Bonnie-Marie and Jamie Yager-Wiggan, and Ben and Ariel Norquist. Love to you all. I'd also like to thank quarterback Josh Allen—let's go Buffalo. Special thanks to Gail Ratzlaff for her generous support of all kinds through these years. My deep gratitude for the blessed memory of George Ratzlaff, who always made it clear how proud he was of his son-in-law. *Requiescat in pace.*

A very heartfelt thank you to Tommy Kidd for his guidance. What a privilege to learn from such a superb historian, and what an honor to call you a friend.

Finally, no one has been a greater champion than Paige, who encouraged and supported me along the way. To her, James, Marianne, and Matthew, all my love and gratitude.

Introduction

Evangelical Protestants are biblicists. Scholars, journalists, and evangelicals themselves agree on this essential characteristic: evangelicals not only believe the Christian Bible is sacred, but consider it their ultimate authority. If the Bible says it, they believe it. Proof of this can be seen in the lengths to which politicians—including US presidents—courting the evangelical vote go to display their own purported esteem of the Bible.

Such regard for the Bible comes from the Protestant ideal of *sola scriptura*, and in this sense evangelicals are not categorically different from other historic Protestants.[1] But in American religion, both scholars and rank-and-file evangelicals contend, *sola scriptura* has morphed from theological principle to exegetical method. Particularly in the nineteenth century, evangelical Protestants rejected other religious authorities and relied instead on a plain reading of scripture. After clearing away the rubble of history and abandoning the old wineskins of tradition, one was left with everything needed to do theology: common sense and the Bible. The effects of this sort of biblicism on the shape of American religion—and, indeed, American history writ large—are difficult to overstate.

Or so the standard story goes. Claims of relying on "the Bible alone" become harder to sustain when biblicists find themselves disagreeing on the meaning of Christian scripture. What do evangelical Protestants do when they differ, for example, about the subjects and mode of baptism? Or on women's roles in church, or sexuality, or marriage? What do they do when one Christian is thoroughly convinced that the Bible is incompatible with race-based slavery, while another is sure that a plain reading of scripture sanctions the institution? After exhausting the available exegetical arguments, where do they turn?

In these moments, evangelical Protestants have often found themselves turning to history. Sometimes they look to past Christians, claiming precedent for their particular stance. Sometimes they make the case that long-standing interpretations were limited by cultural assumptions and should give way to new understandings. In either case, they find themselves drawing

The Old Faith in a New Nation. Paul J. Gutacker, Oxford University Press. © Oxford University Press 2023.
DOI: 10.1093/oso/9780197639146.003.0001

on the Christian past. As it turns out, evangelical Protestants do not avoid tradition as much as the ideal of biblicism makes it seem.

But since the nineteenth century, scholars have largely agreed with evangelicals' self-understanding, portraying them as biblicists with little interest in Christian history. In the 1880s, for example, church historian Philip Schaff complained that "the denominational and sectarian divisions of American Christianity seem to be unfavorable to the study and cultivation of general church history, which requires a large-hearted catholic spirit."[2] Historians since have tended to agree with Schaff. Conventional wisdom holds that tradition and history meant little to American Protestants, who relied on the Bible alone while happily ignoring the Christian past. Compared to their predecessors and their European counterparts, nineteenth-century American Protestants appear more innovative, less tied to precedent, and increasingly biblicist. Indeed, as Nathan Hatch, Mark Noll, and E. Brooks Holifield argue, departure from tradition explains much of the growth, influence, and shortcomings of American Christianity—including the failure of the nation's theologians and churches to resolve the question of slavery.[3]

These interpretations illuminate much about American history in general and the development of evangelical Protestantism in particular. Without question, the Bible was an unrivaled authority for evangelicals. And neither Hatch nor Noll claims that antitradition groups—such as the Disciples of Christ—knew nothing of the Christian past. Both historians recognize that antitraditionalism often included a historical sensibility. Nonetheless, one might easily conclude that those who, as Noll puts it, "deliberately rejected the authority of tradition,"[4] or, in Hatch's terms, made a "decisive expatriation from the past,"[5] dismissed the history of Christianity. The emphasis on antitraditionalism, when combined with little analysis of how evangelicals read and used religious historiography, lends itself to the impression that American evangelicals were ahistoric. Put another way, it seems that evangelical biblicism meant indifference or even hostility toward the Christian past.

This impression has played out in the scholarly literature, which tends to assume that the Christian past was unimportant to those who dominated the early American religious landscape. To take one example, historians treat antebellum debates over slavery as delimited by the supposedly plain meaning of the Bible. As Noll argues, widespread assumptions about scripture and antipathy toward tradition were at least partly responsible for the failure of otherwise like-minded Protestants to resolve the sectional crisis by means other than war.[6] Recent accounts of religion and slavery take for granted

Noll's description of the terms of the debate even if they differ from his assessment.[7] Even as scholarship on Christian pro- and antislavery thought develops or nuances Noll's thesis, it continues to assume that Christian history played little to no part in the controversy. When it comes to slavery and other matters of religious import, it appears that American reliance on "the Bible alone" meant the dismissal of nearly two millennia of Christian teaching and practice.

In fact, hundreds of print sources—sermons, books, speeches, legal arguments, political petitions—show that evangelical Protestants, while claiming to rely on scripture alone, looked to the Christian past when faced with difficult questions. Even when they appeared to be most scornful toward tradition, most optimistic and forward-looking, and most confident in their grasp of the Bible, American Protestants found themselves returning, time and again, to Christian history. They studied religious historiography, wrote about the Christian past, and argued over its implications for the present.

This study maps American memories of the Christian past, or what Jan Assmann names "mnemohistory." Mnemohistory focuses on "the past as it is remembered," attending to the ways the "past is modeled, invented, reinvented, and reconstructed by the present."[8] I trace the sources, narratives, and assumptions that constitute a remembered religious past and show its importance for American Protestantism. My aim is to recover the neglected role of religious memory during the years between the Revolution and the Civil War—to show that American Protestants were not ahistorical or functionally antitradition, but deeply interested in both history and tradition. Indeed, we can only understand American religion when we pay attention to what nineteenth-century Protestants believed about Christian history. Put another way, this study joins other recent scholarship in interrogating the meaning of "biblicism."[9]

As a mnemohistory, this book is not primarily a study of church history in the academy, or of scholarly developments such as the rise of German historicism. While a number of influential scholars appear—Lydia Maria Child, James Pennington, and Philip Schaff, to name a few—more attention is given to the historical imaginations of ordinary educated Protestants. The history of Christianity was of interest not only to scholars and ministers, but also to politicians, lawyers, educators, reformers, and activists, who read religious history, claimed precedent for their causes, and vigorously debated the implications of the Christian past.[10] These found Christian history especially relevant for pressing questions of the day: How should the government relate to religion? Could Catholic immigrants become true Americans? What opportunities and rights should be available to women? To African Americans? Protestants across denominations answered these questions not only with the Bible but also with history.

This last point raises a definitional question. This book centers on evangelicals and biblicism, while also bringing in subjects from across the theological and denominational spectrum, including many not considered evangelicals. Yet my argument refers both to evangelicals and to American Protestants writ large and does so for several reasons. First, regardless of how one defines the boundaries of evangelicalism, by the 1830s American Protestantism was broadly evangelical in ethos and theological approach. Second, and more important, my research shows that there was little difference between American Protestants when it came to engaging with Christian history. The Christian past was a matter of serious interest not only for the usual suspects—Roman Catholics, Episcopalians, or Presbyterians, for example—but also for Baptists, Disciples of Christ, and other evangelicals who would seem less likely to be interested in tradition. I show that even as various Protestant groups differed on the meaning of church history, they shared a common interest in understanding and employing the Christian past. This commonality grounds my claim to say something general about American Protestants.

Sources for Religious Memory

Literate Americans encountered the history of Christianity in a variety of sources: Latin and Greek editions of the church fathers, the history of martyrs by sixteenth-century English history John Foxe, and the thirteen-volume *Magdeburg Centuries*, a sixteenth-century Lutheran history of Christianity.[11] However, the most influential religious histories in America came from the eighteenth century. ·

Perhaps the most foundational source for American religious memory was written by the Lutheran historian Johann Lorenz von Mosheim. A professor of theology at the University of Helmstedt, Mosheim went on to found the University of Göttingen, where he served as chancellor until his death in 1755. But his most significant legacy was the *Institutionum historiae ecclesiasticae*, first published in 1726. Mosheim's *Ecclesiastical History* broke ground in its critical use of sources and stated unwillingness to allow theological biases to dictate interpretation. It was among the most widely used church histories of the eighteenth century and continued to be revised and edited by scholars as late as the 1890s.[12] Seminarians nearly universally read Mosheim, and they encountered the Lutheran's historical material in numerous classes, not only those dedicated to church history.[13] And Mosheim was popular: to take one example, a book salesman traveling throughout Georgia in the 1820s made sure to offer the four-volume *Ecclesiastical History* among other church histories that could be purchased.[14]

A good friend of leading figures of the *Aufklärung*, or German Enlightenment, Mosheim lamented the sectarian and theological biases of even "learned" Protestant historians, who seemed to write history by a faulty logic: "Such an opinion is true; therefore it must of necessity have been adopted by the primitive Christians." In his work, Mosheim intended to liberate church history from dogmatics by tracing events back to their causes, revealing God's providence in such a way that a reader would "find his piety improved, as well as his knowledge."[15] The result was greater attention to human factors and a more complex account of doctrinal and ceremonial developments than prior Protestant historiography.[16]

After Mosheim, the most influential interpretations of Christian history came from the school of historians known as the "philosophes": David Hume's voluminous *History of England* (1754–61), William Robertson's *History of Scotland 1542–1603* (1759) and *Charles V* (1769), Edward Gibbon's six-volume *History of the Decline and Fall of the Roman Empire* (1776–89), and Joseph Priestley's *History of the Corruptions of Christianity* (1782).[17] Each of these historical works included important interpretations of Christian history and each saw extensive readership in America.

Alongside Mosheim and the philosophes, other religious histories circulated in the United States, especially the four-volume church history written by Anglican evangelical Joseph Milner (1744–97). A grammar school headmaster and lecturer at Holy Trinity Church, Hull, Milner wrote his *History of the Church of Christ* to counter what he saw as an increasingly cynical Protestant historiography. Histories that dwelt on schism, heresy, and corruption, Milner argued, were as like a true account of the church as "an history of the highwaymen that have infected this country [were] an history of England." Instead, his account focused on authentic Christianity in every age of the church, celebrating those "men who have been real, not merely nominal Christians."[18] In spite of scholarly criticism, his *History* enjoyed a remarkably long run of popularity, going into a dozen American editions and adaptations over the first half of the nineteenth century.[19]

The histories written by Mosheim, Milner, Gibbon, Hume, and Robertson not only enjoyed wide readerships in the United States but also spread their narratives through a number of derivative sources. Several "elementary histories" relied on the philosophes for their chapters on primitive and medieval Christianity, while a popular guide to teaching Christianity to children reproduced Mosheim in its description of church history.[20] Mosheim's work was also reproduced in Buck's two-volume *Dictionary*, arguably the primary historical reference work for many American ministers.[21] And religious periodicals also frequently reprinted excerpts from these works.[22] Dozens of other examples of adaptation and republication will follow in these pages. In other words, it was largely from this body of historiography, frequently repackaged and revised, that literate Americans derived their understanding of the Christian past.

Organization of the Book

The story unfolds over three topical sections that overlap chronologically. The first two chapters show how the Christian past contributed to political and religious transformations in the early republic. Chapter 1 traces how the most widely read histories provided important justification for distancing civil government from religion. Eighteenth-century historiography presented the Christian past as a fall from apostolic-era purity into medieval corruption and blamed this on the post-Constantine establishment of Christianity. Thomas Jefferson and James Madison commended these histories and used arguments from the Christian past in their most important works on religious freedom; likewise, Isaac Backus and John Leland appealed to Christian history in their sermons and political speeches. American religious disestablishment was achieved in part because of a compelling historical narrative: to disestablish state churches would overturn the great error of Christendom and allow for the recovery of pure, apostolic-era Christianity. As disestablishment progressed on the state level, the same narratives appeared in new American tellings of religious history.

Just as Christian history helped bring about religious disestablishment, it continued to matter in the resulting religious "free market." Chapter 2 shows how upstart Baptists, Methodists, and Restorationists succeeded in part because they tapped into widely held narratives about the history of Christianity. In New England, Baptists published arguments from the Christian past to gain converts from Congregationalism and, after decades of historical controversy, realized the need to invest institutional resources to teaching church history. Likewise, American Methodists required their ministers to study their own denomination's interpretation of Christian history. Leaders of the Stone-Campbell movement, in turn, wrote criticisms of previous religious historiography and urged their constituents to study the Christian past. For early Restorationists, church history was of immediate significance for the religious and national renewal they sought. Rather than the past becoming irrelevant in a time of innovation, history proved vital to the democratization of Christianity.

The second part, chapters 3 and 4, explores historical education in the Jacksonian era. Chapter 3 maps the ways in which pedagogies of Christian history were implicated in the project of national identity. This story begins with the American Sunday School Union, which published a history of Christianity adapted for young readers. Their children's history emphasized the failures of the Catholic past and, by way of contrast, the superiority of the American Protestant present. Religious history also featured prominently in women's education. Female educators assigned Christian history in their curricula and published textbooks on the subject, including Emma Willard's *Universal History*, which stressed the unique place of the United States in sacred history. At the same time, the Christian past offered resources to African Americans. During the 1820s–1830s, Black educators, publications, and institutions frequently appealed to Christian history in their arguments for educational advancement and racial equality. In Jacksonian America, the Christian past encouraged American exceptionalism—the belief that the United States enjoyed a unique, even ultimate place in divine history—and worked both to support and to subvert the construction of the nation as Anglo-Saxon and Protestant.

Chapter 4 turns to Christian history and the education of the Protestant ministerial class. During the first half of the nineteenth century, seminaries navigated a tension between long-standing Protestant historical narratives and newly emerging historiography, some of which appeared more sympathetic toward the Catholic past. This tension can be seen in the careers of three professors: Samuel Miller at Princeton Theological Seminary, James Murdock at Andover, and Philip Schaff at Mercersburg and Union seminaries. Controversies over historical education reflected concern over the future of the nation, particularly in light of rising Catholic immigration. As Catholics built churches and schools, leading Protestant ministers frequently pointed to the Christian past to demonstrate the incompatibility of Catholicism and American liberty. In this context, the next generation of clergy needed just enough church history to bolster their Protestant convictions.

The last section turns to the most significant religious and political debates in antebellum America. Chapter 5 explains how the recovery of women in Christian history shaped the development and contestation of women's rights. In 1835, Lydia Maria Child published a history of women that offered a new female-centric interpretation of the Christian past. Child's argument was enlisted by Sarah Moore Grimké, Lucretia Mott, and Margaret Fuller, who used it to argue for women's rights. At the same time, advocates of domesticity picked up the narrative of women in Christian history for their own purposes. Across the North Atlantic in the 1840s and 1850s, authors increasingly put forward examples of godly motherhood in order to encourage women in their domestic callings. These two diverging interpretations of women in the Christian past were exemplified in works written in the 1850s by Child and Sarah Josepha Hale, respectively. By the middle of the century, scholars and popular authors alike recognized the place of women in Christian history, even as the implications of this past were disputed.

The final two chapters show how Christian history was implicated in the argument over slavery. Chapter 6 reveals how Black abolitionists first produced a powerful antislavery historical argument by associating racial equality with early Christianity and blaming medieval Catholicism for chattel slavery. In the 1830s, white abolitionists also began producing historical arguments that Christianity had effectively abolished slavery in medieval Europe. These histories went uncontested until the 1840s, when controversy erupted over Pope Gregory XVI's encyclical criticizing the slave trade. Abolitionists, proslavery politicians, and Catholic bishops argued over the pope's writings, and in so doing pushed the question of slavery in Christian history to the forefront. By the time Presbyterians, Methodists, and Baptists split over slavery, both anti- and proslavery factions were using the Christian past to condemn their counterparts. At stake in these rival narratives was not only the compatibility of Christianity and slavery, but also the religious and racial character of the nation.

Chapter 7 continues this historical drama. As the sectional crisis heated up, Christianity's historic relationship to slaveholding became all the more controversial. Dozens of proslavery authors, including Catholics, Episcopalians, Presbyterians, Methodists, and Baptists, employed tradition to defend the compatibility of Christianity and slavery, and by the 1850s Christian history was prominent in proslavery arguments put forward by legal scholars and social theorists. Conversely, both white and Black antislavery authors from a variety of denominations used religious history to bolster their cases against slavery. After the South seceded and the Civil War began, the meaning of the Christian past continued to matter for both North and South. For Confederates, church history proved useful in constructing white Christian nationalism, while, in the North, controversy and outrage followed a proslavery account of Christian history written by Episcopal bishop John Henry Hopkins. This chapter shows that the historical dimensions of the argument made it more unlikely to be resolved on theological grounds. American Protestants did not fail to avoid a bloody Civil War because they ignored history or tradition, but because their readings of the Christian past made them all more intransigent.

Together, these chapters tell the story of how American Protestants remembered and used the Christian past. Even as American Protestants maintained they were biblicists, they consistently appealed to Christian precedent that illuminated and underscored the authority of scripture. On questions of church and state, denominational distinctives, education, women's rights, and slavery, Americans read the Bible alongside and in relation to other texts, traditions, and interpreters. Even as they claimed to rely on the Bible alone, antebellum Protestants frequently turned to Christian saints, exegetical traditions, the practices of Christians past, and official church teachings, employing these sources to complement or clarify what they took the Bible to mean. Perhaps this betrays a deeper sense that the Bible was not as self-interpreting as many Protestants hoped. At the very least, it shows the inescapability of tradition. American Protestants never read, or argued over, the Bible alone.

1

Overturning the Past

The Failure of Christendom and the Disestablishment of American Churches

By 1811, William Findley was used to an argument. The congressman was in his second stint in the US House of Representatives, where he tirelessly fought for the principles of Jeffersonian republicanism. But now it was a sermon that raised his ire: "The Two Sons of Oil, or the Faithful Witness for Magistracy and Ministry upon a Scriptural Basis" had been preached by Samuel B. Wylie, a Reformed Presbyterian minister in Philadelphia and published as a pamphlet in 1803. In his sermon, the Reverend Wylie proclaimed that because the US Constitution failed to acknowledge the lordship of Christ, Christians should not give it their allegiance. The Christian obligation to obey divine law, he argued, meant rejecting any political system that refused to submit to this law. Reading this, Findley was appalled. The pamphlet was already in its second printing—it would see a third edition in 1850—and the congressman decided it must be refuted. He wrote a 360-page rejoinder in 1811 and published it a year later.[1]

Both Findley and Wylie were Presbyterians, both ordained ministers, and both immigrants from Ulster, Ireland. There the similarities ended. The two represented very different strands of political thought within the broader Presbyterian tradition: Wylie was a "Covenanter," who believed governments that did not support Reformed religion necessarily rejected divine authority.[2] In 1800, Wylie became the first Covenanter ordained in the United States. Findley, in contrast, came from a long line of "Old Dissenting" Presbyterians, who generally opposed the state establishment of churches.[3] Findley immigrated in the 1760s, served as a Presbyterian chaplain in the War for Independence, and then, for thirty years, represented a western Pennsylvania county in the House. By the end of his career, the venerable congressman had earned the honorary title of "Father of the House."[4]

In 1811, Findley, well practiced at arguing in Congress, now took up his pen to defend Jeffersonian principles against an overzealous East Coast

The Old Faith in a New Nation. Paul J. Gutacker, Oxford University Press. © Oxford University Press 2023.
DOI: 10.1093/oso/9780197639146.003.0002

preacher. But if readers of *Observations on "The Two Sons of Oil": Containing a Vindication of the American Constitutions, and Defending the Blessings of Religious Liberty and Toleration* expected Findley to elaborate the finer points of political theory or refute Wylie's interpretation of scripture, they also encountered something else. Almost the entirety of the work was an explanation of the history of Christianity. In fact, the congressman believed his defense of the Constitution would be especially persuasive "to every true protestant acquainted with church history," and, to readers not yet familiar with this history, he recommended the works written by Edward Gibbon, Johann Lorenz von Mosheim, Joseph Milner, and Thomas Haweis, which would acquaint them with "the corruption and tyranny of [Christian] councils and emperors."[5] Throughout the book, Findley repeated his central point: history showed that the political establishment of the church contradicted genuine Christianity.

To make this case, Findley contrasted the simple faith of early Christians with the "ignorance and credulity" that marked the church after the emperor Constantine's conversion in the early fourth century and the subsequent establishment of Christianity under Emperor Theodosius. He narrated stories of religious persecution enacted "under the tyrannical union of church and state, in the apostate christian church," and castigated that "violent and tyrannical prince" Theodosius, "who completed the establishment of the bloody idol of *uniformity in religion by human authority.*" Following Edward Gibbon's *Decline & Fall*, Findley provocatively suggested that Christian emperors had been more "absurd and inconsistent" in religious persecution "than even the laws of the inhuman monsters Nero and Domitian." After the unholy alliance of church and state, he concluded, the true church of Christ had been found only among persecuted dissenters.[6]

Findley took his history lesson further, arguing that Wylie wanted to return the country to the Dark Ages: those who insisted on religious establishments preferred the "political catholic church" over the church of "the apostolic age." If Wylie represented a regressive return to medieval intolerance, the American experiment in religious freedom was the fulfillment of the Protestant Reformation. Findley acknowledged that Protestant Reformers had indeed established state churches, but wrote this off as a failure to fully recover the practices of the early church. It was up to American Protestants to finish the job—and if they were not up for the task, they might as well become Roman Catholics. Those who wanted to surrender their "own judgment and reason" should go all the way and submit to the infallibility of the pope.[7] Christian history, Findley concluded, fully justified the American political and legal system. The US Constitution, by keeping civil authority apart from religion, fulfilled the Reformation and restored the purity of the pre-Constantinian church.

Findley's *Observations* drew on a long tradition of historical arguments for American religious disestablishment. Like many others, he believed Christian history revealed the problems with religious establishments, and found support for this position in the most influential historiography of the day. With few exceptions, eighteenth-century historical works presented the Christian past as a decline from the purity of the early church into corrupt, superstitious medieval Catholicism, and blamed this largely on the establishment of Christianity as the imperial religion. These historical works were read and cited by leading advocates of disestablishment, who used Christian history to persuade their fellow Americans to disestablish state churches and enshrine religious freedom in the US Constitution.

From the 1770s through the first decade of the nineteenth century, American sermons, political treatises, and petitions show that the Christian past provided a crucial source for religious disestablishment—and one that has gone almost wholly unnoticed by scholars.[8] Eighteenth-century accounts of Christian history appeared to show the sobering consequences of governmental involvement in religion, and this historical narrative was skillfully employed by advocates of religious freedom, including James Madison, Thomas Jefferson, John Leland, and Isaac Backus. As the process of federal and state disestablishment progressed, the same arguments reappeared in new American interpretations of religious history. For authors such as William Findley, Joseph Priestley, and Hannah Adams, Christian history was reaching its fulfillment in America's experiment in religious freedom. Disestablishment, in other words, relied on American memory of the Christian past, as widely held assumptions about the history of Christianity gave Americans confidence to embark on a bold experiment in religious liberty.

Christendom in Eighteenth-Century Historiography

When Americans read eighteenth-century historiography, they encountered a narrative of decline. The most widely read works—Johann Lorenz von Mosheim's *Institutes of Ecclesiastical History*, histories by David Hume,

William Robertson, Edward Gibbon, and Joseph Priestley, and Joseph Milner's *History of the Church of Christ*—offered a variety of interpretations of Christian history. Generally, they agreed that the church fell from its initial purity into medieval intolerance and violence, and they blamed this at least partially, if not entirely, on the fourth-century establishment of Christianity.

In his volumes, Lutheran historian Johann Lorenz von Mosheim narrated the early history of Christianity as a story of corruption: the church was transformed from its apostolic simplicity into an increasingly speculative system.[9] Before Constantine, the democratic governance of the primitive church had already begun to be lost. After second-century councils strengthened the episcopacy, "The ancient privileges of the people were considerably diminished, and the power and authority of the bishops greatly augmented." In Mosheim's telling, establishment was not to blame per se but rather a catalyst for corruption. In particular, after Christianity was established as the imperial religion, the influence of Platonic philosophy led to a number of superstitious practices: the cult of the saints, the idealization of celibacy, worship of relics, and increasingly intricate rituals.[10] Mosheim's *Aufklärung* sensibilities show in his distaste for anything deemed immoderate or unreasonable.[11] He found much in medieval Christianity to criticize, especially scholastic theology, which deepened the "darkness of that cloud that had already been cast over the divine lustre of genuine Christianity." The sixteenth-century Protestant reforms represented the "most glorious of all the Revolutions" since Christ, and Mosheim believed that the Reformers had recovered a measure of Christianity's primitive purity.[12]

If Mosheim emphasized the theme of corruption, his eighteenth-century translator, the Scots-Irish dissenter Archibald Maclaine, amplified it even more. In the original Latin text, Mosheim's account of the Reformation extolled the advantages of a minimal establishment in which the government protected and promoted true religion; Maclaine downplayed this passage while adding a lengthy appendix that recast the Reformation as a struggle for religious freedom.[13] Notably, this reworking of Mosheim's Reformation was appended to most American printings of the *Ecclesiastical History*, including the first, published in Philadelphia in 1797. In Maclaine's translation, Mosheim appeared all the more to offer American readers a historical narrative that strengthened the association between Protestantism and religious liberty.

The historical works by the philosophes went further than Mosheim in highlighting postestablishment corruption—and none more famously than Edward Gibbon's *Decline and Fall*. Gibbon reinterpreted Christian history through the lens of a skeptic: he questioned the number of early Christian martyrs, argued that religious persecution had been worse under Christian emperors than pagan, and expressed disgust at Christian desire for martyrdom. Much could be blamed on the establishment of the church. After emperor Constantine converted to Christianity in the early fourth century, the church's newfound wealth and prestige brought a change from its "primitive freedom and equality" to a model that emulated the despotic hierarchy of the empire. The resulting "dark ages" were the "triumph of barbarism and religion," and Gibbon mocked medieval Christianity for its severe asceticism, elevation of celibacy, and anti-intellectualism.[14] Gibbon's work was as cynical as it was witty, and traditional Christians criticized, edited, and censured *Decline and Fall* in the years after its publication.[15]

But Gibbon was largely in step with other rationalist historians. "Europe had relapsed into the barbarism of the earliest ages," Jean-Jacques Rousseau wrote at the beginning of his First Discourse: "The people of this part of the world . . . lived some centuries ago in a condition worse than ignorance."[16] David Hume closed the second volume of his *History of England* (1754–62) with an apology for so much on the "barbarous ages." His purpose in so doing was to provide a gratifying contrast between these "horrid and deformed" historical periods with the freedom, "science and civility" of the present age.[17] William Robertson was more willing than Hume to acknowledge the humanitarian and legal gains made by the medieval church—but he nonetheless portrayed the Middle Ages as an era of darkness and false religion.[18] Joseph Priestley's *History of the Corruptions of Christianity*, meanwhile, lived up to its title, telling the story of Christianity declining into irrational dogma.[19]

The philosophical school did not write univocally, and these historians varied in their emphases and explanations of the decline of medieval Christianity. Yet even as they quibbled over the relative merits of the apostolic-era church or the accomplishments of the Protestant Reformation, they generally agreed on the link between the post-Constantinian establishment of Christianity and the medieval church's "abuses of power."[20] The philosophes believed that the history of Christianity was a story of established religion leading to centuries of unreasonable, coercive, and violent Catholicism. In fact, no single theme unified this historiography more than a distinctly anti-Catholic portrayal of Christendom.[21]

It was on this point that the Anglican historian Joseph Milner challenged both Mosheim and the philosophers. In a notable departure from his
predecessors, the evangelical minister insisted that Protestant historians
ought not "be prejudiced against the real church, because she then wore a
Roman garb."[22] While Milner's *History* still reflected a degree of eighteenth-
century anti-Catholicism—he believed genuine Christianity grew rare
between Augustine and Luther, and lamented late-medieval "monastic darkness and superstition"—this was mitigated by the desire to present an edifying account.[23] Milner set out to recover as many believers in "Roman garb"
as could be found and, over the course of his first three volumes, was surprisingly successful, including hundreds of monks, bishops, and even several
popes.[24] He defended at length medieval Christians, including Gregory the
Great, Boniface, Anselm of Canterbury, and Bernard of Clairvaux, who had
been unfairly treated by Protestant historians.[25] In this regard, the *History*
departed from the Protestant tendency to exclude Catholics from the lineage
of true spirituality.[26]

Milner also disagreed with other Protestant historians when it came to
explaining spiritual decline. Rather than decline originating with the establishment of the church under Constantine, Milner insisted that it had already
begun through "the common influence of prosperity on human depravity,"
worldliness, and the natural tendency of humans toward sin.[27] Against the
grain of Protestant historiography, Milner placed the Catholic past in judgment over the Protestant present, arguing, for instance, that the so-called
Dark Ages surpassed Protestant Britain in zeal for missions. In contrast to
Mosheim, Gibbon, and Hume, Milner admired medieval Britain, arguing
that the Venerable Bede's eighth-century history of English Christianity
evidenced "a real spirit of godliness" in the land. He reminded his readers
that modern-day Britain owed a spiritual debt to the medieval church.[28]

Milner offered American readers a different take on the history of religious
establishment, but the reception of his work shows the exception proving the
rule. American readers often expressed dislike of Milner's generosity toward
the Catholic past.[29] Those from dissenting denominations tended to be less
favorable: the *Episcopal Recorder* praised Milner's *History* as excellent and instructive, while the Baptist *Christian Review* dismissed it as uncritical and
only "distinguished for its pious strain of feeling."[30] One anonymous student,
writing in the *Evangelical and Literary Magazine*, defended Milner's *History*
against its scholarly detractors. Nonetheless, this sympathetic reader sin-
gled out Milner's account of establishment for disapproval, admitting that

among the *History's* flaws, "The defence of ecclesiastical establishments particularly meets our reprobation."[31] And when American authors adapted Milner's *History*, they typically edited it to appear more anti-Catholic and more antiestablishment.[32]

In contrast, the philosophes earned praise for their representation of the failures of Christendom. Even though theologically traditional readers were troubled by the skepticism of Gibbon and Hume, they acknowledged that the rationalist historians usefully displayed the problems of established religion.[33] For example, in his review of eighteenth-century historiography, novelist and literary critic Charles Brockden Brown lamented that Gibbon's account of the rise of Christianity "attacked the truth of this system with the dangerous weapons of sarcasm and irony," while Hume's corpus showed him to be "the enemy not of any particular form of religion, but of religion itself." Nonetheless, Brown found much to appreciate. He praised Hume's careful explanation of "the effects of superstition and priestcraft" on medieval Christianity, and commended Robertson for distinguishing reasonable religion from "the ignorance and ambition of the middle ages." Reviewers who worried that the philosophes' works eroded belief in divine providence also praised them for illustrating the corruption of postestablishment Christianity.[34]

The History of Such Savage Cruelty: The Christian Past and Religious Dissent

These historical narratives were already well-known when Americans began to challenge colonial-era religious establishments. This process started in 1776, when North Carolina ended tax support of the Church of England, and followed with the disestablishment of state churches in Maryland in 1785 and Virginia in 1786. Not long after, the same arguments worked during the ratification of the US Constitution to commit the nation to religious freedom. By the first decade of the nineteenth century, the tide of disestablishment finally reached New England: in 1807, Vermont became the first state to disestablish its Congregational Church, followed by the other New England states, and culminating in 1833, when the last holdout, Massachusetts, ended tax support of churches.[35] Within a half century, the separation of church and state enshrined in the First Amendment had worked its way throughout the nation and ended the legal and financial establishment of religion.

The process of church disestablishment was neither predictable nor inevitable, but rather the result of political, ideological, social, and religious forces.[36] Leading the cause was an alliance of religious dissenters, particularly Baptists, and politicians such as Thomas Jefferson and James Madison, who worked together to win state and federal religious disestablishment.[37] From pulpits, in assembly halls, and through print, these allies offered their arguments against religious establishment—and quite frequently they used Christian history.

Dissenting ministers often reminded state governments of the lessons of the Christian past. In 1777, William Tennent III gave a speech to the South Carolina assembly in support of a petition put forward by dissenters against the established Church of England. Tennent, a Presbyterian minister and grandson of the revivalist William Tennent, decried the state-enforced penalties for religious dissent. He called assemblymen to learn from the sad episodes of religious persecution throughout Christian history: "You, Sir! look back with horror upon the history of such savage cruelty, the more cruel as it has ever been exercised under the colour of law." If South Carolina ended the establishment of the Church of England, this would be a step forward in historical progress: "*Let the time past suffice.* With the new constitution let the day of justice dawn upon every rank and order of men in this state. Let us bury what is past forever."[38] One year later, Tennent's argument prevailed. When South Carolina ratified its new constitution in 1778, the state gave all Protestant denominations equal rights and freedoms.

Alongside Presbyterians like Tennent, Baptists were the most consistent and vocal advocates for religious freedom, in part because of their experience of religious persecution. In New England, active persecution of Baptists waned following the Toleration Act of 1689, but throughout the eighteenth and into the early nineteenth century, Baptists' tax dollars still supported Congregational churches. In Virginia, persecution of Baptists actually increased in the years leading up to the Revolution, and Baptist ministers were beaten, assaulted while preaching, and imprisoned. Thirty-four Baptist preachers were jailed during the tumultuous decades of the 1760s and 1770s.[39]

One of the most outspoken advocates of disestablishment was Isaac Backus, who in 1751 left the Congregational Church to become a Baptist minister. He then took up the cause of religious liberty, first by lobbying New England governments to exempt Baptists from supporting the Congregational Church with their tax dollars.[40] Backus believed that history provided a compelling case for all Christians to enjoy religious freedom. In a 1773 sermon, *An Appeal to the Public for Religious Liberty*, he reminded his listeners of early Christian history. Jesus Christ "made no use of secular force in the first setting up of the gospel church," but Christians departed from this original plan when the emperor Constantine converted, and corruption quickly followed. One measure of decline, Backus preached, was the rise of persecution: "The same sword that Constantine drew against heretics, Julion [*sic*] turned against the orthodox," and this persecuting spirit would find its apex in the "hellish tyranny" of papal authority. In Backus's telling, the history of Christianity showed that religious establishment led to corruption, persecution, and authoritarianism.[41]

Then Backus widened his historical lens to include the American past. Why did the first colonists come to America? Because, Backus preached, Protestant Reformers failed to go far enough in renouncing medieval ways. When these colonists came to the New World, persecution only continued when the Puritans sought to establish a "Christian common-wealth" with no room for dissent. "The reforming churches flying from Rome," Backus argued, "carried some of them more, some of them less, all of them something of Rome with them, especially in that spirit of *imposition* and *persecution* which too much cleaved to them."[42] By associating New England Congregationalism with the tyranny of the Roman Catholic past, Backus represented it as an Old World holdover—and incompatible with the emerging American commitment to liberty.

In 1774, Backus's interpretations of Christian history came to the attention of several political leaders. When the First Continental Congress met in September, Backus and other Baptists went to Philadelphia to lobby for the cause of religious liberty, distributing copies of Backus's *Appeal* to congressional members. The Massachusetts delegation, including John and Samuel Adams, listened to the Baptists' complaints, but ultimately declined to make changes to the Congregational establishment. But the appeal was not in vain—after this meeting, the active persecution of Baptists in Massachusetts waned significantly. And by bringing a historical case against religious establishments to the attention of the first Congress, Backus and his colleagues planted a seed that would bear fruit in later deliberations.[43]

Like Backus, John Leland was a Congregationalist turned Baptist minister. In 1775, he moved to Virginia, where he fought for religious liberty alongside James Madison, Thomas Jefferson, and other members of the Baptist "General Committee." After successfully campaigning to bring about the disestablishment of the Church of England in that state, Leland worked just as hard to convince Virginians to ratify the new US Constitution and Bill of Rights.[44] In 1791, Leland returned to his birth state of Massachusetts ready to take on the Congregational establishment. He published a sermon, *The Right of Conscience Inalienable*, which articulated the cause he had success-fully fought for in Virginia and in the Constitutional amendments. In this justly famous sermon, Leland made an extended historical case for religious freedom. He traced the error of establishment through Christian history all the way back to Constantine, whose embrace of Christianity represented "the first human establishment of religion." After the conversion of the emperor to Christianity, Leland argued,

> He established it in the Roman empire, compelled the pagans to submit, and banished the christian hereticks; built fine chapels at public expence, and forced large stipends for the preachers. All this was done out of love to the christian religion; but his love operated inadvertently; for he did the christian church more harm than all the persecuting emperors ever did.

The historical results of this "poison" were evident: "From that day to this, the christian religion has been made a stirrup to mount the steed of popularity, wealth and ambition."[45]

Leland made sure to connect the dots: the errors of Roman Catholicism were the result of the Constantinian establishment of Christianity as the imperial religion. In typical anti-Catholic rhetoric of the day, the minister lamented that the church had been "a chaste virgin" for "almost three hun-dred years: but afterwards she played the whore with the kings and princes of this world; who with their gold and wealth came in unto her, and she be-came a strumpet." This adulterous alliance resulted in false religion, Leland explained, as the church began to regard human laws and councils above the word of Christ, and used money and civil force to compel worship. Leland connected this sobering history to the American present: "She is called the *mother of harlots*," Leland wrote of the corrupt medieval Catholic Church, "and all protestant churches, who are regulated by law, and force people to support their preachers, build meeting-houses and otherwise maintain their worship, are daughters of this holy mother."[46]

This historical case would be made again and again by the Baptist min-ister. In 1811, Leland stood in front of the assembled Massachusetts House of Representatives to give a speech on church-state relations. He addressed the issue of state funding for the Congregational Church, which he believed was an unfair burden for taxpayers who belonged to other denominations. He argued that the state legislature should allow religious exemptions to this funding—and made his case by reminding the representatives of the lessons of Christian history, which demonstrated the disastrous results of the state legislating religion. "Under this notion, Mr. Chairman, the crusades were formed in the eleventh century, which lasted about two hundred years, and destroyed nearly two millions of lives," Leland explained. "In view of all this, and ten thousand times as much, is it to be wondered at, that the present petitioners, should be fearful of attaching corporate power to religious societies?" By retelling his listeners about the violence and corruption of medieval Christendom, Leland gave them good reason to distrust religious establishments.[47]

He went on: Christian history also showed that genuine religion did not require state support. In fact, it was Baptists and other dissenting petitioners who organized and funded their churches "in the only way that the Christians did for the first three centuries after Christ." Leland called his audience to remember the early church, when "before the reign of Constantine . . . Christianity did stand and flourish, not only without the aid of the law and the schools, but in opposition to both."[48] The point was clear: genuine religion thrived when free from the support of the state. Or, as Leland put it in an 1804 pamphlet, "Persecution, like a lion, tears the saints to death, but leaves Christianity pure; state establishment of religion, like a bear, hugs the saints but corrupts Christianity."[49]

Repeatedly throughout his career, Leland employed similar historical arguments, highlighting the lessons of Christian history in speeches and publications into the 1830s. Writing in 1815 against sabbatarian laws, Leland argued that

> we look in vain to find any thing like it in the New Testament, and it is generally confessed, that when the event did take place—when Constantine the Great established Christianity in the empire, and forced an observance of the first day of the week, Christianity was disrobed of her virgin beauty and prostituted to the unhallowed principle of state policy, where it has remained in a criminal commerce until the present moment.[50]

In 1820, Leland proposed revising the constitution of Massachusetts, and again he elaborated on the results of Constantine's establishment: "That

Christianity was disrobed of apostolical order, and ravished of her virgin chastity, by this establishment, cannot be confuted. By the *imperial Christian* establishment, arose the shocking monster of *Christian nation.*" In an 1829 dedication of a Baptist meetinghouse Leland reminded his listeners that, since Constantine, "the Christian religion has been an institute of state policy, regulated by the laws of men, and supported by the sword of the magistrate. Whether in a papal or protestant mode, the principle has done incalculable mischief, and drenched the earth in blood." Many more examples from his letters, essays, and sermons could be given.[51] Leland not only expounded the lessons of history, but provided helpful references for other Baptists, who followed his lead in making historical arguments against established denominations.[52]

These arguments made by Backus and Leland did not originate with eighteenth-century historiography. Criticizing Christendom was part of dissenting thought, and there was a long colonial tradition of dissenting ministers citing the lessons of church history in their arguments and blaming Constantine for the fall of Christianity into error. For example, when Roger Williams produced his argument for the separation of church and state, *The Bloudy Tenent of Persecution*, he pointed out that "a civil sword (as woeful experience in all ages has proved) is so far from bringing or helping forward an opposite in religion to repentance that magistrates sin grievously against the work of God and blood of souls by such proceedings."[53] Eight years later, Williams expanded this historical point in *The Bloody Tenent yet more Bloody*, in which he argued that the Roman Empire did not abandon idolatry after the conversion of emperor Constantine, but exchanged it "for more re-fined & beautified *Idols*, painted over with the name of *Christ.*" The church, once the "*wise* and *spouse* of *Christ Jesus*, now degenerates and apostates into an *Whore*, in the times of her ease, security and prosperity."[54]

But if Backus and Leland were writing in a tradition of dissent, they also found that the leading historians of their day—Mosheim, Gibbon, and Hume—were now on their side. In fact, even established ministers recognized the implications of this historiography. For example, in 1773, Izrahiah Wetmore, a Congregationalist minister, preached an election day sermon to the Connecticut general assembly.[55] Wetmore asked if true religion needed civil power or authority "to spread or establish it?" No, Wetmore answered, as "these have generally, if not evermore, been injurious to it; have enervated, obstructed, and . . . greatly corrupted and depraved it—and have robbed it of it's native Beauty, and Glory, and Strength."[56] In other words, when dissenters sought to persuade governmental bodies to defund or disestablish state churches, they used historical narratives that resonated widely.

Almost Fifteen Centuries: Jefferson, Madison, and Antiestablishment History

Leland and Backus had close connections to Thomas Jefferson and James Madison—in fact, Madison's commitment to liberty of conscience emerged after he witnessed the persecution of Baptists in Virginia.[57] Leland convinced Madison to go further than he originally intended in the First Amendment; in turn, Madison persuaded Leland to throw his support behind the ratification of the Constitution and his congressional campaigns in 1788–89.[58] Both Jefferson and Madison knew and appreciated the eighteenth-century historiography that grounded the Baptists' claims about Christian history.[59] In 1783, Madison recommended that the new congressional library include Mosheim, Gibbon, Hume, and Robertson.[60] This interest in the history of Christianity persisted throughout his career. In 1821 he purchased a copy of the first American edition of Mosheim's church history.[61] When, in 1824, Jefferson asked for advice on the new library of the University of Virginia, Madison recommended Mosheim alongside various patristic, medieval, and Reformation authors.[62]

Madison's suggestions must have been well received, as Jefferson had a long-running interest in the church fathers and the history of Christianity.[63] In 1787, he encouraged a young friend to read Mosheim, Hume, and Robertson; twenty years later, he provided another correspondent with a list of recommended books that included Mosheim, Priestley, Gibbon, and Robertson.[64] When Jefferson compiled his wish list for the University of Virginia library, he included twenty-two works under "Histories— Ecclesiastical," including all six volumes of Mosheim, and records show that the library held an 1810 printing of the Maclaine translation.[65]

Above all, Joseph Priestley's historical writings made a significant impression on Jefferson. The two were political and religious allies who exchanged numerous letters on theology, the church fathers, and the degradations of post-Constantinian Christianity. Priestley dedicated his *General History of the Christian Church* to Jefferson; in turn, Jefferson admitted that Priestley's historical writings shaped his religious views more than any other author: "I have read his Corruptions of Christianity, and

Early Opinions of Jesus, over and over again; and I rest on them . . . as the basis of my own faith."[66]

Given their interest in this historiography, it is not surprising that Jefferson and Madison reproduced the historical narratives of these works in their arguments against religious establishment. Jefferson's "Virginia Statute for Religious Freedom," drafted in 1777, grounded its case on historical claims about the corrupting influence of establishment on true religion—and Jefferson's notes on the writing of the statute show just how much he relied on the history of Christianity.[67] In one section, the statute argued that rulers who try to oversee religion "have established and maintained false religions over the greatest part of the world and through all time." In another, Jefferson asserted that religious establishment "tends only to corrupt the principles of that very Religion it is meant to encourage, by bribing with a monopoly of worldly honours and emoluments those who will externally profess and conform to it."[68] In his 1784 *Notes on Virginia*, Jefferson repeated these historical points:

> Millions of innocent men, women, and children, since the introduction of Christianity, have been burnt, tortured, fined, imprisoned; yet we have not advanced one inch towards uniformity. What has been the effect of coercion? To make one half the world fools, and the other half hypocrites. To support roguery and error all over the earth.[69]

These historical arguments helped to bring about the disestablishment of the Anglican Church in Virginia in 1786. Over the rest of his career, Jefferson continued to narrate the struggle over church-state separation in historical terms.[70]

Madison similarly used the lessons of Christian history in his writing. In 1785, he opposed a proposal put forward by Patrick Henry for a plural establishment in Virginia, which would fund preachers of various denominations rather than favoring one.[71] Madison's *Memorial and Remonstrance*, originally published anonymously, argued that the history of the church demonstrated that "ecclesiastical establishments, instead of maintaining the purity and efficacy of Religion, have had a contrary operation." Madison encouraged the state of Virginia to look to the Christian past and see that for "almost fifteen centuries has the legal establishment of Christianity been on trial." What was the result? "Pride and indolence in the Clergy, ignorance and servility in the laity, in both, superstition, bigotry and persecution." Madison insisted that all theologians agreed that Christianity "appeared in its greatest lustre" before it was joined to the state.[72] Similar historical arguments appeared in another petition against Henry's bill, the widely shared Prince George County Petition. These efforts succeeded in killing the proposed tax, and the following year, Virginia established religious freedom.[73]

Madison's *Memorial* and Jefferson's "Statute" are among the most important texts on religious freedom from the founding era, and jurists and scholars have long argued that these documents crucially shaped the writing and ratification of the First Amendment.[74] Both of these foundational texts invoked the Christian past, and did so in ways that evidence the influence of Mosheim, Gibbon, Priestley, and Hume. While Leland and Backus may or may not have read this historiography, they made the same historical claims about the connection between establishment and religious corruption. Despite the theological differences between these statesmen and dissenting ministers, they shared a common memory of the Christian past and its meaning for the American present. Christian history, in other words, contributed to the successful alliance of evangelical Baptists with Madison and Jefferson.

Religious Freedom in Early National Memory

In the years after the ratification of the Constitution, the same historical arguments that worked to bring about national disestablishment continued to matter for Americans in the early republic. The First Amendment did not end the debate over religious freedom, and American Protestants found reason for concern about the religious future of their nation. Abroad, some Europeans predicted that without state support Christianity would all but vanish in the United States. At home, the presidential election of 1800 appeared to some to be a referendum on church-state separation, while others worried about the danger of putting a supposed infidel into the highest office of the land. In this moment American Protestants like William Findley, whose defense of the Constitution opened this chapter, found resources in the Christian past to bolster their commitment to religious freedom. Likewise, American religious historians explored the meaning of the United States within the longer scope of the history of Christianity.

When in 1794 Joseph Priestley emigrated from England, he was fleeing persecution as much as seeking opportunity. Priestley was a polymath—scientist, theologian, philosopher, and historian—who founded the Unitarian movement in England and fought for political and religious rights for dissenters. He also wrote several controversial accounts of Christian history, including works that rejected Trinitarian theology, Calvinism, and eucharistic doctrine.[75] This writing, combined with his political activism, placed Priestley in no small danger. In addition to facing criticism and censure, he also experienced violence—as in July 1791, when an antirevolutionary mob attacked and burned Priestley's home in Birmingham. In light of this increasing peril, he left England for the safety of Pennsylvania.

In Pennsylvania, Priestley finally completed his four-volume *General History of the Christian Church* (1802).[76] The work set the tone for American Unitarianism and, as noted above, significantly influenced Jefferson's religious views.[77] It was a history that developed his earlier arguments against Trinitarian Christianity, while also explicitly connecting the Christian past to his new political and religious context in America. In the opening pages, Priestley dedicated the four-volume work to the newly elected Thomas Jefferson, that "strenuous and uniform advocate of *religious* as well as civil liberty." He added that the first two decades of American national history confirmed that truth prevailed when religion was free.[78]

Throughout the *General History*, Priestley accentuated the achievement of American freedom by placing it against the backdrop of the violent, intolerant Christian past. In his preface, he explained his goal of tracing the rise and fall of religious freedom through the centuries, with special attention to the violent religious persecutions enacted by Christians. Priestley's work highlighted the intolerance of the Catholic Church, which, after Constantine, quickly surpassed that of pagan Rome; sixteenth-century Reformers did no better, as they had been unable to see "the impropriety of the civil magistrate interfering in the business of religion." Religious persecution, Priestley lamented, "has continued with more or less violence to this day, and will continue till the complete downfall of Antichrist." Throughout his history, Priestley contrasted the corrupt Christian past to the superior American present. He advised the reader not to expect those who lived in "what are called the dark ages" to be enlightened. The medieval era merited attention only to make American readers more grateful for the freedom of the present.[79]

Priestley's writings influenced the work of Hannah Adams, a distant relative of John Adams and a groundbreaking female writer.[80] Adams's dictionary, *View of Religions*, made her the first woman writer in America to earn a living solely through her publications.[81] In *View of Religions*, which debuted in 1784 and was expanded in subsequent editions, Adams aimed to present the various religions of the world, including every sect of Christianity, as objectively and charitably as possible.[82] The work was enormously successful: Adams was one of the most widely read authors in New England, surpassing John Bunyan and Benjamin Franklin in popularity.[83]

In the dictionary, Adams wanted to fairly portray every variety of the Christian faith, and although her own biases came through—she despised Calvinism, preferred Unitarian and Universalist theology, and was thoroughly anti-Catholic—her aspiration is still evident.[84] The project required a fair amount of historical material, and for this Adams drew heavily on Mosheim, Robertson, Gibbon, and Priestley, each of whom was cited throughout the work. Her interpretations of the Christian past closely followed Mosheim's and Priestley's, particularly regarding the deleterious effect of pagan philosophy on the faith.[85]

While the dictionary had no driving thesis, religious freedom was a theme that repeatedly came up. In the second part of View of Religions, which surveyed the denominations throughout the world, Adams took care to discuss the question of religious liberty. On France, for example, she lamented that the only kind of religion remaining there after the revolution was "chiefly the Roman Catholic, with an affected display of all the ancient ceremonies. . . . No considerable attempts have been made to promote free inquiry with respect to religion, and to propagate the knowledge of pure Christianity." On the history of America, Adams complained that the Puritans "quitted their native country, in order to enjoy the free exercise of their religion. . . . But the noble principles of liberty ceased to operate on their minds, after they had got the power in their hands." Anglican settlers of Virginia received similar criticism.[86]

This history of religious intolerance underscored the value of American freedom. "It was one of the peculiarities of the forms of government in the United States," she wrote, "that all religious establishments were abolished." According to Adams, by the time of the Revolution, this was a universal desideratum: "The idea of supporting one denomination at the expense of others, or of raising any one sect of Protestants to a legal pre-eminence, was universally reprobated." She praised those states who protected religious freedom, including Massachusetts's "most liberal and tolerant plan" and Connecticut, where "a spirit of liberality and catholicism is increasing." She lauded William Penn for his role in establishing "civil and religious liberty in their utmost latitude," and noted the ongoing harmony between various denominations in Pennsylvania.[87] Adams celebrated religious pluralism, confident that freedom would allow true Christianity to flourish.

Priestley, Adams, and Findley provided explanations of the American present that were rooted in the failings of the Christian past. All drew on well-established narratives about the corruption of post-Constantinian Christianity, and contrasted this history with American freedom. Their construction of Christian history and its meanings for the United States have lived on in the American historical imagination. Recently, Findley's *Observations on the Two Sons of Oil* has reemerged in popular conservative Christian publications. In 2003, *Observations* was picked up by Stephen K. McDowell, founder of a Christian educational nonprofit and author of a series called "America's Providential History." In his book, *Building Godly Nations*, McDowell cites Findley's arguments as evidence that America was founded to be a Christian nation. Other Christian conservatives, including the controversial historian and political activist David Barton, have used Findley's work to show the Christian character of the American founding. Barton is the founder of WallBuilders, an "organization dedicated to presenting America's forgotten history and heroes, with an emphasis on the moral, religious, and constitutional foundation on which America was built."[88] In his 2013 self-published book, *Original Intent: The Courts, the Constitution, and Religion*, Barton reproduced a number of sections from Findley's argument to bolster his case that the Constitution was founded on, and intended to protect, biblical principles. And, in 2007, the Liberty Fund, a libertarian nonprofit, republished Findley's *Observations on the Two Sons of Oil* as an important text in American history on the nature of freedom.[89]

If Findley's recent popularity illustrates the contested legacy of early American constitutional arguments, it also shows the enduring appeal of his historical narrative. Findley's story was supported by the most highly regarded historical works of the eighteenth century, and frequently repeated by those who worked hardest for religious disestablishment. America, in this story, was undoing all that went wrong in Christian history by dissolving the alliance between church and state. For Findley, as well as Madison, Jefferson, and many others, Christian history provided important justification for leaving behind European norms, while also encouraging enduring associations in American historiography between Protestantism and democracy.[90] Statesmen, ministers, and historians alike understood themselves to be overturning the mistakes of the Christian past. Against the dark backdrop of Christendom, the American achievement of political and religious liberty shone brightly. Navigating this new religious "free market," however, would be another story.

2

Restoring the Past

Tradition and the Democratization of Christianity

Until 1804, Daniel Merrill had never written a series of sermons like those he was about to preach. He was going to explain to his Congregationalist church that he no longer agreed with the practice of infant baptism and, further, attempt to persuade the church to join him in embracing Baptist principles. Merrill had been some time in coming to this decision. After serving in the Revolutionary War, he studied at Dartmouth College and was ordained a Congregational minister in 1790. He enthusiastically entered into pastoral ministry, inviting several young men to join a theological discussion group. But as the study group pressed deeper into theological questions and read more on the practice of baptism, Merrill began to doubt Congregationalist tenets. As he and his young cohort discussed the question, he became persuaded that Baptists were correct—that the biblical practice was believer's baptism.[1]

Merrill was by no means alone. Baptists were increasingly persuading New England Congregationalists to their principles, and regional competition between the two denominations was heating up: one Baptist group, the Shaftesbury Baptist association of churches from Vermont, Massachusetts, and New York, grew from twenty-six churches in 1791 to forty-six in 1800.[2] In response, concerned Congregationalists founded the Massachusetts Missionary Society in 1799 to try to keep pace by planting new churches throughout New York and Maine. Now Merrill was attempting to persuade the largest Congregational church in Maine to become the First Baptist Church of Sedgwick. The point of crisis for Merrill was his realization that he could not in good conscience baptize several young children presented by their parents. He revealed his change of mind in a series of sermons that he immediately published afterward, along with an addendum titled *A Miniature History of the Baptists*.[3]

In addition to explaining his theological reasons for affirming believer's baptism, Merrill provided a history lesson. The history of Christianity, he

The Old Faith in a New Nation. Paul J. Gutacker, Oxford University Press. © Oxford University Press 2023.
DOI: 10.1093/oso/9780197639146.003.0003

wrote, showed that infant baptism departed from early Christian practice. In fact, church history demonstrated that Baptists "have been the uninterrupted church of our Lord from the apostles' day to ours." Studying the history of Christianity made it impossible for the minister to continue as a Congregationalist: "The history of the church assures me," he concluded, "that the denomination of Christians to which I have belonged, and to which I do still visibly belong, came through the church of Rome" and was still tainted by the "filth" of this "mother of harlots." However, "The same history assures me, that the Baptists never have submitted to her superstitions and filthy abominations."[4] Merrill's congregation was persuaded. The church approved his continuation as minister and voted one month later to follow his lead and become the First Baptist Church of Sedgwick.

But the controversy was far from over: Merrill's *Miniature History* precipitated a region-wide argument over the history of baptism that continued in print for years. Several prominent Congregationalists wrote rebuttals of Merrill's telling of Christian history, while Baptists published pieces defending Merrill and insisting that leading church historians supported their own position. For several decades, Baptists and their rivals would continue to debate the historical narrative Merrill had written for his congregation.

This was only one of many historical arguments that played out in American sermons and print culture during the era of disestablishment. Yet little attention has been given to Protestant engagement with church history in post-Revolutionary America. Instead, this era is typically represented as overtly hostile toward the Christian past. The years 1780–1830 saw remarkable religious transformations: as the disestablishment of state churches progressed, Presbyterian, Congregational, and Episcopalian churches were quickly surpassed by Baptists, Methodists, and, eventually, the new Stone-Campbell movement.[5] Baptists and Methodists moved from minority sects to the largest denominations in the United States—a remarkable reversal of market share.[6] The religious free market, in other words, favored populist, innovative, and activist groups.

These transformations have been famously described by Nathan Hatch as "the democratization of American Christianity." Evangelical religion took on the ideology of the Revolution, embracing the belief that social and religious progress required abandoning traditional structures and authorities. The remarkable growth of the Stone-Campbell movement, Hatch explains, was premised on its "confidence that one could break the firm grip of custom and precedent," while Methodists and Baptists flourished because they embraced the American disregard for received authority.[7] It seems that this was an era defined by American Protestants knowingly and intentionally breaking from tradition and precedent.[8]

But these dramatic changes encouraged American Protestants to give greater attention to Christian history. The changing of the denominational guard saw older churches and upstart rivals fighting in pulpit and in print: as Presbyterian missionary Timothy Flint put it in 1830, "Nine pulpits in ten in our country are occupied chiefly in the denunciation of other sects."[9] · Denominational rivalry built on and contributed to the dramatic expansion of religious print in the early republic.[10] And these religious publications were inundated with arguments over Christian history. In the context of religious disestablishment, American ministers such as Daniel Merrill were all the more eager to use the Christian past to justify their own denominational particularity.

This argument over the meaning of Christian history modifies how we understand the "democratization" of Christianity in the early republic. The denominations that flourished in the early nineteenth century may have departed from various Protestant teachings and tradition, but they were by no means ignorant of historiography or disinterested in the Christian past. Rather, as denominations competed in the new religious free market, they repeatedly used Christian history to justify their own theological and ecclesiastical positions. American reading of church history fueled denominational competition, while also encouraging the most optimistic attempt at resolving Protestant disunity: Restorationism. As Protestant Christianity took on particularly American modes of theology, organization, and worship, it did not grow further removed from the Christian past, but more engaged with it. The democratization of American Christianity is the story of the ongoing importance of Christian history.

This Ancient and Primitive Church: Baptist History and the Fight over New England

The story of Daniel Merrill's *Miniature History* illustrates how religious memory contributed to denominational competition. The minister's sermon explained the relevant scriptural texts on baptism, and in the addendum he aimed to go further by showing the historical pedigree of his newly embraced Baptist convictions. Merrill relied primarily on Johann Lorenz von Mosheim's *Ecclesiastical History*, which by no means endorsed Baptist teaching—but much could be inferred. He pointed to Mosheim's line that Baptist origins were "hidden in the *remote depths* of *antiquity*," which he and other credobaptists took as a significant concession on the part of the Lutheran historian. According to Merrill, the *Ecclesiastical History* proved that many medieval sects—the Hussites, Wickliffites, Petrobrussians, and, especially, the Waldensians—had been Baptists in principle.[11] In other words, virtually any group persecuted by the Catholic Church should be considered proto-Baptist. Further evidence was provided by the commentary added by Mosheim's translator, Irish Presbyterian Archibald Maclaine. Maclaine argued not only that the Waldensians had been Baptists, but also that this group existed at least as far back as the fifth century if not "to the apostolic age." In another note, Maclaine asserted that pedobaptism was a novelty of the second century. This was enough for Merrill to argue that the Baptists "have been the uninterrupted church of our Lord from the apostles' day to ours."[12]

After offering a historical defense of Baptists, Merrill went on the offensive. He believed that church history was so clear on the dual errors of pedobaptism and religious establishment that Congregationalists could only persist because of historical amnesia. His own historical study left him "somewhat surprised at my own long continued ignorance, and at the yet remaining darkness of my brethren, as to this matter." Congregationalists and all others who opposed the Baptists, "this ancient and primitive church," should heed the lessons of church history: "All the power, craft and cruelty of the wicked, though practised for nighly one thousand eight hundred years, have not been able to prevail against them."[13]

Merrill's treatise sparked an argument over church history. Congregationalists had been long concerned by Baptist growth in the region, and now their largest church in Maine had been lost. Several prominent Congregationalists took it upon themselves to respond to Merrill—and particularly his proto-Baptist narration of Christian history. The Rev. Samuel Worcester, for one example, preached a series of sermons in 1805 that directly addressed Merrill's argument. A graduate of Dartmouth College, Worcester served as minister at Tabernacle Church in Salem, Massachusetts. He was a Hopkinsian or "New Light" Congregationalist—a theology that grew out of Jonathan Edwards's revivalist teaching and adapted traditional Calvinism in light of Arminian criticisms.[14]

In the published form of these sermons, Worcester's rejoinder to Merrill was both confident and condescending. The Congregational minister challenged the idea that infant baptism was a second-century innovation. He pointed out that the lack of controversy over baptism in these early centuries proved nothing, and cited Clement, Justin Martyr, Irenaeus, Tertullian, Origen, Cyprian, Augustine, and many other church fathers who referenced infant baptism. He then targeted Merrill: "An attempt has been made in some late publications, to make the *unlearned and unstable* believe, that the practice of infant baptism had its rise in the dark ages, under the influence of popery." Worcester insisted that infant baptism was the practice of the apostolic and patristic church, and, indeed, of virtually all Christians until the sixteenth century. He added that Merrill "has him-self been brought to acknowledge" the flawed reasoning in his account of medieval Waldensians and other sects, many of whom practiced infant baptism.[15]

In reply, an outraged Merrill denied the insinuation that he had recanted his historical account, responding instead with a vigorous protest against the Congregationalist minister's "great misrepresentations."[16] Over the next few years, the two ministers continued to debate the history of baptism in a series of back-and-forth pamphlets. In 1807, Merrill published a lengthy reply that listed Worcester's historical mistakes, including the accusation of "pervert[ing] and misrepresent[ing] the ancients" while providing no actual evidence that medieval dissenters practiced infant baptism. Such historical distortions were unsurprising, he fumed, given that "Mr. Worcester is . . . in the cause of Antichrist."[17]

Other local ministers weighed in. Thomas Baldwin, Baptist minister in Cambridge, Massachusetts, took up his pen to defend Merrill's historical writings against the "contempt" of Worcester.[18] Having already exchanged arguments with Merrill, Worcester now traded increasingly heated pamphlets with Baldwin—in response to Baldwin's censure, the Congregationalist pointed out that Merrill had called him and other pedobaptists "anti-christ" over forty times. This back-and-forth argument also centered on the conten-tious history of baptism, with Worcester systematically criticizing Merrill's interpretations of church fathers and medieval dissenters, and Baldwin responding in turn.[19] At the same time, Merrill was engaged in a similar back-and-forth with Samuel Austin, a Yale graduate and Congregational minister in Worcester, Massachusetts. Austin, like Worcester a "New Light" theologian, and the future president of the University of Vermont, published a long refutation of Merrill's historical claims; Merrill replied in a series of letters.[20]

The seriousness of this historical debate is evidenced not only by heated letters and sermons but also by institutional responses. Congregationalists demonstrated their concern when the Massachusetts Missionary Society joined the fray. The Society was founded to plant Congregationalist churches in the face of Baptist growth and now recognized the importance of Christian history for this cause. In 1807, the Society's *Massachusetts Missionary Magazine* devoted space to a five-part series offering a "Brief Survey of Ecclesiastical History"—clearly a response to Merrill's telling of Christian history. In this series, the Society showed its determination not to leave its young ministers unarmed but rather to provide them with historical arguments to use against Baptists.[21]

Many of these arguments amounted to both sides accusing the other of distortion and sloppy reading, but some went further in reflecting on the problems of historical interpretation. Merrill's use of sources was questioned by the Rev. John Field, Congregational minister in Charlemont, Massachusetts. In his 1806 publication, Field pointed out that Merrill relied too much on Archibald Maclaine's commentary while ignoring Mosheim's evidence that the early church practiced infant baptism. Field used historical works by Hannah Adams and the English Baptist theologian John Gill to counter Merrill's claim that medieval dissenters should be understood as proto-Baptists.[22]

Field's work persuaded at least one convert: Jabez Chadwick read Merrill's *Miniature History* in 1806, resigned his post as Congregationalist minister in Genoa, New York, and was rebaptized. Just before he was to be ordained to the Baptist ministry, he read Field's *Strictures* and had second thoughts. In the end, he concluded that Merrill's work, "which had had great influence upon my mind," was highly selective in its use of history and ultimately incorrect. Chadwick turned instead to Presbyterian ministry and used his pulpit to defend pedobaptism, preaching Field's anti-Merrill sermon in his own church and republishing it for readers in Utica, New York.[23]

Such criticisms did not prevent Merrill's work from continuing to surface throughout the 1810s.[24] In 1815, Baptists published the *Miniature History* in New Haven, Connecticut, along with a Baptist catechism.[25] The interdenominational argument over the meaning of Christian history reappeared during debates over state religious establishments and church taxes. In 1818, for example, when the state of Connecticut privatized church tithes,

Baptists and Congregationalists engaged in another round of arguments over church history, with Merrill's writings being reproduced and rebutted in turn.[26]

This historical argument in New England was also the impetus for a landmark work of Baptist historiography. David Benedict, a graduate of Brown University, served for twenty-five years as a Baptist pastor in Rhode Island, and knew well of the local rivalry between his denomination and the establishment. He had read much of the back-and-forth debate over Christian history and, in 1813, decided to bolster Baptist defenses with a *General History of the Baptist Denomination*. The work, abridged and republished multiple times, proved to be one of the most influential denominational histories of the nineteenth century.[27]

Benedict sought to prove the antiquity of the Baptists, but was also keen to illuminate the strength of American religion. Like other historians writing in the early republic—Hannah Adams, William Findley, and Joseph Priestley—he contrasted the nation's religious vitality with the many failures of Christendom, devoting over 140 pages to detailing post-Constantinian decline: the loss of godliness, the growth of erroneous theology and popular superstitions, and the lamentable increase in episcopal power and wealth. Benedict blamed church-state alliance for the violence of medieval Catholicism, especially the crusades and the Spanish Inquisition, a spectacle of violence that, by Benedict's calculations, saw 150,000 people executed for heresy. The story of religious persecution followed the established church from medieval Rome, to the Church of England, to New England Puritans. Baptists in the colonies, Benedict explained, "were often fined, and some of them were banished . . . they were of course denounced obstinate hereticks, and suffered accordingly."[28]

For Benedict, the political and religious achievements of the United States represented the undoing of centuries of intolerance and violence. The great accomplishment of the American Revolution was the blow it dealt to this "system of religious oppression." The experience of war itself, he explained, was "peculiarly auspicious to the cause of religious liberty," and its results could be demonstrated in the post-Revolution growth of Baptist churches.[29] The story of Baptists was the story of religious freedom, and throughout the work Benedict reinforced the connection between Baptist principles and the American experiment. "We have happily arrived at an age," he concluded, "in which the spirit of imposition has lost much of its former force." In this new era of freedom, both the Baptists and the nation would thrive.

Benedict's work remained the standard historical account of the denomination until the 1880s, and was frequently invoked by Baptists on church-state matters.[30]

Sifting the Great Mass of History: Christian History and Baptist Higher Education

If debates with established denominations showed the importance of Christian history for Baptists, this was underscored by the prominence given the subject in new Baptist theological institutions. Baptist higher education received a boost in 1817 when the South Carolinian Richard Furman, first president of the national Triennial Convention, gave a passionate speech advocating for greater investment in ministerial training. His speech, and the plans that followed it, led to the formation of Columbian College in 1821 and, in 1826, the establishment of Furman University, the South's first Baptist college. In the 1817 Plan of Education, which began the process of forming these institutions, Furman advised the convention to prioritize church history as a subject second in importance only to theology.[31] Following Furman's advice, church history was built into the curriculum of many new Baptist institutions of higher education: Mercer College (1833), Western Baptist Theological Institute (1845–53), Southern Baptist Theological Seminary (1859), and others.[32]

The limited resources of these institutions, however, often made this priority difficult to enact. Massachusetts's first Baptist seminary, Newton Theological, was founded in 1825 by Francis Wayland and several other Baptist ministers. The seminary intended to include "Ecclesiastical History" as one of "various studies and exercises appropriate to a theological institution," but initially was only able to employ two professors.[33] When in 1832 the seminary hired James D. Knowles as professor of pastoral duties and sacred rhetoric, the need for a church historian moved to the forefront.

In Knowles's inaugural lecture he explained the urgency of filling this position. "A Professor of Ecclesiastical History seems to be specially needed in a Baptist institution," Knowles explained, "since the principles which distinguish the Baptists require them to sift thoroughly the great mass of history and tradition, and extract from the rubbish the pure truth." He suggested that seminarians study ecclesiastical history in their first year and continue throughout the second and third. The study of the history of Christianity would "unfold the progress of truth, and the rise of error, through the long succession of ages, and will thus exhibit to the student the most important lessons for his encouragement, warning and guidance."[34] In spite of Knowles's advocacy, it would be six years before Newton was able to hire a professor of church history.[35]

Similar convictions were shared by another Baptist professor, George W. Eaton. Eaton studied at Princeton Seminary under Archibald Alexander and Samuel Miller, and in the 1830s was invited to join the faculty of Hamilton Literary and Theological Institution, later Madison University.[36] In 1837, he took the chair of ecclesiastical and civil history, a post he held until 1850.[37] Three years into his professorship, Eaton gave a chapel address titled *Claims of Civil and Ecclesiastical History as Indispensable Branches of Ministerial Education*. Church history, he argued, revealed crucial lessons for the student, not least the waning of apostolic Christianity: "What rueful change, what disastrous reverse came over the scene, and dashed this mantling and victorious enterprise, and brought a night of ages over the brightening prospect? Ecclesiastical history alone will tell him the painful and sickening story." He went on: "While theology exhibits the truths of Christianity, as *doctrines*, ecclesiastical history shows them as *facts*."[38] In terms that echoed Knowles, Eaton concluded that "the history of the early corruptions of Christianity ought to be attentively studied by the religious teacher of the present day."[39]

Professor Eaton also pushed back against those Baptists who believed church history "nothing more than the history of religious error and delusion" and thus irrelevant. While he allowed that "the history of the so-called Christian church, from a period not long subsequent to the apostolic age down to the reformation, is not the history of true Christianity," the study of religious error is "of great practical value to the minister of these times." In fact, church history was all the more crucial in this particular moment. Precisely because the American religious scene was so tumultuous, energetic, and active, Eaton explained, Baptist ministers must learn to discern how Satan undermined genuine Christianity through error and novelty. Baptist ministers needed to study church history, he concluded, to learn how to navigate the many religious changes and confusions of the day.[40]

Church History on the Frontier: Martin Ruter and Methodist Historical Education

In comparison to the Baptists, Methodists during the early republic appear not as concerned with church history's usefulness. Methodists had no argument equivalent to Merrill and the Congregationalists, and they were much more slow to establish institutions of higher education. Nonetheless, leading American Methodists were keenly interested in the history of Christianity, and as the denomination formalized its approach to ministerial education, the study of church history took priority. The Christian past was frequently invoked in defense of Methodist revivalism: Lorenzo Dow, famed Methodist itinerant preacher, appealed to the history of Christianity—particularly the post-Constantinian corruption of the faith—when defending his revival methods against critics.[41] Francis Asbury, founding bishop of the Methodist Episcopal Church in the United States, studied the history of Christianity while itinerating through the backwoods. In several addresses made to Methodist conferences, Asbury narrated the lessons of church history: "I am bold to say that the apostolic order of things was lost in the first century, when Church governments were adulterated and had much corruption attached to them," he lamented. "At the Reformation, the reformers only beat off a part of the rubbish." In his private writings, Asbury revealed his conviction that the best ecclesiastical historiography proved the superiority of the Methodist Episcopal system, and he quoted extensively from Thomas Haweis's history in particular.[42]

Even as Asbury was using Christian history to defend Methodist polity, he was under criticism from some Methodists who strained under his authority. After the establishment of the General Conference in 1792, James O'Kelly led a group of Methodists in separating from Asbury's leadership. These self-identified "Christians," also known as Republican Methodists, rejected any creed but the Bible, excluded "all party and sectarian names," and asserted "the right of private judgment, and the liberty of conscience."[43] One of these Republican Methodists, preacher William Guirey, took up the task of defending their dissenting movement. The best weapon he could find for this defense was Christian history.

In 1799, Guirey published a *History of Episcopacy*, which became a key founding document for the Restoration movement.[44] In his retelling of church history, Guirey argued that congregational authority had been the practice of the primitive church, citing a number of historical authorities to make the case, including Mosheim and the church fathers. The rise of episcopacy, he wrote, produced all the corruptions of medieval Catholicism. When viewed against the backdrop of this history, American Methodism could be seen as a continuation of this corrupt church—Guirey compared Methodist class leaders to monks and "Mr. Asbury's power" to authoritarian medieval popes.[45] In this telling, the Christian movement would undo centuries of spiritual tyranny by returning to the democratic norms of the primitive church. Guirey and O'Kelly eventually split over differences regarding baptism, but they continued to agree on this narration of Christian history.[46] When O'Kelly wrote his own *Apology* in 1829, he repeated Guirey's historical arguments, blaming the rise of the episcopacy for all that had gone wrong in church history.[47]

The defection of Republican Methodists did little to slow the expansion of the Methodist Episcopal Church. But even as Methodists grew at an astonishing rate, they lagged behind in higher education, finally founding their first seminary, the Methodist General Biblical Institute in Concord, New Hampshire, in 1847. Before this, Methodist ministers received training not in the classroom but rather as apprentices.[48] The apprenticeship model was supplemented by the Methodist Book Concern, which published texts to promote literacy and knowledge among its ministers. In 1820, the Methodist General Conference asked the entrepreneurial Martin Ruter to found a branch of the Book Concern in Cincinnati in order to address the urgent educational needs on the frontier.[49]

Born in Massachusetts, the self-educated Ruter established New England's first Methodist school, Wilbraham Wesleyan Academy, in 1818. As the academy's first principal, Ruter taught hundreds who went on to be "the educational missionaries of American Methodism," including two future bishops and the eventual founder of Kansas State University.[50] From New England, Ruter went on to found Augusta College in Kentucky and to serve as president of Allegheny College in Pennsylvania. At each of these institutions, the history of Christianity took priority in the curriculum.[51] Yet Ruter's most important contribution to the historical education of Methodist ministers came during his work with the Methodist Book Concern in Cincinnati.[52] In addition to establishing libraries and teaching literacy, Ruter worked on a number of projects related to church history.[53] He decided to adapt and republish a history of the church written by the Anglican clergyman and scholar George Gregory.

The choice of Gregory's *History*, instead of Mosheim's or Milner's, reveals something of the Methodist's goals. Gregory had written his church history in

1790 to acquaint ordinary Christians with "the rise, progress, establishment, corruption, and reformation" of the faith. He intended to narrate this history in a way that was "clear and distinct."[54] These aims were shared by Ruter, who added only one item to Gregory's list of the most important features of ecclesiastical history: "The spread of the Gospel, and the condition of the Church in different ages . . . are by many very imperfectly understood." Ruter hoped that a short adaptation of this history would "place this important branch of knowledge within the reach of multitudes," and prove useful to "the young and rising generation."[55]

For the most part, Ruter left Gregory's narrative intact while bringing the story up to date with more recent American religious history. Perhaps the most significant change was that Ruter gave much greater detail on the history of Christian missions—an unsurprising choice given that his intended readers were itinerating clergy. Otherwise, the *Concise History* followed Gregory closely, reproducing narratives found in much other eighteenth-century historiography: post-Constantinian decline; the deleterious effect of wealth on the clergy; rising ignorance, superstition, and fanaticism from the fifth century on; and above all the horrors of Roman Catholic persecution and the rise of "that most odious of tyrannies, the Inquisition."[56] These lessons of Christian history were well suited to Methodist ministers itinerating across the frontier.

The *Concise History of the Christian Church* was printed in 1832 in Cincinnati and went on to significantly shape Methodist education, in part because of Ruter's other work. In the early 1830s, Ruter, along with fellow Methodist church historian Charles Elliott, headed a committee charged by the General Conference with planning a "Course of Study" for ministers. The committee recommended a curriculum that, according to Methodist historian Robert D. Clark, was considered so "rigorous—much more so than that generally required in Methodism," that it produced significant backlash.[57] Methodist periodicals printed complaints from readers that the course was too burdensome and required ministers to devote far too much time to reading that should be spent preaching the gospel.[58]

Yet denominational leaders believed historical study was too important to water down. In May 1844, the bishops advised the General Convention to adopt the recommendations of Ruter's committee "for the improvement of our ministry." The bishops expressed their concern that Roman Catholics and High Churchmen alike were tirelessly promoting their own accounts of the Christian past. Renewed study was crucial if Methodists "would contend successfully with the great and growing errors of the age."[59] The Conference followed the committee's recommendations, and for the next fifty years Ruter's account of the Christian past was required reading for all Methodist clergy.[60] The *Concise History* was repeated frequently by Methodist publishers, with editions appearing in 1834, 1839, 1840, 1845, 1849, 1852, 1854, and 1865, sometimes with exam questions appended.[61]

Ruter's *Concise History* took part in a significant shift in Methodist life from the 1840s to the 1880s. These years saw Methodists embrace "settling" clergy rather than itinerancy, double the number of clergy relative to church membership, employ higher rates of full-time clergy versus lay preachers, and turn to formal seminary education.[62] These transformations were fueled both by the institutions Ruter helped establish and by the course of study he developed. Virtually every Methodist minister in the century went on to study Ruter's *Concise History*. By 1890, Methodists employed over fifteen thousand ministers, an audience that made his volume one of the most widely read historical works of the time.[63]

Church History and the Rise of Restorationism

Even as Baptists, Congregationalists, and Methodists grappled with each other in the religious free market of the early republic, some turned away from traditional denominationalism to a promising new movement, Restorationism, or the Christian movement. Restorationists proposed a way out of disunity and rivalry: Protestants needed to shed the vestiges of tradition, renounce all man-made creeds and confessions, and return to the simple teaching and practice of the apostolic church. Early Restorationists believed that the restoration of original Christianity would prove so compelling that Protestants of all stripes would abandon their denominations and unite in one genuine church.[64]

It goes without saying that Restorationism was premised on a particular interpretation of Christian history. But little attention has been given to the historical sources that made this interpretation plausible.[65] The Restorationist emphasis is sometimes treated as disinterest in postapostolic Christianity. Put another way, historians have seemed to assume that Restorationist interests mirrored Restorationist principles—that a movement seeking to divest itself of tradition must have had little or no interest in the Christian past.[66] This distinctly American religious movement appears to exemplify early national neglect of Christian history. In fact, the opposite is the case. From its beginnings, Restorationism was steeped in church history, and its leaders believed the Christian past justified their theological and ecclesial project. They took advantage of dominant narratives of Christian history, articulated their vision in historical terms, and frequently cited church historiography in their criticisms of conventional church polity, creeds, and confessions.

The Christian movement gained steam after the Cane Ridge Revival. In August 1801, Methodist, Presbyterian, and Baptist preachers came together for a weeklong camp revival in Kentucky. Flush with the success of their meetings and increasingly dissatisfied with their denominations, some of these ministers began advocating for the recovery of a simple, denominationless Christianity. Nearly every one of these religious pioneers narrated this transformation in historical terms—just as James O'Kelly and William Guirey had several years earlier. Now similar historical reasoning grounded the declarations of ecclesial independence that followed Cane Ridge.

In 1804, a group of Presbyterian ministers published *An Apology for Renouncing the Jurisdiction of the Synod of Kentucky*. Two of them, Richard McNemar and John Thompson, had been censured by their governing body for departing from the Westminster Confession's articulation of the doctrine of grace. In 1803, McNemar and Thompson, along with Barton W. Stone, chose to form the Springfield Presbytery, a break that marked the beginning of the western Christian Church.[67] In the *Apology*, the ministers justified their departure on historical grounds. They argued that one's authority to preach was merely recognized, not granted, by the church—a distinction confirmed "both by the New Testament, and church history." Anyone familiar with Mosheim's *History* "will see that the practice of the primitive church, in such matters, was exceedingly simple; and according to the principles of common sense."[68] The ministers then compared their current crisis to the Protestant Reformation. Quoting Mosheim, the ministers claimed that they stood in the place of Luther, while the Synod played the part of pope: the Synod members "were of different opinion from Dr. Mosheim, as they have acted on the very same principles with the lordly pontiff."[69] McNemar, Thompson, and Stone charged the Synod of Kentucky with departing from the principles of both the early church and the Reformation.

Similar changes were underfoot in the east. Thomas Campbell, a Presbyterian minister from Ireland who immigrated to Pennsylvania in 1807, was suspended two years later by the synod for his views on the doctrine of grace and church discipline. In his defense, Campbell published a *Declaration and Address of the Christian Association of Washington*, a document that chartered the Campbellite wing of the Restorationist movement. And, like his counterparts in the west, Campbell's apology drew extensively on a particular interpretation of Christian history.

The *Declaration* lamented division among Protestant denominations, calling for a return to "that simple original form of Christianity." To return to the practice of the "primitive church," clear, common-sense principles must be set in place of complicated creeds. "Disentangled from the accruing embarrassments of intervening ages," Thomas Campbell explained, "we may stand with evidence upon the same ground on which the church stood at the beginning." Both creeds and denominations must be abandoned. Although the Reformation had done much good, the resulting Protestant denominations had not rid themselves of "the rubbish of ages." He reminded readers that church history was the story of the long, gradual replacement of the clearly expressed will of God with the authority of "human opinions, and human inventions." These traditions, he concluded, "are, and have been, the immediate, obvious, and universally acknowledged causes, of all the corruptions and divisions that ever have taken place in the church of God."[70]

Having located the Christian movement in church history, Thomas Campbell then used the same history to answer potential criticisms. Without creeds, would not churches fall into heresy or rationalism? No, as creeds and "human complications" had never prevented division among Christians. On this point, he advised readers to study "the history of all the churches." But were not creeds necessary? Only if one believed scripture to be inadequate: "Happy indeed, for the church, that Athenasius [*sic*] arose in the fourth century," he sarcastically wrote, "to perfect what the holy apostles and prophets had left in such a rude and unfinished state." Even if unnecessary, were not creeds helpful? "For the confutation of such an assertion," he concluded, "we would again appeal to church history, and existing facts, and leave the judicious and intelligent christian to determine."[71] This founding document made clear that the story of Christian history necessitated and validated the Christian movement.

Thomas Campbell considered the Christian past important, and throughout his career advised the ministers he worked with to consult Mosheim and other church historians in order to learn the lessons of the Christian past.[72] But his son Alexander was even more interested in Christian history. As a young man wrestling with theology, Alexander

Campbell deeply immersed himself in reading ecclesiastical history.[73] By the 1820s, the results of this study were on display when the younger Campbell publicly debated ministers from other denominations. In his first debate, a disputation with the Presbyterian John Walker over baptism, Campbell centered his case on church history. He defended believer's baptism with a host of historical quotations, claiming the support of Clement, Ignatius, Justin Martyr, Jerome, Bede, Anselm, and, surprisingly, Thomas Aquinas.[74] In his second debate, against another Presbyterian minister, Campbell argued that believer's baptism "had its advocates in every century up to the Christian era." He cited church fathers and councils, noting that "even the greatest enemy, among ecclesiastic historians, Dr. Mosheim," conceded that the origins of credobaptism were "hid in the remote depths of antiquity."[75] In his efforts to defend Restorationism, Campbell found the Christian past particularly useful.[76]

When Alexander embarked on his publishing career, this historical interest found a new outlet, first in the monthly journal *Christian Baptist* (published from 1823 to 1830) and then its replacement, the *Millennial Harbinger* (1830–66), which by the 1850s enjoyed fifteen thousand subscribers.[77] The first volume of the *Christian Baptist* included a piece on church history, featuring long extracts from the histories written by Mosheim and by the evangelical Anglican Thomas Haweis.[78] Alexander quoted these "eminent historians" to demonstrate several important points, particularly how pagan ideas and Jewish religion infiltrated early Christianity and gave rise to all sorts of degradations—the connection between church and state, clerical orders, magnificent church buildings, tithes, and more.[79] For those wanting further evidence of corruption, Alexander advised reading Mosheim, Gibbon, and especially the *History of the Waldenses* by William Jones, a Scottish Baptist who wrote several works advocating Restorationism and criticizing religious establishments.[80]

In a number of his editorials, Campbell reflected on the problems inherent to Christian history. He disliked the most popular historians, Mosheim and Joseph Milner, because of their ongoing commitment to Protestant establishments. At one point, he accused Mosheim of hypocrisy, complaining that the church historian continued in the Lutheran church despite knowing that its polity varied from primitive worship.[81] He advised readers to read William Jones over Mosheim or Milner, because the Scotch Baptist was significantly more critical of medieval Catholicism and more willing to identify dissenters as proto-Protestants. In Jones, readers would encounter that true church which had been "persecuted since Constantine," while "that which has been described by Mosheim and Milner as the church of Christ has been the beastly persecutor of his church."[82] Jones provided a historical pedigree that identified Restorationists with persecuted dissenters throughout time. Yet, despite his preference for Jones, Campbell continued to cite Mosheim in articles over the years.[83] Mosheim—as well as the philosophes Gibbon, Robertson, and Hume—remained useful in illustrating the historical corruption of Christianity, and Campbell encouraged his readers to familiarize themselves with this historiography.[84]

Campbell also saw Christian history as crucial in opposing the pernicious spread of Roman Catholicism. In January 1837, in a public meetinghouse in Cincinnati, Ohio, he took the debate stand against the Roman Catholic bishop John Baptist Purcell. The Irish-born Purcell oversaw a diocese that spanned the state of Ohio and was known for his engaging lectures, newspaper articles, and educational initiatives. Purcell invited Campbell to debate after the latter published his concern that Catholic immigration would allow the pope to take over American schools.[85] Their disputation focused significantly on church history, with Campbell contrasting the pure, persecuted church with corrupt Catholicism, and Purcell answering his charges with quotes from Mosheim, that "Protestant church historian."[86]

Before the debate, Campbell published his historical arguments in the January 1837 issue of the *Millennial Harbinger*. He outlined the view of the Christian past he would wield against Catholicism, while also commenting on the problems inherent in Protestant historiography. He complained that there was not yet "a complete narrative" of genuine Christians throughout history. In fact, the "infidel" Gibbon "has almost, if not altogether, written as satisfactory a history of Christianity" as any traditional Christian historian. Protestant historiography was tainted by rivalries and denominational partisanship, such that no "full and perfect history of our religion" would likely ever appear. "We have no standard, no authentic history of Christianity," Campbell lamented.[87]

These difficulties did not mean the Christian past should be ignored; in fact, the flaws of religious historiography made church history all the more instructive. Campbell advised readers to compare the "primitive Christianity" of the Acts of the Apostles with "the various volumes called ecclesiastic histories" to see both the causes and extent of corruption. Such study was particularly crucial in his moment. Those committed to the Restorationist movement must confront a "historic fact of some importance," namely, that

Christianity was corrupted from within by those who "sought to accommodate its institutions, more or less, to the prejudices and capriciousness of the times."[88] Even as church history presented problems, it remained essential for those working toward the recovery of apostolic Christianity.

With his upcoming debate with Purcell in mind, Campbell added that church history was also and "especially" important for "politics, which stand much in need of that peculiar light which a faithful and complete history of the Christian religion . . . would throw upon them."[89] Why would Campbell assert the political importance of church history when he was about to take the debate stand?[90] Because he believed the Christian past was an essential weapon in defending the Protestant nation against the encroachments of Rome.

The priority given to the history of Christianity by Alexander and Thomas Campbell, Barton Stone, William Guirey, and other early Restorationists belies the view that this movement discarded history and tradition. Indeed, other examples could be given.[91] Although Restorationists aimed at getting behind church history, this necessitated greater attention to the Christian past. In fact, Restorationist uses of history explain part of the movement's success. While other denominations continued to argue over their pedigrees, Restorationists offered a way out of denominational pluralism.[92] By reminding Americans of widely accepted narratives about the Christian past—medieval corruption, theological division, and religious persecution—Restorationists presented their primitivist solution as all the more compelling.

When Daniel Merrill sat down to write a historical defense of the Baptists, he simply hoped to win over his congregation. But his argument went much further. In addition to sparking a debate between Congregationalists and Baptists throughout New England, Merrill's arguments resurfaced wherever Baptists were growing: Baptists in Beaufort, South Carolina, reprinted Merrill against local Presbyterian rivals; Pennsylvania Baptist minister David Jones used Merrill in his arguments against infant baptism; and, in Kentucky, Presbyterian minister John P. Campbell published a systematic critique of Merrill's history.[93] Many more examples could be given. Wherever they competed with pedobaptist denominations—throughout New England, New York, New Jersey, Pennsylvania, Kentucky, and South Carolina—Baptists published arguments about the history of Christianity.[94] In fact, Merrill's history continues to be quoted in Baptist literature today.[95]

His pro-Baptist history remains useful for those looking to locate believer's baptism in the early Christian tradition.

The long debate over Merrill's history exemplifies a previously missed aspect of this vital and dramatic era in American religious history. Since Nathan Hatch's seminal work, historians have treated the process of "democratization" as if it entailed a dismissal of Christian tradition. Religious innovation, it would seem, meant a "hostility to the heavy hand of the past," and the groups most willing to depart from precedent grew most rapidly.[96] But the transformation of American religion in the early republic did not rely on indifference toward history, but rather the opposite. Baptists and Methodists invested significant institutional resources in bolstering the historical knowledge of their ministers. The Restorationists, who appear most adverse to tradition, were highly conversant in and engaged with church history. Others numbered among the "democratizers," including the revivalist Charles Finney and the Shakers, were similarly interested in Christian history and used the Christian past to defend their practices.[97]

As denominations competed for adherents, debated theological differences, and developed new forms of organization and practice, they turned time and time again to the Christian past. Certain historical narratives—especially connections between church establishment, corruption, and the persecution of the true church—helped upstart denominations justify their theological or ecclesiastical differences with older, established churches. Innovative, popular religious groups thrived not because they were disconnected from history or tradition but rather because they creatively resourced preexisting historiographic narratives. The democratization of American Christianity proceeded because it drew on the Christian past.

3

Fulfilling the Past

Teaching the Lessons of Christian History to an Exceptional Nation

For several years the Rev. John Bowden had been increasingly concerned about Catholicism. The Episcopalian priest, who taught moral philosophy at Columbia College, was not new to denominational controversy: he had published a defense of episcopacy against Congregationalist and Presbyterian rivals in New York City. But he never expected to take up his pen against Roman Catholicism "in this country, in which the Protestant religion is so generally diffused, and the Bible in the hands of almost every individual."[1] Yet in 1816 he published *Observations, by a Protestant, on a Profession of Catholic Faith*. In the preface to this systematic refutation of Catholic doctrine, he explained that the work had been provoked in part by the recent restoration of the Jesuits, or Society of Jesus, by the Catholic hierarchy. After a forty-year suppression of the order, Pope Pius reinstated the Jesuits in 1814 with the intention of reinvigorating Catholic education.[2]

Protestants across the North Atlantic world sounded the alarm. Bowden expressed a typical fear in the opening pages of his exposé of Catholic teaching, where he warned Americans that one "method of making proselytes to the church of Rome is, by obtaining the education of Protestants." This was not a hypothetical: Bowden shared his horror at observing "several instances of the perversion of Protestant children," that is, their conversion after having been indoctrinated in Catholic schools. "How," he incredulously asked, "can Protestant parents, who are desirous of preserving their children from absurd and corrupting principles, put them within the contagion of popery?"[3]

Much like Alexander Campbell, Bowden saw Catholic education as posing a significant threat to the future of Protestant America. And just as Campbell would in the 1830s, Bowden turned to church history to rally Protestants against the Catholic advance. Rather unbelievably, he claimed that very few Protestants remembered "the corruptions and superstitions of the church of Rome, in the dark ages." The few who did study church history "read of the

The Old Faith in a New Nation. Paul J. Gutacker, Oxford University Press. © Oxford University Press 2023.
DOI: 10.1093/oso/9780197639146.003.0004

treacheries, the frauds, the rapines, the horrors of imprisonment, the tortures of the rack, the murders, and the malice indulged against the souls and bodies of those called heretics."[4] Drawing on the most popular church histories of the day, Bowden recited a long list of the evils of the medieval church while contrasting Catholic teaching with that of primitive Christianity.[5]

Bowden also reminded readers that the history of Catholicism showed how the religion was incompatible with American values: Rome's doctrine "contradicts the testimony of our sense," her pope enjoys "a most intolerable tyranny over the consciences of men," and her inquisitions are "cruel and merciless to the souls and bodies of those whom she calls heretics." Cherished American ideals, including common sense, freedom of conscience, and freedom of religion, were fundamentally at odds with the principles of Roman Catholicism as demonstrated throughout history.[6] American Protestants, and especially parents, would do well to see the danger and avoid it.

Writing in the "Era of Good Feelings," Bowden's anxiety about Catholicism seems out of place compared to the national mood. After successfully holding off Britain in the War of 1812, the United States entered a period characterized by national cohesion and political unity. The nation's growing self-confidence was matched by its ambitions to spread across the continent, as the Louisiana Purchase set off a period of persistent expansion into the west.[7] In politics, the hierarchies of Revolutionary republicanism began giving way to the populism of Jacksonian democracy, as the franchise expanded to include most white men.[8] The significance of the nation and what it meant to be a citizen were dramatically changing.

A generally patriotic mood went hand in hand with religious optimism. The experiment in religious disestablishment seemed a great success, as the awakenings of the 1810s and 1820s set the nation well on its way to becoming a "righteous empire."[9] There seemed much reason to believe in what historians call American exceptionalism—the conviction that the nation enjoyed a unique, even ultimate, place in divine history.[10] And this swelling confidence was reflected in the formation of national institutions: the American Bible Society in 1816, the American Sunday School Union in 1824, and the American Tract Society in 1825, all aimed at evangelizing Protestant America through educational and literacy efforts.[11] By 1830, Protestants across denominations had left behind their competitive rivalry for what Sam Haselby calls "an enduring religious nationalism" that was pan-evangelical, providentialist, and generally affirming of white superiority.[12]

As Haselby suggests, this era of optimism and cooperation also saw hardening racial and religious lines. Even as white male suffrage expanded in the rise of Jacksonian democracy, Black Americans were increasingly disenfranchised. The new state constitutions ratified in these decades—such as New York's in 1821, and Pennsylvania's in 1838—severely limited or completely excluded Black voters. Such exclusion was justified by racial ideologies and enacted through changing definitions of citizenship and political participation.[13] By the 1830s, it was clear that the promises of the Revolution would not be extended to Black Americans.[14]

It was also uncertain if these promises should be extended to the growing number of Catholic immigrants. Between 1820 and 1860, five million immigrants arrived in the United States, over one-third of whom were Irish Catholic, and another 750,000 German Catholic.[15] For John Bowden and Alexander Campbell, these immigrants and their institutions posed an existential threat to the republic. Many other Protestants agreed: in the mid-1830s, Congress seriously considered extending the period of time required before an immigrant could become a citizen. This was in response to a strong lobbying effort by anti-Catholic nativists. For example, in 1837 nearly one hundred nativists in Washington County, New York, signed a petition to Congress expressing that they "view[ed] with deep concern the great influx of Roman Catholics into this country from the various nations of Europe, and their admission to citizenship while they retain their principles, as eminently threatening our civil and religious liberties."[16] A number of Protestant nativist groups formed with the aim of limiting Catholic political participation.

This narration of the emergence of American religious nationalism is now well established in the historiography. But missing from the story is the role played by religious memory.[17] In fact, the story goes, American exceptionalism was ahistorical: it was encouraged by disregard for European precedent, the sense of American newness, and the embrace of an Enlightenment disdain for tradition.[18] Yet during the Era of Good Feelings and through the presidency of Andrew Jackson, Christian history played an important part in constructing religious nationalism and its cousin, American exceptionalism. The importance of the Christian past is especially evident in Protestant educational efforts. Protestant teachers believed that Christian history was vitally important in the American present, especially so for children and women. Accordingly, they wrote historical textbooks, included religious history in their curricula, and used the history of Christianity to bolster arguments for—and, as Bowden's example shows, sometimes against—the formation of new educational institutions.

This chapter explores how Protestants taught Christian history in ways that encouraged belief in the uniqueness of Protestant America. In one sense these uses of history represent a continuation of the story told in chapter 1. The same historical narratives that, during the Revolutionary and early republic eras, brought about the separation of church and state now deepened the sense of American exceptionalism in the Era of Good Feelings. As young Americans read church history in textbooks, memorized it in Sunday schools, and studied it in women's academies, they were strengthened in their conviction that America was exceptional. Protestant memory of the Christian past grounded the belief that the United States enjoyed a special place in sacred history, and had a providentialist "Manifest Destiny" to spread American religious and political ideals across the continent.[19] But similar historical narratives also provided resources for African Americans seeking to develop their own educational institutions. Educators such as James Forten and Lewis Woodson called Black Americans to emulate early North African church fathers, while Black publications and institutions frequently presented evidence from Christian history for educational advancement and racial equality. Religious memory, in other words, both supported and subverted the construction of the nation as Anglo-Saxon and Protestant.

Children's Textbooks and the Christian Past

In 1822, Susannah Rowson published a two-volume history of Christianity for children, *Biblical Dialogues between a Father and His Family: Comprising Sacred History*. The author and educator had long valued history in general, and religious history in particular: history was prioritized in Boston's Young Ladies Academy, which Rowson founded in 1797, and over the next several decades she wrote textbooks designed to make the study of history more accessible and affordable for women and families. These texts would make Rowson one of the most widely read historical authors in antebellum America—and a number of them dealt extensively with the Christian past.[20]

Rowson's writing on Christian history drew on her study of eighteenth-century historiography, including Hume, Gibbon, and Mosheim.[21] Like Gibbon, and in keeping with her commitment to "republican motherhood," Rowson preferred classical Greece and Rome over the Christian past.[22] And her textbooks reflected these influences, especially in her emphasis on the history of intolerance and religious persecution produced by religious establishments. In her first textbook, the *Abridgement of Universal Geography, together with Sketches of History* (1806), Rowson used both geography and history to critique Roman Catholicism and to document the problems of Christendom. The land itself reflected the irrationality of Catholicism, Rowson wrote, noting that ecclesiastical territory in Italy had been reduced to unfruitful swampland through centuries of "monkish tyranny and indolence." She highlighted Catholic violence against Protestants, especially in the Spanish Inquisition, which she described in detail before assuring readers that "these execrable receptacles of Monkish superstition and bigotted tyranny are in a great measure abolished."[23]

Similar themes returned in Rowson's 1822 work, *Biblical Dialogues between a Father and His Family.* The book drew material from the most popular Protestant church histories of the day—Joseph Milner's *History of the Church of Christ*, along with Mosheim's history—but in the form of a familial conversation. The work aimed to distill the most important lessons of the biblical and Christian past and make them accessible to young readers.[24] Rowson's editorial choices show her priorities. Although a moderate Anglican and regular attendee at Boston's Episcopal Trinity Church, Rowson preferred Gibbon's interpretations of Christendom to those of the evangelical Anglican Milner. For example, Rowson agreed with Gibbon that religious persecution was greater under the "papal government" than it had been under pagan Rome. When Rowson did use material from Milner's *History*, she usually revised it to be less favorable toward the Catholic past, adding more criticism of medieval Christians and more praise of medieval dissenters.[25]

These editorial choices worked to emphasize the achievement of American religious disestablishment. Rowson blamed the loss of primitive Christian purity on Constantine aligning the church with the state, a change that brought the church wealth, power, and, inevitably, corruption. She catechized readers in the long list of medieval degradations that resulted from church-state alliance: the savagery of these "darkest times," the "horrid massacres" and "mutual cruelty" of the crusades, and the "despotic sway" of Catholic clergy. She also traced the legacy of religious intolerance in the American past, lamenting the sectarianism of seventeenth-century Puritans and detailing how "the ignorant and bigotted of each sect, in the blind fury of their zeal, persecuted, reviled, and even plundered each other."[26] The American children who read Rowson's *Biblical Dialogues* learned the value of religious freedom by way of contrast with the corrupt, tyrannical Christian past.

A similar pedagogy was at work in *Letters on Ecclesiastical History*, a two-volume history published in 1832 by the American Sunday School Union. Founded in 1824 as a pan-denominational organization, the ASSU was determined to Christianize the nation through Sunday schools and an expansive publication program.[27] Early on, the ASSU declared that "the objects of this Society are alike interesting to the Christian and the Patriot."[28] In addition to its vigorous efforts to plant Sunday schools around the country, the ASSU published tracts and children's books designed to provide moral instruction, an initiative that was one of the most significant means of religious education in the early republic.[29]

The ASSU sought to unite American Protestants by avoiding denominational particularity, printing only "those plain and simple gospel truths, which are peculiar to NO sect, but of vital importance to ALL."[30] Among these truths were the lessons of church history. The ASSU publication committee took Milner's *History*, shortened the narrative, supplemented it with details from Mosheim, and edited the amalgamation into letters from the fictional Mrs. Lyman to her children. This epistolary form tapped into cultural ideals of maternal religious instruction while also rendering the history accessible to a young audience.[31]

The *Letters* used the Christian past to teach nineteenth-century social and ethical norms, converting church history into lessons appropriate for young readers.[32] Children received instruction in the morals to be learned from the past: keep the Sabbath, remember their prayers, do not neglect scripture reading. How should nineteenth-century American children imitate early Christian martyrs? "Sometimes the young suffer a kind of persecution from their gay companions," Mrs. Lyman ventured, "being the subjects of satirical remarks, and undeserved ridicule. Now this same spirit would teach you to meet this ridicule with a calm and equal temper." Similar applications appeared throughout the *Letters*, with Mrs. Lyman translating history into axiomatic morals. For example, Gregory the Great's care for the poor offered Mrs. Lyman the opportunity to exhort her sons to fair business practices and honest bargaining in "their intercourse with one another."[33] In the ASSU edition, the saints of the Christian past functioned as instructors in nineteenth-century Protestant social and ethical norms.

Even more than Rowson's *Biblical Dialogues*, the ASSU's editorial choices reinterpreted church history in ways that bolstered the Protestant nation. While Milner's original work used Christian history to critique the shortcomings of eighteenth-century Protestant Britain, the ASSU used this history to showcase American exceptionalism, repeatedly comparing the Christian past unfavorably to nineteenth-century American democracy and freedom of religion. For example, the fourth-century Arian controversy "ought to make us grateful that the government of our country has no control over its religion. You, my dear sons, will, I hope, grow up with an abhorrence of any plan or principle which shall lead to a connexion between the church and the government of the country." While Milner used stories of persecution to criticize the apathy of his day, Mrs. Lyman told of horrific martyrdoms to inspire thanks "for our happy government, and that freedom of thought and expression, which is enjoyed by the most obscure member of our republic."[34]

For the ASSU, church history proved the superiority of disestablishment and cultivated patriotic gratitude for the American political and religious system. The ASSU Letters also reoriented the Christian past in a more decidedly anti-Catholic direction, consistently modifying the evangelical Anglican's charitable reading of various Catholic saints.[35] After disparaging medieval piety and devotion, Mrs. Lyman turned to the present, warning her children that Catholicism "may yet prevail to a great extent in the United States, unless the people are enlightened by an early acquaintance with the word of God."[36] If the young reader did not devote herself to Protestantism, the nation might fall back into the dark ages. The ASSU's reconstruction of Milner's History, in other words, mobilized children to defend the Protestant nation against the threat of the Catholic past and, along the way, reversed Milner's direction of critique in order to demonstrate the superiority of Protestant religion.[37]

Suited Both to Their Sex and Education: Christian History and Female Academies

Susanna Rowson's publication career did much to instruct American children in the meaning of Christian history. But she also led the way in promoting the historical education of women. After founding the Young Ladies Academy in 1797, Rowson faced criticism from those who believed that women and men were not intellectual equals. She responded with a vigorous argument that American women needed proper education in order to fulfill their role of raising children into virtuous citizens of the republic.[38] Years later, Rowson insisted that historical study was particularly important for republican mothers, advising young women that this subject imparted a true, rather than romantic or illiberal, knowledge of the world.[39] Rowson's belief in the particular importance of history for women was one she shared with David Hume, whose advice to female readers was reprinted in several early national periodicals: "There is nothing I would recommend more earnestly to my female readers than the study of history, as an occupation, of all others, the best suited both to their sex and education."[40]

Hume would have been pleased with the reading habits of American women. Throughout the early republic and antebellum eras, history was a regular subject in female academies and promoted as an important topic of study for women.[41] Antebellum women devoured history: their journals, letters, and literature abound with historical references and allusions, evidencing, as Nina Baym puts it, "the wide currency of history among women across a range of literacies."[42] Women were not only readers but also writers of history: by one count, American women published over 150 historical narratives between the Revolution and the Civil War.[43]

But women educators differed on which historical works would be most useful for women to read. Susannah Rowson celebrated "Hume, Gibbon, Robinson, and Mrs. M'Cauley" as exemplary British historians, while Mosheim was named as one of the "learned and pious men" of Germany.[44] Similarly, in *The Female Student* (1836), Almira Hart Lincoln Phelps advised reading "Hume, Robertson, and Gibbon" but warned readers of Gibbon's "hostility to the christian religion." Phelps concluded, however, that Gibbon's historical writing posed "little danger [to] any one educated and settled in a religious faith."[45] In 1847, Sarah Josepha Hale would recommend to readers of *Godey's Magazine and Lady's Book* that they read Gibbon and Robertson, but not Hume.[46]

Others preferred a more evangelical account of the Christian past: in 1817, Rebecca Eaton published an abridgement of Joseph Milner's *History*. "An acquaintance with history is highly conducive to the improvement of the mind," the schoolteacher wrote.

If attention to history in general be useful, will not a particular attention to a history of the church be peculiarly so? Will not all, especially the young, delight in . . . looking through the ages of time, and amidst convulsion, devastation, and overthrow, in beholding the rising glory of Zion?

Eaton's work adapted Milner's *History* with the intention of "exciting the attention of young ladies" to church history. She understood that few had the time or money to read Milner's four volumes, and reducing this vast amount of material to an affordable volume would make more accessible this evangelical—and explicitly providential—narration of Christian history. And, for the aid of teachers, Eaton also added "questions for examination" of the reader.[47]

Religious history also featured prominently in women's educational institutions. The first several decades of the nineteenth century saw remarkable growth in educational opportunity for women in the founding of hundreds of academies, or "seminaries."[48] Frequently, these schools prescribed the study of Christian history.[49] Courses of study varied greatly between these institutions, but leading female seminaries, including Ipswich, Byfield, Charleston, and Holyoke, required church history in their curricula.[50] Mt. Holyoke Female Seminary, a premiere institution, prescribed ecclesiastical history in its three-year curriculum through the 1850s, and kept this requirement when in the 1860s it expanded to a four-year course of study.[51] Pioneering educator Mary Lyon assigned ecclesiastical history in the final year of study at Ipswich Female Seminary, where students used John Marsh's *Epitome of General Ecclesiastical History*, a popular abridgement of the histories of Mosheim and Milner.[52] Similarly, a female academy in Jacksonville, Illinois, required ecclesiastical history as a subject for its middle class in its 1845–46 catalog.[53] The institutions preparing American women to be mothers, teachers, and missionaries prioritized the study of the Christian past.

Exactly how the history of Christianity mattered for American women is evident in the writing of Emma Willard, another pioneering educator in this era. As a twenty-year-old, Willard launched an experimental female academy in Vermont; in 1821, after lobbying New York governor De Witt Clinton on behalf of female education, she founded Troy Female Seminary with city funds. In the 1820s, she also began producing geography and history textbooks, first coauthored with William C. Woodbridge and later written on her own.[54] These books enjoyed remarkable popularity, in part because of their innovative use of maps and charts as memory aids.[55] Among Willard's most successful works was her *Universal History*, first published in 1835 and reprinted twenty-four times over the next half century.[56] She began writing it after returning from a grand European tour.[57] Armed with new confidence and a global perspective, Willard told of the rise and fall of kings and empires in a sweeping narrative that combined both liberal and classical strands of republican thought.[58]

Although Willard preferred Greek and Roman history to the history of Christendom, the *Universal History* gave significant space to interpreting the Christian past.[59] The textbook reproduced typical eighteenth-century narratives: "Since the reign of Constantine, Christianity had been rapidly declining from its primitive purity," Willard lamented, "and ambitious men sought, through its medium, to gratify the unhallowed lust of power." She associated the church hierarchy with violence, religious persecution, and political instability, decried the subjection of kings and emperors to bishops, and praised those civil authorities who sought to mitigate clerical influence. Above all, she criticized "popery" as "the wicked ambition of man to hold an unjust sway over his fellow," and a tyranny that turned the Christian religion from a blessing into the "direst curse."[60]

Like Rowson, Willard valued moderation in all things religious, a sensibility in keeping with her adult conversion to an orderly, conservative Episcopalianism.[61] The *Universal History* castigated all who appeared religiously excessive, and throughout the narrative, Willard showed how misguided piety could produce violence, intolerance, and coercion—chiefly seen in the crusades, which she blamed on religious enthusiasm. Willard honored victims of religious persecution as martyrs for the cause of freedom, such as the twelfth-century dissenter Arnold of Brescia, who "advocated the principles of civil liberty" and was first banished and later burned at the stake. She praised the Albigenses, whom the pope persecuted in spite of their "pure and harmless lives," and she commemorated the "ten thousand bleeding corpses of the protestants" killed on St. Bartholomew's Day.[62]

In the *Universal History*, proto-Protestants appeared as proto-republicans. Medieval dissenters reincarnated the greatness of classical Greece and Rome: for example, Willard described medieval Italians who in "remembrance of the glory of their ancestors . . . often burst forth in resistance to the power of the pope." Forerunners of the Protestant Reformation such as John Wycliffe (1330–84), Jan Hus (1369–1415), and Jerome of Prague (1379–1416) appeared as early advocates of liberty, men who "burst from the thralldom of superstition, and asserted their right to freedom of opinion."[63] Willard narrated Europe's escape from the "dark ages" and into the era of "Modern History" by beginning the latter with the discovery of America, "the most important event recorded in profane history."[64] Her narrative conflated Protestant, humanistic, and national progress, as, for

Willard, the expansion of the nation also meant the extension of genuine Christianity.[65]

Willard's textbook, much like Rowson's before her, comprised one of the most important sources of historical knowledge in the early nineteenth century. In these decades, popular histories were frequently written by and for women, who drew on leading European historiography, repackaged their narratives about the Christian past into affordable texts, and published them for use in homes, academies, and Sunday schools. Even as these works reproduced historical material from the standard European historiography, they adapted the narrative not only to their particular audiences, but also in light of the American political and religious context. When they founded academies for women, these educators continued to prioritize the study of Christian history, ensuring that the lessons of the past would be learned by the nation's "republican mothers."

The Enlightened Nations Consider Them Cornerstones: Religious Memory and Black Education

The same year Emma Willard founded a women's academy in Vermont, Jacob Oson gave a lecture in New Haven, Connecticut, titled *A Search for the Truth; or, An Inquiry for the Origin of the African Nation*. Oson addressed an audience of free African Americans, explaining to them the history of Africa with an eye to present-day questions of Black identity and racial equality. He aimed at proving that Africa was neither barbarous nor ignorant by naming a number of the continent's "literary characters": "Divinus, Turtulian [*sic*], Cyprian, Julius, Africanus, Armobius, Saetantins, and St. Austine [or Augustine]." Oson argued that to remember these theological giants as African was at the same time to demonstrate the cultural and religious debt owed to Africa by Europe and America. "These were all of them bishops of the church," Oson argued, "and, therefore, may I not say that the enlightened nations consider some of them as corner stones?"[66] Oson, who went on to be ordained an Episcopalian priest, gave this lecture again in New York City before publishing it with the help of Christopher Rush, bishop in the African Methodist Episcopal Zion Church. *Search for the Truth* would be at the cusp of a flourishing of historical work by African American intellectuals.

As Oson's lecture proved, the history of early Christianity offered resources to African Americans striving for inclusion in a national community that increasingly defined itself as Protestant and white.[67] Just one year before Oson's lecture, the American Colonization Society was founded, an enterprise that, even though supported by some African Americans, also reflected the growing desire among white northerners to create a racially unmixed nation.[68] The national consciousness emerging in these decades only included those who, in the words of Liam Riordan, fit with the values of "respectability, whiteness, partisanship, and evangelical Protestantism."[69] History was involved in this racial exclusion: Anglo-American historical writing was defined by racial ideology and contributed to the construction of the white republic.[70]

But a counterhistoriography was emerging. In the early nineteenth century, African American intellectuals picked up a thread that stretched back to Revolutionary-era abolitionists such as Lemuel Haynes. Haynes, the first Black minister ordained in the United States, helped to birth a "liberation historiography" that contrasted the equality of the early church with the intolerance and inequality of Christendom.[71] Like other classically trained ministers of the day, Haynes knew his eighteenth-century historiography, frequently referencing Voltaire, Hume, Gibbon, and Robertson in his sermons and essays.[72] Haynes used these historians to present slavery as belonging to the worst era in Christian history. By associating racial inequality with post-Constantinian decline, medieval corruption, and the rise of Islam, Haynes cast slavery as incompatible with genuine Christianity.[73] In a context when anti-Constantinian and anti-Catholic assumptions governed American Protestant historical imagination, this was an incisive point, and one that permeated early Black abolitionism—and continues to persist in Black liberation theology today.[74]

In addition to associating slavery with the corrupt Catholic past, African American historians also recovered the ancient African roots of orthodox Christianity. This interpretation belonged to a broader trend of highlighting the classical legacies of ancient Africa. Following the arguments of French historian Comte de Volney, African American intellectuals such as David Walker and Maria Stewart argued that Western civilization began in Egypt rather than Greece or Rome.[75] Other African Americans added a religious dimension to this classicist argument, pointing out that not only Western civilization but also Christianity itself grew out of Africa.[76] These authors noticed the importance of North African theologians and churchmen to the development of Christianity and celebrated them as examples of Africa's intellectual and religious contribution to the world.

For example, in 1789 the Methodist minister and missionary John Marrant pointed to postapostolic Christianity as evidence for racial equality.[77] Marrant, an early abolitionist in Boston, argued that "ancient history will produce some of the Africans who were truly good, wise, and learned men, and as eloquent as any other nation whatever." As examples, Marrant listed a number of North African church fathers: "Tertullian, Cyprian, Origen, Augustine, Chrysostom, Gregory Nazianzan."[78] These leaders of the early church exemplified the intellectual and religious capabilities of Africans and, as such, challenged racial hierarchies. Likewise, in 1792, Prince Hall, the founder of the African American Masonic lodge in Boston, gave a speech. that celebrated Cyprian, Augustine, Fulgentius, and Tertullian as African church fathers.[79] Jacob Oson, in other words, followed the lead of Marrant and others in making a powerful case for Africa's robust religious history—a heritage that influenced European and American theology and church life down to the present.

As nineteenth-century Black educators built their own institutions, they recognized African church fathers as powerful symbols of the promise of education. Among the most influential was the abolitionist James Forten, a stalwart proponent of African American belonging in the nation. Forten was among those wealthy Black Philadelphians who protested the loss of their prior voting rights under the new, explicitly discriminatory state constitution of 1838. He would go on to influence William Lloyd Garrison's anticolonization views and serve as vice president of the American Anti-Slavery Society.[80]

For decades prior to this political disenfranchisement, Forten had already been at work in the establishment of Black religious and educational institutions. In 1817 he joined Richard Allen in forming the African Methodist Episcopal Church; one year later, Forten and other prominent Philadelphians founded a school for African Americans. For their patron they turned to early church history, naming the institution the "Augustine Education Society." As his biographer, Julie Winch, explains, "In the minds of Forten and his friends, St. Augustine united piety, intellectual endeavor, and 'African' achievements. And when it came to finding a suitable speaker to inaugurate their lecture series, they looked to a descendant of Africa who was devoted to both learning and religion."[81]

Similarly, the first Black Masonic lodge in west Pennsylvania was named St. Cyprian Lodge.[82] Augustine's and Cyprian's names appeared often in African American literature, particularly in relation to the question of education and intellectual advancement. The nineteenth century saw Cyprian, in the words of Jared Hickman, become "something like a racial saint" who reappeared at various important moments in Black intellectual life and in African American print culture.[83] *Freedom's Journal*, the first American newspaper owned and operated by African Americans, regularly included articles from a pseudonymous "Cyprian" who urged readers to devote themselves to "the Improvement of the Coloured Population."[84]

African church fathers were also appreciated by Lewis Woodson, an African Methodist Episcopalian minister and educational pioneer. Woodson founded a number of educational institutions, including the African Education Society in Pittsburgh, the African Educational and Benevolent Society in Ohio, and Wilberforce College in Ohio, which in the 1860s became the first college in the country to be owned by Black Americans. For four years, he wrote letters for the *Colored American* urging readers to found Black churches and schools. These letters influenced Martin R. Delany and Henry Highland Garnet to develop a robust African American nationalist and emigrationist tradition, leading one scholar to argue that Woodson should be called "the father of Black nationalism." Tellingly, Woodson wrote all of these letters under the pseudonym "Augustine."[85]

These African American periodicals also featured articles that drew on popular historical narratives—particularly the superiority of the pre-Constantinian church—to bolster their arguments for inclusion in American life. In the 1820s, *Freedom's Journal* published several articles on the history of early Christianity, one of which cited Augustine's *City of God* to prove the religious and cultural debt that Europe owed to ancient Africans.[86] In 1827, John Brown Russwurm, abolitionist and cofounder of *Freedom's Journal*, published a three-part essay on historical change, citing early church history as leading evidence of African intellectual and spiritual capacity.[87] Two years later Russwurm, a supporter of the American Colonization Society, moved to Liberia to help establish colonies for free African Americans.

Similar articles appeared in the *Colored American*, arguably the most influential African American newspaper during its run from 1837 to 1841. Published by prominent Black intellectuals—including Samuel Cornish, Charles Bennett Ray, and James McCune Smith—the *Colored American* enjoyed a national readership and played a pivotal role in uniting abolitionists in the Northeast.[88] The paper's mission was to work toward "the *moral, social* and *political* elevation of the free colored people; and the peaceful emancipation of the slaves," a goal it pursued by disseminating information on African American abolition efforts, educational institutions, and cultural societies.[89]

An early issue of the *Colored American* included an article encouraging African Americans to emulate the intellectual achievements of great saints of the Christian past. "The pinnacle of earthly glory, with all its shining attractions is before them. What Cyprian, Augustine, Origen, Tertullian, and others, in the Church were, colored men may be again."[90] The *Colored American* also used church history to push back on biblically sourced arguments for racial subordination, particularly the notion that Africans were descended from Canaan and thus inheritors of the curse of Ham.[91] In March 1837, an article titled "Prejudice Against Color in the Light of History" noted the self-contradictions of white Christians' arguments for their own racial superiority. The article castigated the "learned man" who in one breath argued for race-based chattel slavery on the basis of the curse of Ham, and in another proudly quoted from Cyprian, Cyril, or Augustine to make a theo- logical argument—even though "they were negroes!" The article complained of white Christian hypocrisy: "Does this learned disciple expect to sit down with them in heaven? And will he continue to speak of their countrymen as being of a degraded caste?"[92]

The final chapters of this study will trace further connections between religious history and Black abolition. But even in the first decades of the nineteenth century, as African Americans wrote race histories, formed educational societies, launched newspapers, and founded schools, they sought resources in the Christian past. Drawing on arguments made by an earlier generation of authors, educators such as James Forten and Lewis Woodson called Black Americans to emulate the religious and intellectual achievements of Augustine, Origen, Tertullian, and other North African church fathers. During the 1810s–1830s, Black publications and institutions frequently presented evidence from Christian history for educational ad- vancement and racial equality.

When John Bowden warned his Protestant readers of the threat posed by Catholic education, he was ahead of his time. By the 1830s, Protestant leaders would pull out the stops in opposing Catholic schools and institutions, pro- ducing what Mark Massa calls "a vast anti-Catholic publishing tradition that flourished . . . at every level of U.S. society."[93] This literature included best- selling sensations such as Rebecca Reed's *Six Months in a Convent* (1835) and the *Awful Disclosures of Maria Monk* (1836).[94] At times, anti-Catholic sentiment turned violent, most famously in the burning of the Ursuline convent in Charlestown, Massachusetts in August 1834. After the convent and school opened in 1827, local Protestants were alarmed by the prospect of young girls, including some Protestants, being indoctrinated by nuns and priests. As rumors spread of abuse in the order, anti-Catholic publications and sermons contributed to the hostile mood in town.

Several of these sermons were preached by Presbyterian minister Lyman Beecher, just returned from Ohio to raise money for Lane Theological Seminary.[95] Beecher wanted to warn Protestants of what he was witnessing in the west. In Cincinnati, where Beecher taught, the Catholic bishop Edward D. Fenwick had opened a Catholic grammar school in 1824, founded a seminary in 1829, started a Catholic college, and launched a weekly Catholic newspaper.[96] Beecher returned east to urge Protestants to step up their investments in education on the frontier. His message was distinctly anti-Catholic. On August 10, he visited three churches in the Boston area, preaching at each on the danger of Protestant children being educated at Catholic institutions. The next evening, a Protestant mob broke into and ransacked the convent before burning its buildings to the ground.[97]

Afterward, Beecher condemned the mob and tried to distance himself from the violence. Yet he doubled down on his main point only a few months later when he published his *Plea for the West*, an extended case that Catholic education and proselytization posed a serious threat to American liberties. Beecher's argument relied thoroughly on church history. Like Bowden before him, Beecher urged Protestants to learn well this history, as it served "to show that [Catholics] always have been hostile to civil and religious liberty." Beecher also echoed Bowden's worry about American Protestant forgetting. He reminded readers of the "deeds of persecution and blood" of the Catholic past and worried that a religion that had been "so enslaving and terrible in its recorded deeds" now appeared "mild, meek, unassuming" because "the records of its history [were] denied, or forgotten."[98] The same church that had gone on crusades and overseen the Inquisition was now seeking to destroy American religious and political liberties.

Beecher's *Plea* shows how much continuity existed between Bowden's 1816 treatise and the nativism of the 1830s. Years before rising immigration fanned anti-Catholicism into flame, the embers of prejudice were kept alive by Protestant historical memory. But if Bowden fretted that Protestants had forgotten the sordid history of Catholicism, he need not have worried. In the decades to follow, educators stayed busy publishing textbooks and assigning curricula that taught young Americans the lessons of the Christian past.[99] As Roman Catholicism spread westward, Protestants became all the more concerned to publish religious histories that purported to demonstrate the incompatibility of Catholicism with American ideals.

Already in the first third of the nineteenth century, the important place given by Protestant educators to anti-Catholic history challenges the notion that the Era of Good Feelings saw a lack of concern with Roman Catholicism.[100] Indeed, an anti-Catholic telling of the Christian past helped Protestants move past the rivalries of the early republic. As new nondenominational groups such as the ASSU took on the task of missionizing the nation, they also published histories of Christianity designed to foster patriotism. These textbooks and pedagogies suggest that anti-Catholicism was a feature, not a bug, of early American nationalism.

Further, the ways in which Protestants remembered the Christian past encouraged American exceptionalism. Against the backdrop of the history of Christianity, the United States appeared as a land where the simplicity of primitive Christianity could be restored, the principles of the Protestant Reformation fulfilled, and the last vestiges of medieval darkness left behind. The historical narratives in American textbooks, scholarly histories, sermons, and popular literature worked together to fortify the belief that the nation was unique in Christian history, lending considerable credibility to claims of America's "Manifest Destiny." Put another way, American exceptionalism derived some of its strength from the stories Americans told themselves about Christian history.

But these historical narratives could push in a variety of political directions. For some white Protestants, church history proved a useful tool in constructing the nation as both Protestant and Anglo-Saxon. Conversely, those on the margins of the imagined national community found an ally in the same church history. African Americans reworked Protestant historiography, using anti-Catholic narratives to criticize race-based slavery and arguing that the early history of Christianity supported their full participation in American religious and political life. From both the center and the periphery, Americans used church history to negotiate the limits and boundaries of national belonging. Religious memory, in other words, worked both to support and to subvert American exceptionalism: the same histories that justified antebellum nativism and violent anti-Catholicism, on the one hand, provided resources for African Americans seeking full participation in the national community, on the other.

4

Protecting the Past

The Troubled Place of History in Protestant Seminaries

For his introductory speech to the students of United Presbyterian
Theological Seminary in Monmouth, Illinois, Professor David R. Kerr chose
the topic "Church History—What It Is—How It Should Be Studied—And for
What Ends." He urged students to devote themselves to this subject. "There
is just now a special reason why Church History should receive more than
ordinary attention," Kerr proclaimed. "There never was a time when it was
so much abused, when its simple narrations were so much perverted, and
when its true and more important uses were so completely overlooked in following fanciful theories and false deductions; and such as seriously threaten
the interests of Protestant Christianity." He warned students to beware of
two "fanciful theories": the "Mercersburg theology" taught by Philip Schaff
and John Williamson Nevin, which appeared to depart from traditional
Reformed views of the sacraments and of church history, and the Oxford
Movement, a group of High Church Anglicans whose writings in the 1830s
and 1840s gave birth to Anglo-Catholicism. These errors could not be countered merely with scripture, Kerr argued, but required careful attention to
church history, which alone could "correct the gross perversions and false
glosses."[1]

One year later, Baptist minister James P. Boyce sounded a similar note in
an address given in Greenville, South Carolina, at Furman University. Boyce
stressed the importance of Baptists educating their own clergy, especially as
other seminaries became enamored with German historiography—a trend
embodied in the work of Philip Schaff. "The history of religious literature and
of Christian scholarship has been a history of Baptist wrongs," he complained.
"Historians who have professed to write the history of the Church have either utterly ignored the presence of those of our faith, or classed them among
fanatics and heretics." In order to defend their principles, Boyce urged, Baptists
must build theological libraries, invest in the study of philology, and train
students to do the difficult work of historical criticism.[2] When, three years

The Old Faith in a New Nation. Paul J. Gutacker, Oxford University Press. © Oxford University Press 2023.
DOI: 10.1093/oso/9780197639146.003.0005

later, Boyce founded Southern Baptist Theological Seminary, he followed his own advice: the curriculum included church history as a foundational course.[3]

These speeches were given at a time when Protestant denominations in the United States had never devoted more resources to seminary education. Religious higher education had proliferated since the early republic: out of the forty colleges and universities established between 1780 and 1829, twenty-nine were denominational, and twenty of these belonged to Presbyterian, Episcopalian, and Congregational churches.[4] Then the Second Great Awakening produced an explosion of growth, so that by 1840 the ministry outpaced legal practice as the chosen profession of graduates.[5] In 1844, thirty-eight seminaries and theological departments were educating approximately 1,500 seminarians.[6] Initially, older denominations dominated: in 1831, 234 students were enrolled in Congregational seminaries, 257 in Presbyterian, 47 in Episcopalian, and 107 in Baptist.[7] But upstart denominations were gaining ground by the middle of the century. In 1859, fifty-one seminaries enjoyed rising enrollment, with Congregationalist seminaries instructing 275 students, Presbyterians 632, Episcopalians 130, Baptists 210, and Methodists 51.[8]

Even while much changed, much remained the same. Seminarians across denominations typically read the same historical works in use since the eighteenth century: Joseph Milner's *History*, the voluminous *Magdeburg Centuries*, and Latin editions of the church fathers.[9] Above all, Mosheim's *Institutes* remained the standard. Episcopalian, Baptist, and Presbyterian educators recommended and assigned Mosheim's history to their young seminarians.[10] Even as Mosheim's Lutheranism consternated many—Quakers, Episcopalians, and Restorationists all published critiques of the *Institutes*—his work remained the standard for the first half of the nineteenth century.[11]

Yet, as Kerr's and Boyce's addresses suggest, by the 1850s new historiographic developments were disturbing the status quo. The immediate cause of these two lectures was the theology emerging from Mercersburg Seminary, where Nevin and Schaff taught. Schaff's writings seemed to undermine traditional Protestant understandings of church history, and both Kerr and Boyce considered his German methods a grave threat to be countered by a renewal of historical education. Ironically, if Schaff provoked his contemporaries to invest more in church history, he has since led scholars to assume that the subject was relatively unimportant in his day. "The denominational and sectarian divisions of American Christianity," Schaff lamented, "seem to be unfavorable to the study and cultivation of general church history, which requires a large-hearted catholic spirit."[12] Subsequent historiography has tended to agree, presenting most Protestant educators as largely uninterested in the Christian past or treating the subject as a precursor to the emergence of the discipline of religious studies.[13]

But church history was an important, if highly contested, subject in American seminaries. During the first half of the nineteenth century seminaries navigated a tension between long-standing Protestant historical narratives and newly emerging historiography, some of which appeared more sympathetic toward the Catholic past. This tension is illustrated in the careers of three professors: Samuel Miller at Princeton Theological Seminary, James Murdock at Andover, and Philip Schaff at Mercersburg and Union Seminaries.[14] Each of these scholars wrestled with teaching Christian history in light of denominational commitments, institutional limitations, and textual questions. At times these controversies spilled over—as when Schaff's theories about church history not only brought accusations of heresy from within his Reformed denomination but also convinced both Baptists and Presbyterians to devote greater resources to teaching church history. Schaff's theories appeared to challenge what might be called "Protestant exceptionalism"—the idea that everything wrong in Christian history was due to Roman Catholic corruptions, while everything good could be traced to Protestant, or proto-Protestant, principles.

The veracity of Protestant exceptionalism as a historical narrative was not a purely academic question. The meaning of the Christian past mattered not only to those ensconced in an ivory tower but also to the many Protestant ministers worried about the changing religious character of the nation—especially in light of the growing presence of Catholic immigrants and institutions. At the very time seminaries increasingly invested resources in historical education, nativist Protestants loudly insisted that the lessons of Christian history proved the incompatibility of Catholicism and American freedoms. Arguments over how to teach church history were at the same time arguments about the future of the Protestant nation.

"Witnesses for the Truth": Samuel Miller and History at Princeton Seminary

Few nineteenth-century professors of church history had a greater influence than Samuel Miller, whose life bridged the early republic and antebellum eras. Miller was taught by Charles Nisbet, good friend of John Witherspoon and Benjamin Rush, and his education bequeathed to him the optimism of the Revolutionary generation. In his most widely read work, *Brief Retrospect of the Eighteenth Century* (1803), Miller reviewed the progress made in "science, arts, and literature" and celebrated "the course of improvement which the human mind has exhibited," including the historiographic achievements begun by Voltaire and continued by Hume and Robertson.[15] But Miller combined this enthusiastic republicanism with a moderate Old School Presbyterianism.[16] He was first and foremost a Presbyterian churchman: before joining Princeton Theological Seminary, Miller pastored the Presbyterian Church in Wall Street, New York City. Miller's devotion to the ministry made it a difficult decision to leave the pastorate to be a professor.[17]

But Miller's experience in New York City also pushed him toward teaching church history. He found himself entering into controversy with local Episcopalians, especially the High Church bishop John Henry Hobart, who argued that clerical authority was derived from bishops who stood in the line of apostolic succession.[18] Hobart's publications provoked Miller, who worried that this Episcopalian interpretation of church history might undermine Presbyterians' confidence in their own polity. Miller wrote a rebuttal that began with the church fathers, drew on the historical works by Mosheim and Gibbon, and made an extensive case for the venerable roots of Presbyterianism. These historians, according to Miller, showed a clear declension from the congregational freedom of the early postapostolic church into later episcopal authoritarianism.[19]

This published debate clearly influenced Miller's interest in teaching church history to his denomination's future leaders.[20] He joined Princeton Theological Seminary upon its formation in 1813 and remained professor there for over three decades. The original faculty was comprised by Miller and Archibald Alexander, who taught an initial class of twenty-four students. To Miller fell the subject of church history, at the time only taught in the second year of study.[21] His inaugural lecture showed Miller's priorities: "Witnesses for the Truth during the Dark Ages." The talk reproduced a typical Protestant narrative of the Middle Ages as a struggle between proto-Protestant dissenters—including the Waldenses, Albigenses, and the fifteenth-century Hussite movement—and a corrupt church establishment. But Miller was not entirely satisfied by the lecture, declining to publish it, according to his biographer, "on the ground that it was hastily written, and that some of its statements would require to be fortified by numerous references and quotations."[22] Twenty years later he felt more confident in the basic argument, employing the "witnesses for the truth" in an essay against critics—both "zealous and high-toned Prelatists" and "some Independents"—who asserted that ruling elders were innovated by John Calvin. In both his 1813 lecture and 1832 essay on the topic, Miller argued that the history of medieval dissent supported the Presbyterian model of church governance.[23]

Much like his view of the "Dark Ages," Miller's approach to teaching church history remained relatively static over his thirty-six years at Princeton. Unenthused with newer historiography, Miller reluctantly relied on the typical eighteenth-century texts. He cautioned young seminarians that Mosheim, as a Lutheran, was "not very friendly to our religion"; Milner, for his part, was not much better—though his plan was pious, he "was still an Episcopalian." Miller concluded that a history "tolerably adapted to the views of a Calvin: of a Presbyterian; [and] well adapted to the use of seminarians, is yet a desideratum in our church!"[24] In the meantime, seminarians might profitably read Mosheim for historical context, and Milner for a sense of the "real spiritual church of Christ."[25]

If Miller gave little attention to developments in historiography, he did reflect on his pedagogical approach, which centered on lectures and student recitation.[26] He told students that his task as professor was "to excite [you] to think" and be able "to state leading facts, rather than the minuter items of history." He believed it crucial for future ministers to study "the opinion and practice of our Fathers in all past ages."[27] This historical study should not be cursory. In one lecture, Miller urged seminarians not to be satisfied with "a careful perusal of the Bible, of some one systematic work on theology . . . and of Mosheim and Milner on Ecclesiastical History," but rather to expend significant time and energy on each of these topics.[28]

In his lectures and notes alike, Miller explained the importance of historical training for future clergy. His opening lecture in the ecclesiastical history class, first given in 1815, argued that studying the Christian past produced greater confidence in divine power. A properly conceived history of Christianity "will always be grateful, instructive and consolatory, to them who live by faith." Even the medieval era proved edifying to the Protestant reader: "To see the church emerge from long depression, break off the yoke of superstition, dispel the thick cloud which enveloped her, and wash away the pollution of ages, gladdens the heart of every friend to truth and happiness." Miller called students to mix appreciation and criticism toward the past: history ought to cultivate gratitude for the sacrifices and martyrdoms of past Christians, while at the same time providing a warning of how the church falls into heresy and corruption.[29]

For Miller, rightly interpreting medieval Christianity was a matter of particular importance. He thought that patristic and medieval theology had little value—except for Augustine of Hippo, whom Miller recommended among the church fathers because he was "in sentiment a Calvinist, [although] for justification he mistakes inherent sanctification."[30] But students could benefit much from understanding the extent and reasons for the corruption of medieval Christianity. Student notes taken in 1821 show how Miller narrated this decline: by the fifth century, "Rites and superstitions increased much. Monkery was extended. This was the source of all the superstitions." According to these notes, Miller believed that both the evangelical Milner and the skeptic Gibbon underestimated the superstition of Roman Catholicism and the piety of medieval dissenters.[31] Learning this declension narrative was essential for the future leaders of the Presbyterian church.

It is difficult to overstate the influence of Miller's teaching over thirty-six years as professor of ecclesiastical history and church government (1813–49). He passed on his vision of the Christian past to hundreds of seminarians— 537 during his first two decades alone. Among his students were prominent theologians and historians, including Charles Hodge, Robert Baird, Francis McFarland, Albert Barnes, and John Williamson Nevin.[32] Many others went on to become Baptist, Reformed, Presbyterian, and Congregational pastors and educators. They, in turn, would diffuse Miller's historical vision through countless sermons, lessons, and lectures.[33]

Essential for an Educated Ministry: James Murdock and History at Andover Seminary

About the same time Miller was penning his response to Bishop Hobart, he was pleased to hear about a newly forming Congregational seminary. He and other Reformed educators, including Timothy Dwight and Charles Hodge, hoped that this new institution would preserve orthodox Calvinism while also taking the lead in serious scholarship and specialized training.[34] At Andover Seminary's opening in 1807, Dwight, then president of Yale College, called the fledgling institution to train future ministers in natural theology, dogmatics, preaching—and church history.[35] The seminary quickly grew, educating 514 students within its first twenty-five years.[36]

Yet the early history of Andover illuminates the difficulties surrounding church history and ministerial training in this era. First and foremost, limited resources were available for the subject, and, in spite of the planned curriculum, for its first decade the seminary lacked a professor of church history.[37] This changed when Moses Brown, a wealthy patron, funded a new professorship of church history in 1819. But the existing faculty of Andover— Ebenezer Porter, Moses Stuart, and Leonard Woods—successfully petitioned Brown to expand the parameters of this position also to include "sacred rhetoric," which they deemed a more urgent need than historical training.[38] Thus began a seven-year-long controversy over the professorship and its first occupant, James Murdock.[39]

Murdock was a Congregational minister who had studied theology with Timothy Dwight at Yale. He possessed a noteworthy talent for ancient languages and was eager to teach history to future Congregationalist ministers through a lecture-based pedagogy that focused "on the formation, history, and contents of both ancient and contemporary creeds."[40] However, Murdock quickly grew frustrated with his colleagues' insistence that he focus on sacred rhetoric, a subject he had little expertise or interest in. Within a year of Murdock's appointment, Porter, Stuart, and Woods recommended he resign.

The struggle continued when, in 1825, proposed curriculum revisions exposed the extent of the faculty's differences when it came to historical pedagogy. On one side, Murdock argued that church history, presently relegated to several public lectures, must be built into the ordinary course of study, given as much time as other subjects, and in fact precede theology. On the other side, Porter, Stuart, and Woods sought to keep church history marginal in the curriculum. Their plan gave church history half of the time designated to sacred rhetoric, and relegated the subject to the summer term of seminarians' final year. Murdock saw this as an attempt to render his teaching irrelevant.[41]

All accounts of this struggle agree that there was a profound degree of distrust between the faculty. But, in addition to personal animus, this contest involved a real question of how and why to study church history. According to his son-in-law, Nathaniel Smith Richardson, an Episcopalian minister and editor of the Church Review, Murdock found popular church histories simplistic and overly apologetic. His commitment to historical exactness, Richardson wrote, could be seen in the marginalia in his personal library: "He rarely read [popular histories]; and when he did, his marginal notes and references showed with what unsparing fidelity he sat in judgment on their loose, unguarded, or perverted narratives." Familiar with developments in German historiography, Murdock appreciated newly emerging "scientific" approaches to historical inquiry even as he continued a "strict Congregationalist" with orthodox theological views.[42] For example, Murdock admired the work of Wilhelm Münscher, a German historian whose work mediated Lutheran orthodoxy and German rationalism, and also English cleric Henry Hart Milman, who wrote a relatively sympathetic account of medieval Christianity.[43]

By contrast, the other faculty worried that church history, if encountered too early, might undermine students' confidence in the very system of theology the seminary existed to preserve. Institutional historian Leonard Woods recounts their position: "It is necessary therefore that all men, particularly the young, should have their minds informed and settled in regard to the doctrines of our religion, by carefully searching the Scriptures themselves, before they can with profit, or even with safety, go through the labyrinth of opinions and controversies found in the history of the church."[44] Or, as Ebenezer Porter warned the trustees, if seminarians studied the Christian past too much they might fall into theological uncertainty or, worse, "blind acquisience [sic] in human authority."[45] In other words, Murdock's colleagues believed that the murky waters of church history should only be navigated by students already confident in their theology.

Students, however, disagreed. In January, 1827, a majority of the seminarians at Andover put their names to a "Memorial" protesting the fact that ecclesiastical history was "nearly ignored in the course of study." According to Murdock's son-in-law this petition was almost unanimously signed by students and evidenced "the position which Dr. Murdock occupied in the Seminary, the strong hold which he had upon the confidence of the students, and the high estimate in which both he and his department were now regarded by them."[46] The petition failed. Andover's trustees sided with Murdock's colleagues, relegated church history to the final year of study, and, by that September, released Murdock.[47]

Andover eventually gave church history a place in the curriculum—but the controversy with Murdock reveals fault lines between seminary education and historical study.[48] The seminary's aim of producing confidently orthodox, Calvinist ministers fit uncomfortably with Murdock's interest in historical complexity. But the professor's work was not done. In his retirement, Murdock went on to translate and abridge works by Mosheim, Münscher, and Milman, and wrote several historical articles, including a refutation of Gibbon's account of early Christianity.[49] In his preface to the Mosheim translation, Murdock noted the "great need of such a work at the present day, when every other branch of theology is much cultivated." He believed that Mosheim's history was "the best adapted to the wants of this country, and the most likely to meet general approbation among the American clergy," and hoped the new translation would provide "the more intelligent and especially the younger clergy, with a comprehensive history of the christian religion and church."[50] Murdock's translation enjoined praise from scholars and preserved Mosheim's place as the standard in many Protestant seminaries.[51]

"The Treasures of Past Centuries": Philip Schaff and History at Mercersburg

No scholar influenced the study of church history in America more than Philip Schaff. Born in Switzerland, Schaff studied in German universities under luminaries F. C. Baur, August Tholuck, David Strauss, and August Neander. In 1843, the German Reformed Church in America invited Schaff to the Professorship of Church History and Biblical Literature at its seminary in Mercersburg, Pennsylvania. After twenty years at Mercersburg, Schaff went on to teach church history at Andover (1862–67) and Union Theological Seminary (1870–93). Other contributions to the guild include his *History of the Apostolic Church* (translated in 1853) and the eight-volume *History of the Christian Church* (1858–90), the edited *Nicene and Post-Nicene Fathers of the Christian Church* (1886–1900), and, in 1888, the founding of the American Society of Church History.

But Schaff's work in America got off to a rocky start. In his inaugural address at Mercersberg, *The Principle of Protestantism*, Schaff argued that American Protestantism needed to reject its antihistorical, sectarian tendencies and recognize its place within the historic church, which had organically developed through time.[52] Schaff's address challenged several typical Protestant narratives, even going so far as to assert that the Protestant Reformation was "the legitimate offspring, the greatest act of the Catholic church." Against those who sought to get behind the medieval era to a pure "primitive" Christianity, he insisted that Catholicism had been one stage in the church's historical development. Further, Protestantism was penultimate, representing only a phase of church history that would eventually give way to a new era of what he called "Protestant Catholicism."[53] Schaff's understanding of church history called Protestants to see themselves as belonging to the entirety of the Christian past.

The speech drew serious criticism. In reply, Schaff sought to further explain his views in a set of lectures published as *What Is Church History? A Vindication of the Idea of Historical Development* (1846). Here he argued that American ministers suffered from a "Spirit of Puritanism" and a "low esteem for history and tradition [that] has itself stiffened long since into as tyrannical a tradition as is to be met with in any other quarter." Schaff explained that American antipathy toward history had been cultivated in the age of revolution, when two impulses, sectarianism and rationalism, gained steam through an "overthrow of all previous History." Both impulses were opposed to church history, and both undermined proper churchliness. Those who sought to build up the church, Schaff taught, must seek "fondly to look after and collect the treasures of past centuries."[54]

Then Schaff explained why it was so important that ministers study church history. First, the history of the church was rightly understood as an "organic development" from Christ's divine revelation.[55] A corollary of this was that knowledge of the "rise and progress of the Church of God in all ages" was necessary in order to understand the present and work toward the future.[56] Schaff believed that a proper conception of the Christian past was immensely practical: it inspired genuine interest in every part of church history; it offered comfort in Christ's ongoing presence with and guidance of his church; it encouraged ministers that their work was not vain; it tended "to overthrow all *narrow party spirit* and *intolerant party zeal*," particularly violent anti-Catholicism; and, most importantly, it contributed to the work of "Christian Union," or the necessary movement of various denominations toward visible unity.[57] For Schaff, the very progress of the church hinged on a proper understanding of the Christian past. Put another way, an objective history of Christianity went hand in hand with the theological truth about the church of Christ.[58]

Schaff's belief in the significance of church history played out not only in his publications but also, and perhaps primarily, in his work as a teacher. After twenty years at Mercersburg, Schaff went on to teach church history at Andover and Union Theological Seminary. In each institution Schaff argued that church history ought to be taught in every year of the curriculum. He offered courses on patristic, medieval, and Reformation church history, introduced the "seminar method" of discussion and research, and taught his students to learn from primary sources rather than rely on later historians.[59] Over five decades, Schaff taught hundreds of seminarians, work he considered central to his vocation as a historian.[60] In fact, his historical writing was driven by a concern to prepare students for ministry. In *History of the Apostolic Church*, Schaff discussed his desire to convert his lectures into a longer church history "for the theoretical and practical benefit especially of ministers and students of theology."[61]

Schaff wanted to see not only increased study of church history, but also study of a different kind. He was particularly bothered that seminaries continued to assign Mosheim's *Institutes* rather than utilizing more recent German historiography, which he had been trained in. He acknowledged Mosheim's achievement—the Lutheran "performed all that it was possible to perform in his time"—but found it absurd that British and American historians continued to rely on an account written in the 1720s.[62] In fact, he suggested that the use of Mosheim was one reason that seminarians found church history uninteresting.[63] According to student notes from 1860, Schaff enjoyed pointing out that Princeton Seminary still used the "dry and undigestible" Mosheim.[64]

Instead, Schaff recommended the work of August Neander, whom he studied with at the University of Berlin. Neander's work encapsulated the themes of German Romanticism, including an appreciation for the particularity of the past, an emphasis on historical context, and a concept of history as organic.[65] Schaff praised the qualities of this historiography: a "spirit of *catholicity*," attention to all eras of church history, "freedom from prejudice," and a "purely *scientific* spirit."[66] He recommended that his mentor's work replace Mosheim in American seminaries.[67] But this took time. Neander's *History of the Planting and Training of the Christian Church* was first translated and published in the United States in 1844, and the *General History of the Christian Religion and Church* in 1849.[68] Schaff wished a scholar would revise Neander's volumes into "a judicious compilation or epitome as a manual for students of theology, [rather] than a literal translation."[69] He continued to recommend Neander into the late 1870s.[70] The eventual acceptance of Neander as the standard text in seminaries marked a turning point in American theological education. If earlier Protestant teachers of church history emphasized the decline of genuine piety after the apostles, Elizabeth

Clark points out, "Those professors whose vision of early Christianity had been shaped by Neander doubted the early church's precipitous drop into darkness."[71]

Antiscriptural and Anti-Protestant: The Controversy over Schaff

Unsurprisingly, this development was not welcomed by all, and Schaff's career was marked by controversy within and without his denomination. After his inaugural *Principle of Protestantism* lecture, Schaff was tried for heresy.[72] Joseph Berg, pastor of First German Reformed Church in Philadelphia and editor of the anti-Catholic publication *Protestant Banner*, brought charges against Schaff. Although acquitted, Schaff's theories provoked sharp criticism from several Presbyterian pastors, including Amasa Converse and George Cheever, who castigated Schaff's portrayal of the medieval church in their reviews.[73] J. J. Janeway, a Presbyterian minister and friend of Samuel Miller and Charles Hodge, also took exception to Schaff's portrayal of the medieval church. Janeway, professor of theology at Western Theological Seminary and eventual vice president of Rutgers, published several works against Schaff's subversion of traditional Protestant historical narratives.[74] Even some of Schaff's students registered their offense: when he assigned in his class at Mercersberg the reading of Counter-Reformational theologian Robert Bellarmine and the Oxford Movement's John Henry Newman, six students withdrew from the seminary in protest of his "Romanizing" pedagogy.[75]

Interestingly, Princeton Seminary's faculty offered a more measured response to Schaff's work. Charles Hodge, who taught Schaff's colleague John Williamson Nevin, disagreed with his protégé's departures from Reformed principles in the newly emerging Mercersburg theology.[76] However, Hodge's review of the *Principle of Protestantism* was far more appreciative than other Presbyterian criticisms. In fact, Hodge agreed with Schaff that the Reformation developed out of late medieval Christianity, and dismissed those who charged Schaff with "Puseyism" or being a closeted Roman Catholic. But he also criticized Schaff for being overly concerned with external unity and, what's more, mistaken about the animating spirit of evangelical denominations; he also expressed doubts about Schaff's view of progress and use of German theology. On the whole, however, Hodge found

Principle of Protestantism praiseworthy, lauding the "evangelical character of the leading doctrines of his book."[77]

As Schaff continued to clarify the principle of organic development in his later works, Protestant scholars expressed varying degrees of disagreement. Joseph Addison Alexander, who occupied the chair of biblical and ecclesiastical history at Princeton Theological Seminary from 1851 to 1859, praised *What Is Church History?* for encouraging "a spirit of historical inquiry," particularly since he agreed with Schaff that the American tendency was "to slight the past and overrate the present." Yet Alexander worried that Schaff's principle of development was suspiciously similar to Newman's theories, and concluded that Schaff's learning was "rather superficially extensive than profound."[78]

When Hodge reviewed the English translation of Schaff's *History of the Apostolic Church*, he concluded that the idea of development included much that "is new, anti-scriptural, and anti-protestant." Yet he also believed that Schaff's theories differed importantly from Nevin's explicitly anti-Protestant, Romanizing theology. Hodge observed a promising trajectory in the *History of the Apostolic Church*, which he recommended to readers as a "noble history [that] reveals only here and there traces of principles which are made offensively prominent in his earlier works."[79]

By the 1850s, Schaff's contributions to the study of church history were clearly evident, and even readers who were staunchly Reformed offered his works qualified praise. The *History of the Christian Church*, for example, was celebrated by the *Bibliotheca Sacra* for its wide-ranging scope and fresh, enthusiastic interpretations, although with a cautionary word about its "Sacramentarian and High-church tendencies."[80] Henry Boynton Smith recommended the same in the *American Theological Review*, arguing that its theories rightly dealt with error and corruption, and, in this regard, surpassed Mosheim's narrative. Smith, who also played a role in introducing German historiography to American scholars, assured his readers that Schaff was "far enough from being a Romanist."[81]

Not all were so sure, however, and Schaff's project became for some Protestants a clarion call for renewed investment in historical study—as evidenced in the opening examples of this chapter. James P. Boyce's speech shows how plans for Baptist theological education were explicitly designed to counter the influence of Schaff. Boyce argued that Baptists needed to invest in graduate study precisely so they might develop an Anglo-Saxon alternative to the errors of German scholarship.[82] Likewise, David R. Kerr argued that Schaff advanced "one of the falsest theories of Church History, that of 'historical development,' a dreamy speculation of the German mind." The worst threat posed by Mercersberg was a retelling of history, which "makes the Romanism of the dark ages, with all its corruptions, a genuine representation of Christianity for the time, and anything there is more excellent in Protestantism, but a higher development of that abominable system!" He warned his students that, via Schaff and the Oxford Movement, the German fallacies "are felt in our own land, and have already well nigh Romanized . . . the German Reformed Church." He urged students that historical study of the Christian past, not scriptural arguments alone, was needed to counter these dangerous trends. It was up to the discipline of history, Kerr argued, "to correct the gross perversions and false glosses" within its own purview.[83]

These responses to Schaff's project demonstrate the threat he posed to Protestant understandings of church history. Such concerns may have been justified—as Clark argues, the German historiography mediated by Schaff led, over time, to scholars reconsidering several age-old Protestant assumptions.[84] This not only caused controversy within his own denomination, but also spurred other denominations to invest in their own study of church history. As his influence spread, Schaff inspired Presbyterians and Baptists in particular to devote resources to the historical training of their ministers, deepening their institutional commitments to an anti-Catholic account of Christian history. In other words, Schaff threatened a historical narrative of Protestant exceptionalism, the notion that the spiritual and social goods of Christianity grew out of Protestant values, while all that was misguided or false was due to Romanist corruption. The importance of Protestant exceptionalism is evidenced by the robust institutional response to scholarship that appeared to undermine it.

"Every Page of the History of That Church": Protestant Clergy and Anti-Catholic Nativism

But this response to Schaff also took place in a shifting demographic and political milieu. To challenge Protestant exceptionalism was to call into question well-established historical narratives that, to many, appeared more relevant than ever before. Already by the 1830s, many Protestant ministers were quite concerned with the growing presence of Catholic immigrants and institutions.[85] If Samuel Miller began his professorial career concerned by Episcopalians, two decades later he was much more worried about a different threat. In 1834, Miller hastily penned an introduction to an anti-Catholic *History of Popery*—a book he confessed that he had not time to fully read—and stressed the urgency of its content: the Catholic Church in America was at that very moment being "strengthened by large emigrations from the old world." He warned Protestants to arm themselves with scripture and history. "He who brings the corruptions of the Papacy to the test of God's unerring word, and presents a dispassionate and unvarnished history of their rise, progress, and practical influence," Miller promised, "cannot fail of convincing candid and intelligent minds of their pestiferous character."[86]

One of Samuel Miller's students, Robert Baird, shared these concerns. In his landmark work *Religion in America*, Baird worried about the rising numbers of Catholic immigrants and the growth of parochial education: "Of all forms of error in the United States, Romanism is by far the most formidable, because of the number of its adherents, the organization, wealth, influence, and worldly and unscrupulous policy of its hierarchy."[87] Like his mentor, Baird believed that church history provided resources to combat Catholicism. In 1845, he published *The Life of Ramon Monsalvatge*, a narrative of a Spanish monk who converted to Protestantism. In the preface to this conversion narrative, Baird contrasted Catholic "bigotry, ignorance, and ferociousness" with the light of "this Protestant country." He then rehearsed the typical historical episodes that proved the corruption of the Catholic Church: the violence of the Inquisition, the martyrdom and persecutions of countless Protestants, and the "Black Legend" of Spanish cruelty in the Americas.[88]

Baird and Miller were not alone in using Christian history to raise concern about Catholicism. By the mid-1830s, the Christian past was a regular feature of anti-Catholic polemics. The same year that Lyman Beecher published his *Plea for the West*, another well-known Protestant produced a book warning Americans of the quickly growing Catholic threat: Samuel F. B. Morse, famed artist and inventor. One year after the burning of the Ursuline convent in Charlestown, Massachusetts, Morse's birthplace, he published *Foreign Conspiracy against the Liberties of the United States*. The book argued that the Catholic hierarchy, in alliance with Austria, was plotting to colonize America's west through a tide of immigration and Jesuit-led Catholic education. Morse did not rest with words alone: in 1835 he helped found the Native

American Democratic Association, and the next year stood as the nativist candidate for mayor of New York City.[89]

Morse's argument in *Foreign Conspiracy* shows the connections between church history and political activism, as he relied significantly on historical arguments to galvanize Protestant opposition to Catholic immigration. In fact, Americans whose friendly experiences with Catholics led them to believe the religion was tolerant were, according to Morse, historically naive: "No one can be deceived by evidence so partial and circumscribed, while the blood of the persecuted for opinion's sake, stains with the deepest tinge every page of the history of that church."[90] These horrors of medieval Catholicism were alive and well, as the methods of the "dark ages"—chains, soldiers, and Inquisition—were still in use in Austria. In a creative retelling of national history, Morse urged Americans to remember how their ancestors, the Puritans, fled from "Popish usurpation" to enjoy their religious rights in the new land. Morse implored his readers not to become the generation that saw America's hard-won liberties undone by the reestablishment of Catholic tyranny.[91]

Tellingly, Morse's anti-Catholic screed was endorsed by prominent Protestant leaders. *Foreign Conspiracy* was prefaced by a letter from ministers from four denominations—the Episcopalian James Milnor, the Presbyterian Thomas De Witt, the Methodist Nathan Bangs, and the Baptist Jonathan Going—each of whom recommended the book. In their recommendation the ministers clarified that although they "disapprove of harsh, denunciatory language toward Roman Catholics, their past history" meant that Americans ought to be "jealous of their influence, and to watch with unremitted care all their movements in relation to our free institutions."[92] It was a shared Protestant memory of the Catholic past, in other words, that justified anti-Catholic nativism.

Other Protestant ministers agreed that historical memory was politically important. In 1836, William Craig Brownlee published *Popery, an Enemy to Civil and Religious Liberty; and Dangerous to Our Republic*. A Scottish-born clergyman who taught ancient languages at Rutgers College, Brownlee also served in Associate Presbyterian and Dutch Reformed churches. And he was a tireless opponent of Roman Catholicism: the same year that he wrote *Popery*, one of his several anti-Catholic publications, Brownlee founded the American Society to Promote the Principles of the Protestant Reformation. He wrote *Popery* to warn America's men about the army "annually pouring in upon us," made up of "prelates, priests, monks, nuns, and hundreds of thousands of the very offscourings of the European Catholic population!"[93]

Like Morse and Beecher, Brownlee grounded his nativism on religious history.[94] Over two hundred pages Brownlee narrated the history of Catholicism as a story of persecution, violence, and oppression. He spared no rhetorical expense, recounting "agonies, and moanings, and shrieks of the oppressed" during the Spanish Inquisition, which, he told, "cost Spain in all TWO MILLIONS OF LIVES!" The history of Christianity proved that Catholic principles were incompatible with republicanism and religious freedom. What was more, Rome was particularly interested in keeping people from knowing about their sordid past: the histories written by Locke, Milton, Mosheim, and Robertson, he claimed, had all been banned by the Catholic hierarchy. The modern Catholic Church, Brownlee concluded, was "the same evil, as in the Dark Ages."[95]

Brownlee's rhetoric was too strong for some—one reviewer conceded that the book was "hot and impetuous." But even so, this anonymous critic writing in the *Christian Review* appreciated the argument Brownlee was making and used the book review as a launching point to discuss a number of questions surrounding American religious freedom and the dangers posed by corrupt Christianity. Again, religious history grounded the reviewer's anti-Catholicism: he contrasted the genuine religion that flourished in America with "the mixed Christianity that began its career at an early period in the history of the church" and came to its full fruition in "the intolerance of edicts . . . bloody persecutions . . . sacrifice[s] to the incensed spirit of bigotry."[96] In other words, even those who disliked the pitch of anti-Catholic rhetoric agreed with the historical justification for anti-Catholic concern.

These anti-Catholic uses of history fueled the nativism that eventually culminated in the Know Nothing Party of the 1850s. In the face of rising immigration and growing Catholic institutions, American Protestants found reasons in Christian history to limit Catholic participation in national life. The nativism that emerged by the 1830s was not merely a matter of popular prejudice or salacious literature, but was encouraged and propagated by serious Protestant historiography. While anti-Catholicism was driven by economic, ethnic, and gender-based concerns, the history of Christianity also played a significant role in the Protestant ministerial class's crusade against Rome.[97] Religious memory made anti-Catholic fears more believable, bolstered the informal establishment of Protestantism, and constructed the boundaries of Protestant national identity.

Whether in the halls of Andover Seminary, on the frontier in Ohio, or among German Reformed ministers in Philadelphia, the pages of church history proved a battleground. Baptist, Reformed, Congregational, and Presbyterian educators alike worried about historiographic developments that appeared to undermine Protestant exceptionalism. As a growing Catholic population built churches and schools, these ministers pointed to the Christian past to demonstrate the incompatibility of Catholicism and American liberty. From the 1830s on, anti-Catholic historical narratives were central to nativist arguments against Catholic voters and institutions. According to leading Protestants, anti-Catholicism was not paranoid or prejudiced, but, in light of the history of Christianity, eminently reasonable. The ministers who worked to make evangelical Protestantism an informal establishment had been educated in an anti-Catholic, defensively Protestant historiographic tradition. In turn, they passed this Protestant exceptionalism on to ordinary churchgoers who imbibed history over the course of many hundreds of sermons.[98]

The need to maintain Protestant exceptionalism explains why the teaching of church history was controversial. Samuel Miller's concern with historical sources, the interpersonal conflict over the place of church history in the Andover curriculum, and the controversy sparked by Schaff's historiography that inspired "more than ordinary attention" to the Christian past, all centered on the question of Protestant exceptionalism. For some educators, historical complexity undermined denominational claims; others rejected theories of historical development as ultimately un-Protestant. By these lights, the next generation of clergy needed just enough church history to maintain their Protestant convictions. Antebellum historians who challenged this approach, particularly Schaff, only served to encourage the institutionalization of anti-Catholic historiography—at least in the short term.

5

Rewriting the Past

How Women Recovered Their Place in Christian History

Already the author of several books, Sarah Josepha Hale published her most ambitious literary project to date in 1853: *Woman's Record; or, Sketches of All Distinguished Women, from "The Beginning" until A.D. 1850.* The poet, novelist, and longtime editor of *Godey's Lady's Book* aimed at presenting the lives of women throughout recorded time and, along the way, to offer her own interpretation of Christian history.[1] "Wherever this Gospel was made known, women were found ready to receive it," Hale explained. "Queens became the nursing mothers of the true Church, and lovely maidens martyrs for its truth." Beginning with Constantine's mother, Helena, Europe's queens and princesses converted their countries by converting their husbands, sons, and fathers. "It was the influence of women," she concluded, "that changed the worship of the greater part of Europe from Paganism to Christianity."[2] While many histories of the Christian past left women out, in Hale's telling, church history became a triumphal narrative of the world-changing power of female domestic piety. Christ's promise to build his church had been fulfilled by its many "nursing mothers."

Woman's Record emerged during a debate over the meaning of Christian history for women. This was a rather new question: prior to the mid-1830s, historians both male and female tended to pay little attention to the women of the Christian past. While Hannah Adams, Susannah Rowson, and Emma Willard produced innovative accounts of Christian history, these rarely focused on their own sex. This changed in 1835, when Lydia Maria Child published a history of women that offered a new and influential interpretation of their place in the story of Christianity. Child's narrative was picked up by leading activists in the women's rights movement, such as Sarah Moore Grimké, Lucretia Mott, and Margaret Fuller, who used her history to bolster their arguments for women's equality. At the same time, advocates of women's domesticity took up the same historical narratives and represented them in books that cast female saints as exemplars of women's proper calling.

The Old Faith in a New Nation. Paul J. Gutacker, Oxford University Press. © Oxford University Press 2023.
DOI: 10.1093/oso/9780197639146.003.0006

Hale also had read Child and wanted to make her own contribution. She opposed sexual equality—historian Ann Douglas called her the "chief exponent of the doctrine of the feminine sphere"—but as a widow who raised five children, she also staunchly advocated for female education, women's advancement, and married women's property rights.[3] She first made her living by writing poetry and short stories, breaking through in 1827 with a bestselling novel, *Northwood*. One year later, she founded *Ladies Magazine*, which proved so successful that in 1837 it was purchased by publisher Louis Antoine Godey simply so he could acquire Hale's editorial services. Over the next forty years, her editorship made *Godey's Lady's Book* one of the most influential periodicals in the United States. Hale published authors as wide-ranging as Lydia Sigourney, Nathaniel Hawthorne, Oliver Wendell Holmes, and Washington Irving.[4]

Since childhood, Hale had loved history, and she considered historical study particularly crucial for women's advancement.[5] In 1847, *Godey's* published a serial "Course of Reading" that explained what women should study and why. "After a systematic reading of the Bible," Hale advised, "we would recommend that of the history of our religion." Hale suggested a long list of religious histories, including Henry Hart Milman's *History of Christianity*, Robert Baird's *View of Religions in America*, and Gibbon and Robertson among eighteenth-century historians. Women needed to study these to "be able to compare the past with the present and judge of the improvement of the world since the days when woman was a born serf to her 'lord.'"[6]

But while there were many histories to recommend, including a growing number of books on the women of Christian history, by the early 1850s Hale concluded that none "contains the true idea of woman's nature and mission." *Woman's Record* meant to fill the gap. It would contribute to women's advancement by clearly showing "what God intended woman should do; what she has done; and what farther advantages are needed to fit her to perform well her part." She explained this design: women were to be "the preserver of infancy, the teacher of childhood, the inspirer or helper of man's moral nature in its efforts to reach after spiritual things."[7] Over nearly nine hundred pages, *Woman's Record* illustrated this vocation, while also making a case for the symbiotic relationship between Christianity and women. "Wherever the Bible is *read*, female talents are cultivated and esteemed," Hale concluded. Christianity promoted women; in turn, women spread Christianity.[8]

Hale offered commentary on the meaning of Christian history, often contrasting the faithfulness of women with men's failures. While early Christian women spread the "simple teaching and believing" of apostolic faith, Hale wrote, "truth was perverted by selfish men." She was particularly critical of clerical celibacy and monasticism, developments that downgraded marriage and contributed to the subjugation of women. Hale's own experience of impoverished widowhood gave an edge to her critique of Catholic teaching on celibacy.[9] But if medieval Catholicism departed from Christianity's progressive liberation of women, the Protestant Reformation recovered it.[10] In other words, she not only argued that Christianity encouraged the education and advancement of women, but also that women's domesticity was at the heart of Christianity's progress. And through an array of female saints, readers saw that their work as mothers, sisters, and wives would also prove central to the unfolding of Christian history.[11]

Hale's *Woman's Record* belongs to a mid-century wave of interest in the women of Christian history.[12] If historians in the 1810s and 1820s left women out of their accounts of the Christian past, the next generation gave them increasing attention. By the 1850s, scholars, biographers, and ministers alike recognized that women played no small role in the history of Christianity, even as they disputed the implications of this past. This was largely due to women who recovered the importance of their sex in Christian history, women like Hale and Child, who produced diverging historical narratives that would contribute to the expansion and contestation of women's advancement and rights. The story of mid-century women rewriting the Christian past sheds light on the relationship between female authorship and conventions of female domesticity and piety.[13] When women wrote history, they subverted the boundaries between private and public spheres.[14] And the lines between private and public were nowhere blurrier than in the pages of church history.

"Perhaps More Conspicuous": The Missing Women of Christian History

As chapter 3 explained, in the early republic, history was considered an important subject for American women. Women with varying degrees of literacy read history widely, as evidenced by many historical references and allusions in their journals, letters, and literature.[15] Women were not only readers but also writers of history: Mary Kelley counts over 150 historical narratives written by women in the early national and antebellum eras.[16] And the history of Christianity was of particular interest. Female academies prioritized religious history in their curricula, and educators promoted church history as a highly important subject for women.[17]

But when women read the leading accounts of the Christian past, they encountered few examples of their sex.[18] Almost no women appeared in Johann Lorenz von Mosheim's history, and the Lutheran historian had little to say about the role of women in the early church—other than a complaint that women made up many of those who considered learning "injurious and even destructive to true piety and godliness," and thus contributed to early Christian anti-intellectualism.[19] Edward Gibbon, who preferred the masculine virtues of ancient Rome over Christian piety, was even more disparaging: he noted the importance of "female devotion" to the rise of the faith, while closely associating effeminacy with the luxury and weakness that undermined the Roman Empire and lamenting the loss of "manly virtues" in the church as monasticism rose.[20]

The Anglican evangelical Joseph Milner made a more promising start in his introduction, in which he explained that "the female sex, almost excluded from civil history, will appear perhaps more conspicuous in ecclesiastical. Less immersed in secular concerns, and less haughty and independent in spirit, they seem, in all ages, to have had their full proportion, or more than the other sex, of the grace of the gospel."[21] If Milner's intention was to highlight the women of Christian history, however, this ideal went unrealized in the volumes that followed. Blandina and Perpetua, early Christian martyrs, received extended treatment from Milner, but he otherwise neglected women except for a passing mention of notable relatives of church fathers: Augustine's mother Monica; Marcellina, sister of Ambrose; and Macrina the Elder, grandmother of Gregory of Nyssa and Basil the Great.[22]

Some American editors of Milner tried to correct his neglect. When Milner's *History* was revised for female readers in the early nineteenth century, women appeared more prominently. Schoolteacher Rebecca Eaton, who adapted Milner's church history to "excit[e] the attention of young ladies," made several adjustments in order to emphasize female piety. She noted that under Roman persecution Christian women "distinguished themselves by a patient course of suffering." The patience and fortitude of martyrs such as Blandina represented a "Christian triumph." Eaton also went beyond Milner's passing notice of the female relatives of church fathers, describing

Monica, Marcellina, Macrina the Elder, and John Chrysostom's mother as the primary influences on these pillars of early Christianity.[23] Women also stood out in the American Sunday School Union's adaptation of Milner's *History* printed in 1832. As a series of letters from the fictional "Mrs. Lyman" to her sons, the ASSU's church history tapped into cultural ideals of maternal religious instruction while also making Milner accessible to a young audience.[24] Along with emphasizing young piety in figures such as Origen and Ephraim the Syrian, the *Letters* paid attention to examples of godly motherhood, particularly Monica.[25]

However, if male historians in the eighteenth century largely ignored the women of Christian history, women writing history in the early republic, including those whose histories were discussed in chapters 1 and 3, did little to remedy this. While Hannah Adams paved the way for other women historians with her influential *View of Religions*, she gave virtually no attention to questions of gender or women in religious history. A similar neglect characterizes the work of Susanna Rowson, one of the most widely read historians in the first half of the nineteenth century. Rowson believed that women needed to read history in order to fulfill their role as "republican mothers"—educating their children to be virtuous citizens.[26] Her 1811 work, *A Present for Young Ladies*, included a number of biographical sketches of historically significant women. But these "exemplary women" included none before the sixteenth century except for Hypatia, the fifth-century pagan scholar who was murdered by a Christian mob.[27]

By the early 1800s, Rowson had abandoned her early conviction that women should participate in the political sphere, concluding instead that the right of woman was simply "in all domestic matters to preside."[28] The boundary between public politics and private domesticity was especially clear in the pages of history: Rowson believed that republican mothers needed to know the past, but the past they learned was a story of great men. This was also true of Christian history. When Rowson published a two-volume history of Christianity, *Biblical Dialogues between a Father and His Family: Comprising Sacred History* (1822), she left women out almost entirely. This adaptation of Milner's and Mosheim's history, designed for family reading, focused on male theologians, church leaders, emperors, and reformers.

Likewise, the women of Christian history hardly appeared in Emma Willard's *System of Universal History, in Perspective*.[29] After returning from Europe in 1830, Willard, head of Troy Female Seminary, wrote the *Universal History*, a textbook that went on to be reprinted twenty-four times.[30] When it came to the history of Christianity, Willard was less interested in tracing women throughout the story than she was in offering an account of the progress of religious freedom.[31] Like other historiography of the day, Willard's widely read work overlooked women in the Christian past.

"The Influence of a Believing Queen": Lydia Maria Child's *History of the Condition of Women*

The same year that Willard produced the *Universal History*, another publication made significant strides in recovering the women of the Christian past: Lydia Maria Child's *History of the Condition of Women, in Various Ages and Nations*. The daughter of a Congregationalist minister, as a young woman Child rejected her father's strict Calvinism. She studied at a female academy before continuing her education under the tutelage of her older brother, Convers Francis, a Harvard-educated Unitarian minister who introduced her to Ralph Waldo Emerson, Henry David Thoreau, and Margaret Fuller. After experimenting with Swedenborgianism in her twenties, Child converted to Unitarianism and, with the encouragement of Boston's literati, began work as a journalist and author. By the early 1830s she enjoyed fame as a novelist, poet, and editor of a popular bimonthly, *Juvenile Miscellany*. When her strong abolitionist stances led to the closing of the *Juvenile Miscellany* because of canceled subscriptions, Child turned her attention to writing a history of women.[32] The book was a remarkable synthesis of classics, church histories, encyclopedias, and the latest European scholarship.[33] In it, Child described the customs and treatment of women from ancient through modern times, while offering considerable commentary on Christianity and the female sex.

In her *History*, Child argued that early Christianity helped women by challenging "diseased" Roman gender relations and marriage practices. She noted the difference that Christianity made for wealthy Roman women, who, after converting to the faith, abandoned "the seductive allurements of worldly pleasure" and devoted themselves to lives of service to the poor and sick. And she highlighted the role Christian women played in the early medieval conversion of pagan countries. In fact, Child argued that the Christianization of European nations was largely due to the spiritual sensitivity of women: "It is an undoubted fact that most nations were brought into

Christianity by the influence of a believing queen."[34] This was a historical point Child gleaned from an 1809 essay by Henry Card, an English cleric and author of several historical works. Card noted that after the fall of Rome, Christianity in Europe "was almost uniformly introduced by the female sex," adding that "most nations are indebted for their conversion to the charms of a believing queen." His essay was reproduced in the *American Review of History and Politics*, and the similarities between Card's wording and Child's make clear that she read it. But in Child's work this historical point would go much further.[35]

If the successes of early Christianity were due to its women, many of the unfortunate developments in medieval Europe could be blamed on sexual inequality. For example, Child criticized the ways in which the feudal system subjugated women and left them vulnerable to abuse: "There was a vast amount of ignorance, degradation, corruption, and tyranny," Child wrote, "as there ever must be where one portion of the human family are allowed unrestrained power over the other." She was particularly critical of the elevation of celibacy, lamenting that "a life closely secluded from [female] society was deemed the surest road to heaven," and critically describing various saints' "abhorrence of women."[36] While acknowledging that medieval convents provided women with education, Child portrayed religious orders as institutionalizing unnatural gender relations. In rhetoric that echoed other anti-Catholic literature of the day, Child described priests using their access to nunneries to do that "which might have been expected from people bound by unnatural vows."[37] In Child's telling, Catholic mistreatment of women, and especially the hypocrisy and abuse produced by clerical celibacy, set the stage for reform.

In turn, the Protestant Reformation represented significant gains for women. Child was by no means a proponent of traditional Protestant doctrines, so her account of the Reformation stressed intellectual and cultural changes rather than theological developments.[38] Child celebrated the Renaissance as a force for gender equality: early modern women "preached in public, supported controversies, published and defended theses, filled the chairs of philosophy and law, harangued the popes in Latin, wrote Greek, and read Hebrew." The progress of women was driven by the twin forces of print technology and the Protestant emphasis on reading scripture. She concluded that Protestant countries, which had a "tendency toward a universal dissemination of knowledge," were noted for their well-educated women.[39]

"The Destiny of the Sex": Child's *History* and the Women's Rights Movement

The History of the Condition of Women did not make any explicit argument for women's rights, but rather narrated the past in a way that associated the advancement of women with genuine Christianity. For the most part, Child avoided comment on present-day concerns, a decision that reflected her disinterest in taking a leading role in the emerging woman's movement. While her work frequently challenged gender stereotypes, Child's writing and activism alike focused more on slavery than women's rights.[40] Nonetheless, the *History* associated the elevation of women with the purity of the apostolic church, while conflating gender inequality, ecclesiastical authoritarianism, and Roman Catholic superstition. This was a narrative that tapped into longstanding American Protestant memories of the Christian past. And unlike previous historians—Adams, Rowson, and Willard—Child's narrative placed women in the center of the story of Christianity.

But some found Child's reticence disappointing. In her review, Sarah Josepha Hale complained that Child's *History* included a "vast amount of information" but rather less than desired in terms of "philosophy of history." Hale wanted more commentary, more explanation of historical cause and effect, and more clear and distinct comparisons "between the character of women, in different ages, and among different nations instituted." Above all, she worried that Child failed to properly emphasize "the great and blessed influence which the Christian religion has exercised on the condition of the female sex." These criticisms made, Hale still recommended Child's *History*, which "possesses much merit, and deserves a place in every 'Ladies' family Library."[41]

Other readers saw that Child had filled a significant historiographic gap, and a number of women used the *History* as a source for their arguments for women's rights.[42] Years later, Elizabeth Cady Stanton and Susan B. Anthony maintained that Child's *History* "was the first American storehouse of information upon the whole question, and undoubtedly increased the agitation."[43] The importance of Child's book was immediately evident. In 1836, Almira Phelps, the former vice principal of Troy Female Seminary, borrowed from Child's account in her defense of female education. She explained to readers that church history demonstrated that Christianity resulted in an "improvement in the condition of women." The teaching of Christ, Phelps concluded, freed women from being "servile" and the "property of man."

Since the dawn of Christianity, "Our sex have been honoured wherever the name of the Redeemer is worshipped. Many, like Lois and Eunice . . . have been honoured instruments of promoting the cause of true religion, and their praise has been heard in the churches."[44]

Similarly, Child's *History* influenced Sarah Moore Grimké, the outspoken abolitionist and women's rights activist. In her 1838 *Letters on the Equality of the Sexes*, Grimké frequently cited Child, reproduced her accounts of Renaissance women, and quoted her on Christianity's influence on marriage.[45] Repeatedly throughout the *Letters*, the Quaker Grimké distinguished corrupt "traditions of men" from the practices of the primitive church, which offered women a much greater degree of dignity and equality. "We learn also from ecclesiastical history," Grimké argued, "that female ministers suffered martyrdom in the early ages of the Christian church." She went on: "If women were permitted to be ministers of the gospel, as they unquestionably were in the primitive ages of the Christian church, it would interfere materially with the present organized system of spiritual power and ecclesiastical authority, which is now vested solely in the hands of men."[46] Grimké borrowed historical arguments from Child and connected this history to present-day concerns.

Another leading intellectual in the women's movement, the Transcendentalist literary critic Margaret Fuller, also drew on Child's *History*.[47] Fuller's landmark feminist work, *Woman in the Nineteenth Century* (1845), reproduced Child's description of the progress of Christianity and noted that "the empresses who embraced the cross, converted sons and husbands." Fuller agreed with Child that Christianity had a remarkable influence on the elevation of women, particularly emphasizing the importance of the doctrine of Mary as the mother of Christ. The Madonna brought about

> an immediate influence on the destiny of the sex. . . . Whole calendars of female saints, heroic dames of chivalry, binding the emblem of faith on the heart of the best-beloved, and wasting the bloom of youth in separation and loneliness, for the sake of duties they thought it religion to assume, with innumerable forms of poesy, trace their lineage to this one.

According to Fuller, Europe was transformed by Mary's example and by Christian teachings, especially the doctrine that "women are in themselves possessors of and possessed by immortal souls," a crucial philosophical development in the history of women, and a principle that "undoubtedly received a greater outward stability from the belief of the church that the earthly parent of the Saviour of souls was a woman."[48] Fuller's point was well received by a reviewer in the *Southern Quarterly*, who concluded that "the introduction of the worship of the Virgin Mary and the female saints and martyrs, must, necessarily have tended to elevate man's opinion of the gentler sex, of whom, these objects of adoration were such bright exemplars."[49]

Likewise, Quaker minister and activist Lucretia Mott drew on Christian history to argue for women's rights. In a number of sermons, Mott argued that history offered evidence of women ministers well into the third or fourth centuries; she believed that the historical record showed women subjected to male authority only after the development of "priestcraft" and the rise of a Christian establishment. In one sermon given in 1849, Mott argued that the history of Christianity showed how scripture could be twisted to support dogma, superstition, priestcraft, and church-state alliances. The Christian past, Mott preached, showed the Bible being used "to prove the rightfulness of war and slavery, and of crushing woman's powers, the assumption of authority over her [and] all the evils under which . . . humanity has groaned from age to age."[50] While Mott did not directly quote Child's *History*, its narratives are implicit throughout the Quaker's sermons. And the two women were friends and allies in the abolitionist cause. In 1839, Mott and Child were elected together to the executive committee of the Anti-Slavery Society—an election that was the occasion for the society's split.

In the hands of Grimké, Fuller, and Mott, Child's account of women in the Christian past became a strong point in favor of women's equality. As women's rights coalesced in the late 1840s and early 1850s, the platform of the national movement reflected Child's historical narrative. Beginning with the Seneca Falls Convention in 1848, and in other national conventions in the early 1850s, women networked across state lines to advocate for legal and economic equality, property rights, and suffrage.[51] These conventions frequently were resourced by the historical accounts of Christianity written by women. For example, Seneca Falls' famous *Declaration of Sentiments* drew heavily on the religious arguments made by Grimké, which, in turn, drew on Child's *History*.[52] And the history of Christianity took center stage at the National Women's Rights Convention in 1854, when Mott answered a critic with a historical distinction made by Child: "It is not Christianity, but priestcraft that has subjected woman as we find her. The Church and State have been united, and it is well for us to see it so."[53] Mott associated gender inequality not with scripture but rather with the corruptions and intolerance of medieval Catholicism, turning widely shared understandings of Christian history into arguments for women's rights.

"Patterns of Genuine Wives and Mothers": Domestic Hagiography and the Christian Past

At the same time women's rights activists began employing church history in their cause, a growing body of literature used the Christian past to encourage women to live out their domestic role. Authors increasingly noticed and celebrated the female relatives of influential Christian men—and none more than Monica, the mother of Augustine of Hippo, whose piety was famously chronicled in her son's classic text, *Confessions*.[54] For some time Monica had enjoyed a reputation among American preachers. She was a favorite subject of Puritan ministers Increase and Cotton Mather, who in several sermons set her forth as the embodiment of the virtuous woman.[55] The revivalist George Whitefield advised godly parents to imitate Monica and "pray and still hope for the Conversion of their Children."[56] By the nineteenth century, Monica had become a kind of patron saint for evangelical mothers. Her story was told and retold widely: in the United States and England nearly fifty articles on Monica were published in religious periodicals from 1800 to 1860.[57]

Early in the nineteenth century, Monica appeared to be the exception, as few other women appeared in literature on the Christian past. A new trend began in the 1830s and accelerated throughout the 1840s and 1850s, as, across the North Atlantic and in a variety of genres, the female saints of the Christian past became more prominent. At the same time that the international women's rights movement was emerging, historians, educators, ministers, and popular authors gave unprecedented attention to the women of the Christian past, elevating examples of godly motherhood to encourage women in their callings.[58]

Female saints began to populate the latest ecclesiastical histories from Europe. Unlike prior church historians, German professor August Neander dealt with women in his scholarly work, histories that eventually replaced Mosheim's *Institutes* as the standard ecclesiastical history text in American higher education.[59] In Neander's *History of the Planting and Training of the Christian Church*, written in 1832 and published in the United States in 1844, the German historian noted that "many eminent men in all ages who have been great blessings to the Church, have been indebted to their pious mothers" for their early religion.[60] Neander's emphasis on the importance of maternal guidance in Christian history was in part autobiographical, as his own mother had a profound influence on his young religious life.[61] This point was expanded upon in Neander's *General History of the Christian Religion and Church*, which appeared in 1829 and went into its first US edition in 1849. Neander argued that the spread of Christianity was due in large measure to the devotion and witness of its women. "Pious Christian females, presenting patterns of genuine wives and mothers," he wrote, contrasted notably with the depravity and luxury of pagan women. He went on to produce examples of women's religious influence on important church fathers: Nonna on her husband Gregory and son Gregory of Nazianzus, Anthusa on her son John Chrysostom, and Monica, who influenced not only her son Augustine but also her pagan husband.[62]

As these "patterns of genuine wives and mothers" appeared in cutting-edge historiography, they also proliferated in popular print. An 1849 pamphlet printed by the American Tract Society instructed Christian women to compare the state of "females of Turkey, of India, and of our Western wilderness" to their own position. "For the females of Christendom the Son of God has done every thing. He has called you forth from obscurity, and lifted you up from degradation." The tract then explained women's role in this sacred history: "Pious women have always done much in the kingdom of Christ. . . . Indeed, in every age, the progress of the Gospel has been essentially aided by their pious and devoted labors."[63] In other words, according to the ATS, women spread Christianity, and in turn the faith elevated women. Protestant Christianity and women's advancement went hand in hand.[64]

American Protestant ministers also drew attention to female saints. In 1852, Jesse Ames Spencer edited a volume of *The Women of Early Christianity; a Series of Portraits*. Spencer worked as book researcher for the General Protestant Episcopal Sunday School Union, and for this project he recruited notable clergymen such as Episcopal bishop W. Ingraham Kip and Presbyterian minister W. B. Sprague to contribute chapters. These chapters, each preceded by "original designs engraved expressly for this work," focused on seventeen holy women, including Helena, Monica, Bertha, Hilda of Whitby, and Felicity, the second-century martyr who was much celebrated in Protestant histories and whose engraving is reprinted on the cover of this book.[65]

Spencer was aware that such a project might raise concerns among some Protestants, and in his introduction he expressed his own doubts about the historicity of these women's lives and the "legendary character of most of what is preserved." He apologized that the collection included women as late as the seventh and eleventh centuries, worried that the inclusion of medieval women might offend "the sensitive feelings of Protestant readers."[66] But Protestants would have no qualms about Monica, whose chapter in the volume was written by Rev. William Adams, a Presbyterian minister in New York City and future president of Union Theological Seminary. Adams recounted the familiar story of "this holy woman," whose "ceaseless prayer" was "Oh God, convert my son." After telling of Augustine's conversion, the happy years mother and son spent together, and Augustine's grief after her death, Adams came to his conclusion: "Let no Christian mother despair, however unpromising or profligate her child," he wrote, "while the example of Monica . . . shines in its clear radiance to teach the impressive lesson of faith, fidelity and prayer."[67]

Adams was not the only one to connect Monica's story with the mid-century trope of young men sowing their wild oats. America's growing cities, and above all New York City, appeared as dens of sin where young and impressionable men lost their virtue and their faith.[68] The *New York Evangelist* addressed these fears in a piece titled "The Absent Son," which told Monica's and Augustine's story to encourage Christian parents concerned with the specter of rising urbanization. Parents should remain hopeful even "when they send forth their sons to encounter the sharp temptations of life," remembering that "Monica thought Rome the worst of all places on earth for her son." Yet it was in that "guilty city" that Augustine encountered Christ and became "that eminent defender of truth."[69] Similarly, "The Mother's Cares," an 1856 piece first printed in the *German Reformed Messenger* and reprinted in the *New York Observer and Chronicle*, urged anxious mothers whose children were "ill, or absent, or in danger" to follow the "well known" example of Monica and devote themselves to fervent prayer.[70] In a rapidly changing society, parents worried for their wayward children should imitate Monica's faithfulness and trust God's providence.

Monica also served as a useful example of the importance of domestic religion. An article in the *German Reformed Messenger* titled "The Christian Home" (1856) encouraged Christian parents to emulate the "teaching and prayers of [Augustine's] mother Monica," comparing her to the parents of George Washington and John Quincy Adams.[71] Others stressed the importance of female domesticity for husbands, and pointed to Monica's trials with a pagan spouse. Joseph Parrish Thompson, Congregationalist minister in

New York City, celebrated Monica in a series of lectures on Christian virtues. In his discussion of patience, Thompson noted that the Christian woman more often embodies this virtue, as "her sphere gives more occasion for the passive virtues than for active and noisy heroism." Monica endured "in her own household the most bitter trials," particularly in a pagan husband who "would not only annoy her by all manner of heathen orgies in the house, but being a man of most violent temper, would turn upon her the fury of his passion." Thompson lauded Monica's forbearance: "But through all this Monica was so gentle, so kind, so meek, so patient, so faithful, that at length she softened the tiger to a lamb." His depiction of Monica's patience was reproduced in religious periodicals.[72]

The sentimental appeal of Monica's story earned her inclusion in mid-century collections of women's biographies on both sides of the Atlantic. She enjoyed her own chapters in Jabez Burns's *Mothers of the Wise and Good* (1846) and William King Tweedie's *The Early Choice: A Book for Daughters* (1855), each a widely read work of advice literature.[73] While many of these hagiographies were written by men, the stories of Monica, Macrina, and other female saints also spread throughout a growing network of female readers and authors.[74] Sarah Stickney Ellis celebrated Monica in her bestselling *Mothers of Great Men* (1859),[75] while Lydia Huntley Sigourney opened with Monica in *Examples of Life and Death* (1852), a book that epitomized the "domestication of death" in nineteenth-century sentimental literature.[76] "If any anxious and pious mother, agonized by the wanderings of a beloved child, should be ready to sink in despair," Sigourney wrote, "let her remember the perils, and the rescue of the son of Monica."[77]

Feminine Christ: Lydia Maria Child's *Progress of Religious Ideas*

This literature, which I call domestic hagiography, rarely went beyond offering examples. While these authors and works gave unprecedented attention to the female saints of the past and offered commentary on the meaning of Christian history for women, they did not produce a new narrative of the Christian past. This would be left to Lydia Maria Child, who, twenty years after her groundbreaking *History of the Condition of Women*, produced a three-volume opus, *The Progress of Religious Ideas, through Successive Ages* (1855). Child disliked how Christian historiography portrayed other religions and aimed "to show that *theology* is not *religion*; with the hope that I might help to break down partition walls."[78] While she believed in the superiority of Christ's teachings, Child intended to emphasize commonalities and promote religious tolerance. The result was an account of Christian history that excoriated formal theology and religious hierarchy alike.

Throughout the work, Child's dislike of theology drove her narrative. She argued that Constantine's conversion meant a "rapid degeneracy" due to growing clerical wealth and power.[79] Not long after the alliance between church and empire, Christians found themselves violently persecuting harmless pagans as well as any Christian sect that varied from imperial doctrine. She described fourth- and fifth-century controversies over Christian doctrine as meaningless "scenes of outrage," lamented that Arians and Athanasians fought over "such abstract questions," and speculated that bishops on both sides had been "influenced, more or less unconsciously, by ambition to win a game where the patronage of emperors was the prize." On the Trinitarian and Christological controversies, Child concluded that "nothing did so much injury to Christianity, as the numerous sectarian contests." Perhaps the worst example of Christian persecution was the murder of Hypatia. Child had mentioned Hypatia in her 1835 work but not described her death; now, she held up Hypatia as an example of Christian intolerance and anti-intellectualism, particularly pointing out that the emperor Theodosius refused to punish the murderers.[80]

Child's *Progress of Religious Ideas* associated all that she considered oppressive—slaveholding, intolerance, sexual asceticism—with religious authoritarianism and the codification of Christian theology. Such an interpretation belonged to a longer Protestant tradition, and Child's reading of Christian history was indebted to the eighteenth-century declension narratives written by Gibbon and Priestley. But if Child's primary concern was to challenge Christian dogma, along the way she made several arguments about women. In fact, she gave the typical narrative of decline a gendered twist: those most to blame were male professionals—priests, theologians, and monks—while the success of genuine Christianity was largely due to female piety and activism.

As in her earlier work, Child pointed out the mutual connection between women's advancement and the best aspects of Christianity. She noted the central role played by women in the growth of early Christianity: women "formed so large a proportion of the converts, that the most common sarcasm of the Pagans was that Christian assemblies were filled with women and slaves." Her pages were filled with those converted or influenced by mothers, sisters, or wives, including Macrina, Anthusa, and Monica. Like many others writing in the 1850s, Child could not resist sharing Monica's tale in all its detail.[81]

Child found plenty to criticize in Christianity's history with women, especially the rise of monasticism and the idealization of celibacy, which she blamed on long-standing Jewish and Eastern associations between the material world, evil, and femininity.[82] But she also argued that basic Christian teachings, particularly the affirmation of spiritual equality, represented a vast improvement for women. Importantly, this teaching was not the invention of male theologians, Child argued, but rather a response to female agency: "By proving such efficient missionaries with husbands, sons, and brothers, women acquired an importance in the church, which they had never possessed in connection with the old worship. There was *spiritual* equality between slaves and patricians, between men and women." Spiritual egalitarianism, in turn, "ennobled" and transformed marriage into a partnership of companions.[83]

After hundreds of pages detailing the greed, rivalry, and authoritarianism of men throughout Christian history, Child closed her three volumes with an ode to the selfless ministry of Jesus. She approvingly quoted a friend's description of Christ as "gentle, affectionate, and feminine" in his spirituality. Child believed this truth about Christ had been borne out in church history: "The gentle and compassionate character of Christ was peculiarly attractive to the feminine nature," Child concluded, and "therefore, the number of proselytes was always much greater among women than among men."[84] By focusing on Christ's teaching, Child argued that the essence of Christianity was a timeless, feminine spirituality that should be freed from the husks of tradition and custom.

Surprisingly, reviews of *Progress of Religious Ideas* largely ignored Child's gender as well as the gendered elements of her argument. Instead, reviewers focused their concern on her atheological treatment of Christianity. The *Boston Recorder*, for example, appreciated the "immense amount of curious and valuable information" on various religious systems, yet registered the reviewer's apprehension that Child did not think it necessary to commit to one religion.[85] The *New York Evangelist* lamented that Child treated Christianity as "simply a higher expression of the [human] religious sentiment," reducing the faith to Christ's "spirit of love" while leaving behind doctrines such as the incarnation, atonement, and Trinity.[86] The *Christian*

Register worried that although "educated and reflecting" readers would benefit from Child's work, "another class however, might get evil instead of good, might be led by such painful exhibitions of Christian superstition to suppose the religion they deform to be no better than any human invention."[87]

One reviewer who highlighted Child's conclusion still missed its gendered implication. John A. Gurley, a Universalist pastor and editor of the Cincinnati newspaper *Star in the West*, worried that Child's history "will prove a source of much injury to the cause of Christianity, by multiplying skeptics, especially among her own sex." Gurley insisted that genuine Christianity had nothing to do with the corrupt traditions that Child traced. "Romanism and Calvinism are not Christianity," Gurley explained. "Here is where Mrs. Child mistakes. Human creeds, filled with the omnipotent wrath of God, and endless hell torments, are *not* Christianity. To find Christianity we must find Christ. Christ, the gentle, the lowly, the compassionate." Child, of course, had described Christ in these terms and named them feminine—a point that Gurley failed to notice even as he worried about Child's account damaging the faithful hope of pious women.[88]

Child was not the only woman whose work was misread by contemporary reviewers. Hale's *Woman's Record*, which opened this chapter, intended to show the importance of education, opportunity, and advancement for women. But if Hale hoped to show the historical significance of her sex, male reviewers read her book as proof of their own superiority. The *Evening Post* took its review of *Woman's Record* as an opportunity to belittle women: "From the creation to the present day . . . the 5,857 years which have passed have only bequeathed to us 2,500 distinguished women—less than half a distinguished woman per annum." The review suggested that many of the women included hardly deserved such commendation, pointed out that even the "most brilliant . . . are sadly behind their masculine rivals," and speculated that a work that compiled every distinguished man since creation would make the woman's record appear a trifle.[89]

Other reviews were more positive in their assessment, but stressed that this was because *Woman's Record* would help bolster opposition to the growing women's rights movement. For example, the *North American Review* criticized the proportions of *Woman's Record*, but praised Hale for having "too much good sense to advocate the movement for emancipating the sex from all the restraints, whether of legal enactments or of fashionable garments, which are now imposed upon them."[90] In a generally positive treatment of the work, *Southern Quarterly Review* assured men that it "may well be read with satisfaction by thousands, who, while giving the sex their full hearts, are rather slow to accord it the right of suffrage."[91] Hale's work, according to these men, made a case against and not for the equality of the sexes.

Even if misunderstood, Hale's and Child's respective publications show how much had changed by the 1850s. The most prominent historians writing in the early republic, both male and female, had largely ignored the role of women in the Christian past. As notions of women's superior spirituality gained cultural currency, this began to change, in large part because women historians wrote their sex into Christian history. From 1835 to 1855, women adapted and reprinted European historiography, revised narratives of the Christian past in their own historical writing, used female Christian saints for their own purposes, and produced innovative reinterpretations of church history. At the same time, leading historians and Protestant ministers increasingly highlighted the importance of women throughout the history of Christianity. While women authors were not solely responsible for this shift, they drove the historiographic recovery of women's place in the long Christian past.

This recovery worked in several directions. On the one hand, it played a key role in the women's rights movement, as activists such as Sarah Moore Grimké, Lucretia Mott, and Margaret Fuller appealed to the Christian past as offering evidence of women's intellectual and spiritual equality. On the other hand, advocates of women's domesticity used the same historical narratives to encourage women to be godly wives and mothers. By attributing the progress of Christianity to the devotion of Christian women, these works promoted female domesticity while at the same time problematizing a stark divide between the public and private spheres.[92] If, as Hale put it, women were "the nursing mothers of the true Church," then one could not tell the history of Western civilization without them.

6

Liberating the Past

Christian History in the Debate over Slavery

Like other abolitionists in the 1840s, James W. C. Pennington wrote with a sense of urgency: "I must start with the question, who and whence are the colored people?" With this he opened the *Text Book of the Origin and History of Colored People*, offering an answer to this "vexed and vexing question," and, along the way, a historical challenge to race-based slavery. Pennington knew the necessity of this history in 1841. The abolition movement had been growing since the early 1830s, and, in response, defenders of slavery were doubling down on their insistence that the institution was both biblically and historically justified. As the inheritors of the biblical "curse of Ham," so the proslavery argument went, persons of African descent were destined to serve—or, as Pennington summed it up, Black men and women were "enslaved because they are fit only for slaves."[1]

Pennington knew of what he wrote. Born on a plantation in Maryland, Pennington was enslaved until 1827, when, as a nineteen-year-old, he left behind eleven siblings and his parents to seek his freedom. Escaping to Pennsylvania, the fugitive Pennington was taken in by Quakers, who taught him to read and write and encouraged his love of learning. After moving to Brooklyn, New York, Pennington educated himself in his spare time, learning Greek and Latin with the help of tutors. He found spiritual community in a Presbyterian church, as well as a growing sense of a call to ordained ministry.[2]

But when Pennington applied to Yale Divinity School, where he planned to pursue both his education and his ministerial call, he was turned down. Yale informed him that he could only attend if he sat in the back, remained silent, and did not participate as a student. So the undaunted Pennington audited courses instead. He became a proficient reader of several languages, was ordained a minister, and gave himself to a number of activist causes: he helped found the Union Missionary Society, lectured on the abolition circuit, and served as a delegate to an international antislavery conference in

The Old Faith in a New Nation. Paul J. Gutacker, Oxford University Press. © Oxford University Press 2023.
DOI: 10.1093/oso/9780197639146.003.0007

London. He wrote several important antislavery works, including his widely read autobiography, *The Fugitive Blacksmith* (1849).

It was in Connecticut, while working as a newly installed minister at a Congregational church, that Pennington decided to write and publish his *Text Book*. He aimed to narrate Black experience throughout sacred history, while constructing a powerful historical case that slavery was incompatible with genuine Christianity. Pennington's work was motivated in part to undo the damage done to African Americans by racialized arguments: "I have met with not a few colored persons who held historical views as prejudicial to the truth in our case as the whites do." To counter this, he addressed head on the "curse of Ham" argument, tracing biblical genealogies and parsing Greek and Hebrew to disprove the theory.[3]

Pennington then traced the historical development of African enslavement, coming to a powerful conclusion: "Slavery is an institution of the *dark age!*" He explained that African slavery in the New World began under the emperor Charles V: "This great patron of the mother of abomination; this stoutest of the co-workers with the Pope of Rome, in his persecution of Luther and the reformers," Pennington wrote, "*was also the first patron and patriarch of the institution which is so peculiar at the south.*" He explained that Spanish colonizers, the first to practice slavery in the New World, enslaved natives until "the bishop of Chiapa," Bartolomé de las Casas, suggested to Charles V that they enslave Africans instead. And thus "The Africans took the place of the aborigines in the institution of slavery."[4] Pennington saw much meaning in this origin of the transatlantic slave trade. He made its significance clear:

> Have the apologists for slavery ever thought of this? They are apologizing for the dark age. Have the ministers of the sacred office at the south, who interpret the Bible in support of slavery, ever thought that they are preaching a doctrine first invented by a bishop of the Romish church!? Let this point then, stand in bold relief to the view of the world. And let it be fairly understood that the American slaveholder and his apologists are patrons of *Rome* and the *dark age!*[5]

It was an incisive historical point. Pennington's history associated chattel slavery with that which was anathema to American Protestants, while implying that the Protestant Reformation and abolition efforts were one and the same movement of Christian freedom.

Pennington's book was not the only antebellum work to pose this provocative question: what was the standing of slavery in the history of Christianity? As the abolition movement gained steam, this question and its various answers grew in significance. From the 1830s, both white and Black antislavery authors frequently used religious history to bolster their case against the peculiar institution, with African Americans leading the way in developing an antislavery account of the Christian past. Conversely, dozens of proslavery authors, including Catholics, Episcopalians, Presbyterians, Methodists, and Baptists, employed tradition to defend the compatibility of Christianity and slavery.

Yet relatively little attention has been given to the place of Christian tradition in antebellum slavery debates.[6] In fact, the conventional wisdom holds that antebellum debates over slavery were characterized by reliance on the plain meaning of the Bible. As Mark Noll explains, the arguments made by Christians on both sides featured a common-sense, biblicist, and antitraditional approach to theology. The hermeneutical assumptions of the day meant that simpler, more straightforward interpretations of scripture carried the argument. Because abolitionists and antislavery theologians were forced to offer more complicated exegetical arguments, they were necessarily less persuasive. In other words, it appears that an untraditioned approach to theology was at least partially responsible for the failure of otherwise like-minded Christians to resolve the sectional crisis by any means other than war.[7] Recent accounts of religion and slavery take for granted Noll's description of the terms of the debate even if they differ on his assessment of why it failed.[8]

Antebellum pro- and antislavery literature complicates this picture. Black abolitionists associated racial equality with early Christianity and blamed medieval Catholicism for chattel slavery, offering a powerful historical critique of race-based slavery. Likewise, in the 1830s, white abolitionists published historical arguments that Christianity had once limited, and effectively abolished, slavery in Europe. Defenders of slavery realized their need to respond, and proslavery Protestants and Catholics produced works that purported to show the untroubled place of slavery in the history of the church. By the mid-1840s, the question of slavery in Christian history had become a matter of significant ecclesiastical importance. As Presbyterians, Methodists, and Baptists split over slavery, Christianity's historic relationship to slaveholding became all the more controversial. Although antebellum Protestants are typically represented as uninterested in or overtly hostile toward church history, the Christian past played a significant role in the debate that first divided the church and then ruptured the nation.

"Adverse to Slavery": Abolitionists and an Antislavery Christian Past

For the most part, religious histories in the early republic gave scant attention to the history of Christianity and slavery. Slavery hardly appeared in the two most widely read church histories, German Lutheran Johann von Lorenz Mosheim's *Institutes of Ecclesiastical History* and the Anglican Joseph Milner's *History of the Church of Christ*.[9] Other historical works made passing commentary on slavery in the Christian past. Edward Gibbon's *Decline and Fall of the Roman Empire* attributed the decline of slavery in Europe to "the prevailing influence of Christianity"; William Robertson, another of the philosophes, concluded in his bestselling *Charles V* that the "humane spirit of the Christian religion . . . contributed more than any other circumstance to introduce the practice of manumission."[10] Yet even as these historians agreed that Christian principles produced a decline of slavery in Christendom, the question of slavery in the Christian tradition remained relatively undeveloped in the historiography read by Americans in the early nineteenth century.[11]

But from the Revolutionary era on, Black historians saw Christian history as directly addressing the question of slavery and racial inequality.[12] As chapter 3 explained, authors such as Lemuel Haynes and John Marrant developed what John Ernest calls a "liberation historiography" that associated slavery with the corruption of Christendom.[13] African American intellectuals, such as Jacob Oson, Peter Williams Jr., and James Forten, appealed to the Christian past to push back on their exclusion from the Protestant nation. By invoking North African church fathers, Black historians not only made a strong case for the religious and intellectual capability of ancient Africans, but also associated racial equality with early Christianity. By implication, inequality and slavery were later developments that left behind the apostolic ideal.

By comparison, white antislavery authors lagged behind when it came to recognizing the resources available in the Christian past. The British activist Thomas Clarkson noticed that leading historians attributed the decline of European slavery to Christianity, and in his account of British abolition he connected that long history to the modern-day movement.[14] But the history of Christianity did not emerge as a central plank in antislavery discourse until the early 1830s. In 1831, William Lloyd Garrison founded *The Liberator*, and the following year he, Arthur Tappan, and David Lee Child founded the New England Anti-Slavery Society. A more radical phase of abolitionist activism had begun.[15]

On the first anniversary of the society's founding, David Child gave a speech. Journalist, lawyer, and husband to Lydia Maria Child, David sought to show the horror and hypocrisy of American slavery and did so by situating the institution within the history of Christianity. His speech highlighted the achievements of past Christians, arguing that modern slavery was far worse than the relatively humane slavery of Greece and Rome, and pointing out the fate of the latter: "Christianity abolished it." According to David, early Christians recognized the incompatibility between freedom in Christ and enslaving other persons and voluntarily "set their bondsmen free."[16] The history of early Christianity, in David's speech, shamed American Christians and inspired them to fervently oppose slavery.

David's historical point reached a broader audience when it was reproduced by his wife. Lydia already enjoyed a wide readership through her periodical, *Juvenile Miscellany*. In 1833, she produced her first antislavery work, *An Appeal in Favor of That Class of Americans Called Africans*, calling for immediate emancipation and racial equality. In the *Appeal*, Lydia made the point that the laws surrounding slavery showed that it was incompatible with Christianity, not least in the ways in which these laws worked against the Christian instruction and worship of the enslaved. In fact, Lydia argued, slaveowners rightly saw Christianity as posing a danger. The spread of Christianity among the enslaved might cause them to question "whether slavery could be reconciled with religious precepts, [especially] that all men are children of the same Heavenly Father." She pointed out that West Indian slaveowners were more consistent than southern Americans, as the former at least recognized "that slavery and Christianity could not exist together" and fined or imprisoned the Methodists who sought to evangelize the enslaved. She then quoted from her husband's speech:

In Rome, the introduction of "Christianity abolished slavery; the idea of exclusive property in our fellow men was too obviously at variance with its holy precepts; and its professors, in the sincerity of their hearts, made a formal surrender of such claims. In various ancient instruments of emancipation, the masters begin by declaring, that, 'for the love of God and Jesus Christ, for the easing of their consciences, and the safety of their souls' they set their bondmen free."[17]

Like early Christians, Lydia argued, abolitionists recognized that the teaching of Christ required manumission. The work provoked such a widespread negative reaction that shortly after its publication Child was forced to close the *Juvenile Miscellany* due to canceled subscriptions.[18]

If Lydia and David Child brought Christian history to the attention of white abolitionists, Bela Bates Edwards provided the cause with substantial historical ammunition. Trained to be a Congregational minister, Edwards had a short but productive career as a scholar, editor, and professor at his alma mater, Andover Theological Seminary. He founded the *American Quarterly Observer* and in 1844 took over the *Bibliotheca Sacra*, one of the leading theological journals of the era.[19] Edwards was also an energetic activist, founding the American Missionary Society and the Society for Ameliorating the Condition of the Slave. Two years before he began his professorship at Andover, in the fall of 1835, Edwards produced an article titled "Roman Slavery"; the following January, he wrote another on medieval slavery. Both appeared in a periodical edited by Edwards, the *Biblical Repository*, a predecessor of the *Bibliotheca Sacra*. Edwards was a lifelong abolitionist, and his reading of religious historiography convinced him that there was a substantive case to be made for the antislavery trajectory of historic Christianity. In these articles, he aimed to bring together everything that could be known about the history of Christianity and slavery from the teaching and practices of early Christians, Gibbon, Robertson, other European historians, and scholarship on slavery in ancient Rome.[20]

In the first article, Edwards contrasted slavery in the Roman Empire before and after the rise of Christianity. After explaining how slavery was treated in the writings of the New Testament, he acknowledged that Christianity did not abolish ancient slavery "by direct precept." Nonetheless, "Its whole spirit and genius are adverse to slavery, and it was the most powerful of all the causes . . . which finally extinguished the system throughout Europe." Edwards quoted from early Christian writings—including the Apostolic Canons, Ignatius's letter to Polycarp, and the epistle of Clement—to show the "warm sympathy" of early Christians toward slaves, and pointed out that various bishops and church fathers sold off the goods of their church to redeem slaves. "After the establishment of Christianity, under Constantine, slaves partook of all the ordinances of religion," Edwards explained, "and their birth was no impediment to their rising to the highest dignities of the priesthood." He also highlighted laws that were passed by Emperor Constantine, which provided more equal treatment of slaves, and traced the increase of manumission after the legal establishment of Christianity.[21] Even if early Christianity did not end slavery, Edwards believed that Christian teaching set in motion the process of emancipation.

The second article explained the next stage of this process, when, throughout the medieval era, Christianity continued to work against slavery. "In the darkness and confusion which reigned from the 4th to the 12th century," Edwards allowed, "we might expect that such an institution as slavery would flourish." But even if forms of servitude persisted in feudalism, medieval Christians slowly recognized that slavery was incompatible with their faith. Edwards believed that the strongest evidence of this was the increasing prevalence of the rites of manumission: "Christians became so sensible of the inconsistency of their conduct with their professions, that to set a slave free was deemed an act of highly meritorious piety." Historians agreed, according to Edwards, that Christian convictions were primarily responsible for the numeric decline of slaves in Europe.[22]

Edwards ended the series with a summary of his findings: first, although there had been "no royal edict" in Christendom that destroyed slavery in a single blow, nonetheless "its contrariety to the precepts of the New Testament was gradually seen." Quickly after the Christianization of the empire, conditions improved, and the rights of the enslaved were upheld by clergymen and codified in slave laws. Second, even if the feudal system perpetuated forms of slavery, this was also undone by Christian principles: "In the abolition of the servitude of the middle ages, Christianity again performed her work of mercy." Edwards made sure his readers understood the historiographic consensus: "All contemporary and subsequent history conspires to attribute the gradual abolition of the system to her beneficent but effectual aid."

In these two articles, Edwards presented a well-documented account of early and medieval Christianity working to slowly dismantle slavery. Several editors in the region noticed the weight of his argument, and excerpts from the second article were reprinted in two religious newspapers with antislavery sympathies, the *Boston Recorder* and the *Connecticut Observer*.[23] Although Edwards received no direct responses from proslavery historians or theologians, his research would be frequently cited by antislavery authors throughout the 1840s and beyond—including several of the figures treated below: Albert Barnes, John Gregg Fee, Francis Wayland, Jonathan Blanchard, and Alexander Campbell.[24]

As white abolitionists developed historical arguments against slave-holding, African American intellectuals continued to produce works that clarified the meaning of Christian history for racial equality. In the 1830s, Robert Benjamin Lewis, a mixed-race Indian and African American, contributed to this literature with an ethnological history. Lewis's life remains obscure in the historical record, but he appears to have been educated by a Congregationalist missionary society with the intent of becoming a missionary to Africa. He was an entrepreneur who held patents on several inventions, including a highly successful hair oil. He was also fascinated with classical history and, in 1836, produced the first edition of *Light and Truth: From Ancient and Sacred History*. Lewis sought to reveal "truths which have long been concealed from the sons of Ethiopia" about the history of various ethnicities.[25] Drawing on scripture, ancient historians such as Eusebius and Josephus, and eighteenth-century authors, including Gibbon and Joseph Milner, Lewis historically demonstrated the intellectual and religious equality of Africans.[26]

Lewis reminded readers of the African character of early Christianity. He pointed out that the church in Africa "abounded with Christians in the 2d and 3d centuries" and then introduced leading Africans, including the third-century bishop Cyprian, whose "sacred writings were very valuable, and his labor in the gospel of Christ our Lord"; Athanasius, the hero of Trinitarian orthodoxy and "the celebrated St. Augustine [who] was an African bishop of Hippo."[27] Along with naming dozens of other African bishops and martyrs, Lewis described the crucial role played by Africans in preserving the gospel:

> The Christian religion was ably defended by Origen, Dionysius, and Cyprian. In the third century, St. Chrysostom and St. Augustine, learned and eloquent fathers in the church, were bishops of Africa. In the fourth century the Christian religion was externally advanced, but internally corrupted. It had, however, many able and pious apologists, besides Lactanius, Chrysostom and Augustine. The pens of Athanasius, Basil, the Gregories, Jerome, Cyril and others were employed either in the defence or illustration of the doctrines of Christianity.[28]

Lewis also informed his readers that Africans had bravely endured mar-tyrdom. In his description of the Decian persecution in the 250s, he cited figures from Joseph Milner's history, which had sought to counter Gibbon's more cynical assessment of Christian martyrdoms: "In Egypt alone no less than 144,000 Christians died by the violence of their persecution—besides 700,000, that died through the fatigues of banishment etc." To make his point clear, Lewis added, "All that search history will find these were black people."[29]

When Lewis republished the work in 1844 as *Light and Truth . . . the Universal History of the Colored and the Indian Race* (1844), he further empha-sized the African heritage in Christian history. His list of literary Africans expanded to a greater number of church fathers, including Cyprian, Origen, Eusebius of Caesarea, the historians Victorinus and Sulpicius Severus, the apologists Apollinarius and Optatius, and theologians such as Theophilus, Hilary, and Vigilius. In this edition, Augustine merited more than a men-tion. Lewis added a detailed account of Augustine's writings, closely fol-lowing Joseph Milner's interpretation of the fifth-century bishop of Hippo and reproducing long excerpts of Milner's summary of the twenty-two books that made up the *City of God*.[30] By celebrating these North African church fathers, Lewis made the case that Africa was the source not only of Western civilization, but also of the Christian church.

"Unworthy of the Christian Name": Pope Gregory XVI and the Proslavery Response

By 1840, Christian history had become a common feature of religious an-tislavery arguments. African American authors appealed to the early church—particularly to North African church fathers—both to demonstrate their intellectual and spiritual equality with Anglo-Americans and to asso-ciate racial equality with primitive, pre-Constantinian Christianity. White abolitionists drew on eighteenth-century historians to argue that Christian principles slowly worked their way out in the early and medieval church to limit, if not completely abolish, slavery in Europe. These antislavery narratives went generally uncontested until the early 1840s, when proslavery authors began to realize the importance of attending to slavery in Christian history.[31]

These proslavery accounts of the Christian past emerged in response to the publication and reception of *In supremo apostolates*, an encyclical of Pope Gregory XVI (pope from 1831 to 1846). Written in 1839, Gregory XVI's letter strongly condemned the modern slave trade while making several claims about Christianity's historical opposition to slavery. The pope declared that it was his pastoral duty to "seek to turn the faithful altogether from the unfeeling traffic in negroes, or any other human beings." He explained that "when the light of the Gospel first began to diffuse itself," enslaved men "felt their condition among Christians very much alleviated." According to the Roman pontiff, early Christians—such as Gregory of Nyssa and Clement of Rome—worked for the manumission of slaves, and some were even compelled "by a more ardent charity [to deliver] themselves into bonds that they might redeem others." The result of Christian principles working their way through European society, he concluded, was that "for successive ages, no slaves existed among many Christian nations."[32]

Gregory XVI then castigated the rise of the modern slave trade, lamenting that Christians had been among "those who, shamefully blinded by the lust of sordid lucre, in scattered and remote lands, reduced Indians, negroes, and other unfortunate beings, into slavery." He noted that a long list of his predecessors had condemned the slave trade: Pius II in 1462, Paul III in 1537, Urban VIII in 1639, Benedict XIV in 1741, and most recently, Pius VII, who, "impelled by the same spirit of religion and charity . . . employed his influence assiduously with the powerful" against the trade in African slaves. But this record was no cause for pride, "since the traffic in negroes, although diminished in some parts, is still practiced by many Christians."[33] After tracing this history, the pope issued his charge:

By our apostolical authority [we] admonish and conjure earnestly, in the Lord, the faithful of Christ, of every condition, that hereafter they do not unjustly molest Indians, negroes, nor any other race of men, nor spoil them of their goods nor reduce them into slavery . . . nor carry on that inhuman commerce by which negroes, as though they were not men, but mere brutes, held in any manner of servitude, without distinction, against the laws of justice and humanity, are bought, sold and devoted to cruel and sometimes intolerable labor. . . . Verily, all these practices, as altogether unworthy of the Christian name, we reprobate by our apostolical authority; and by the same authority we strictly prohibit and interdict any ecclesiastic or layman from defending the traffic in negroes as lawful.[34]

The encyclical quickly stirred up controversy in the United States. It was reprinted in the *United States Catholic Miscellany*, the *Pennsylvania Freeman*, and the *Massachusetts Abolitionist*, as well as in a collection of antislavery writings edited by the Quaker abolitionist Benjamin Lunday—earning Gregory XVI the rare distinction of being a pope praised by Quaker activists.[35] William Lloyd Garrison published the encyclical in the March 13, 1840, edition of the *Liberator*; fourteen years later he quoted the encyclical, pointing out that to America's shame, even "Papal-ridden Italy" opposed slavery.[36]

The encyclical also found its way into congressional arguments. William Slade, US representative and eventual governor of Vermont, cited it in his 1840 speech to Congress on abolition. An antislavery Whig, Slade called the United States to join "the great movement of Christendom against slavery which has been going on for centuries." He argued that those who defended slavery set themselves against the emancipatory power of Christianity in history—a historical movement most recently expressed in Gregory XVI's encyclical—which he hoped would have a "tremendous effect against slavery . . . in Brazil, the Spanish West Indies, and the United States."[37]

While antislavery northerners celebrated the pope's account of Christian history, others saw the encyclical, and its publication by abolitionists, as a portent of rising fanaticism.[38] Secretary of State John Forsyth attached the entirety of the encyclical to an electioneering address sent to Georgian voters on the occasion of William Henry Harrison's presidential nomination by the Whigs in August 1840. A Jacksonian Democrat and slaveholder, Forsyth speculated that the British government was acting as the "agent of the Pope, in presenting an apostolic letter on slavery to some of the Spanish American States." With the 1833 British abolition of slavery in recent memory, Forsyth feared that Rome and Britain were building an antislavery faction in US politics. British interference in the slave trade in the Americas, Forsyth explained, gave northern abolitionists the courage to nominate Harrison despite the protests of southern Whigs. According to Forsyth, these British machinations and the papal encyclical—together "a compound of ignorance, folly, and insolence"—represented nothing less than a foreign intrusion into American party politics.[39] He warned Georgia's voters that a Harrison presidency would see such fanaticism brought into power.

Proslavery authors realized they could not let Gregory XVI's historical claims go unanswered. Faced on one side with abolitionist enthusiasm for the encyclical and on the other with nativist concern that Roman Catholics would subvert American rights, southern Catholics quickly argued that their religion did not and never had opposed slavery.[40] Most notably, John England, the first Roman Catholic bishop of Charleston, South Carolina, entered the fray. As historian Patrick Carey puts it, Bishop England was "a national spokesman and apologist for the compatibility of Catholicism and American democratic traditions" over the twenty-two years of his episcopacy—founding the first Catholic newspaper with a national reach, addressing Congress in 1826, and establishing a number of religious orders and educational institutions.[41]

The bishop was bothered by slavery as practiced in the South and thought the institution needed reform, but was vocally opposed to abolitionism. And he had already spent considerable effort assuring Catholics that the pope was not condemning slavery itself—only the foreign slave trade.[42] When in March 1840 he printed *In Supremo* in the *United States Catholic Miscellany*, a publication he founded and edited, he paired it with an editorial that made this clear. That summer, England worked hard to ensure that the pope's letter did not take center stage during the provincial council of Catholic bishops held in Baltimore. So when England, who leaned Democratic in his politics, read Forsyth's speech, he took great offense.[43] In October 1840, he published several letters to the secretary of state in the *Catholic Miscellany*. Even after Harrison won the election, rendering Forsyth's address moot, the undeterred bishop kept writing: by the following April, he had published eighteen letters responding to the charge that Catholicism opposed slavery.

England's letters aimed to prove that slaveholding, in the abstract, was at odds with neither tradition nor scripture.[44] He insisted that Gregory XVI's castigation of "inhuman commerce" only referred to "what our laws condemn as the 'slave trade,' and not that sale and purchase which must frequently occur in domestic slavery." In other words, US law already forbade what the pope condemned. This rather conveniently ignored the ongoing trade of slaves in and between southern states. From 1790 to 1860, over one million slaves were sold between the upper and lower South, with another two million sold locally—but England insisted this did not come under the pope's denunciation of Africans being "bought, sold and devoted to cruel and sometimes intolerable labor."[45] The pope, he claimed, was concerned with the inhumane conditions on slave ships—the practices currently of Portugal and Spain, which England related several gruesome stories about—but was unbothered by domestic slavery, "which rests upon a totally different basis, as it is perfectly unconnected with cruelty such as is above described."[46]

Having explained away the pope's condemnation, England then endeavored to clarify exactly what the Catholic Church had taught and practiced regarding slavery. This meant a brief introduction to the Catholic tradition of natural law: citing St. Thomas Aquinas, the bishop insisted that "the existence of slavery is considered by our theologians to be as little incompatible with the natural law as is the existence of property." According to Catholic theologians, he explained, slavery was granted by God as a consequence of humanity's fall into sin, and toward this end England quoted Augustine, Ambrose, Chrysostom, and the fifth-century Pope Gelasius I, each of whom described slavery in these terms. Book XIX of Augustine's *City of God*, he added, "argues at length to show that the peace and good order of society, as well as religious duty, demand that the wholesome laws of the state regulating the conduct of slaves, should be conscientiously observed." In other words, even if slavery were not the ideal, it was a reality of life in a fallen world, and one that needed to be respected by the church.[47]

England then turned to sacred history. He described the status of slavery in the Christian tradition, devoting most of his letters to the history of Christianity, which "show[ed] the canonical legislation of that church during a series of ages, in every region, predicated upon the legal and correctly moral existence of the relation of master and slave." England mustered an impressive list of references to slavery from theologians, councils, and popes from throughout the first five hundred years of Christian history. These showed that the church never sought to abolish slavery, but rather to "plead for morality and to exhort to practice mercy." As Christianity expanded throughout Europe, he concluded, it only made slavery less severe, not less common.[48]

In fact, England went on, it was heretics who taught abolitionism. He pointed out the church's response to fifth-century Gnostic "fanatics," who, in addition to condemning the consumption of meat and wine and the institution of marriage, denounced slavery and encouraged slaves to run away. Pope Symmachus, in a council around 500, decreed that anyone who "teaches a slave to despise his master, and to withdraw from his service" would be "Anathema." This brought England to the question of manumission. From the second century on, there was an extensive practice of Christians freeing their slaves, and "in several particular churches, it was agreed that if a slave became a Christian, he should be manumitted on receiving baptism." He allowed that "from the encouragement of manumission and the spirit of Christianity, the number of slaves had been greatly reduced and their situation greatly improved." However, England insisted that this did not change the fact that the church in principle had always recognized the "moral and religious legality of holding slave property." He argued for the perpetuity of Christian slaveholding throughout the Middle Ages, pointing out that the church never officially condemned ownership of slaves but only cruelty.[49]

After tracing nine centuries of teaching, canonical rule, pastoral advice, and conciliar documents, England summarized "my argument of tradition":

> And of what does that body of evidence consist? Of the admonitions of the earliest and the holiest pastors of the church; of the decrees of her councils, repeatedly made upon a variety of occasions; of the synodical condemnation of those who, under the pretext of religion, would teach the slave to despise his master; of the prohibition to her prelates to interfere with the slave property of any one, without his full permission, for the purpose of ordination or of monastic profession; of the sanction and support of those laws by which the civil power sought to preserve the rights of the owner; of the deeds of gift or of sale by which the church acquired such property for the cultivation of her lands, for the support of her temples, for the maintenance of her clergy, for the benefit of her monasteries, of her hospitals, of her orphans, and of her other works of charity. All this testified that she continued to regard the possession of such property as being fully compatible with the doctrine of the gospel that she was commissioned to proclaim. . . . Thus, by the testimony of the church, and not by our own conjectures, we learn that doctrine which was originally delivered by God, and then handed down, without alteration, through successive generations.[50]

The remainder of his letters explained medieval developments—England pointed out that Islam "did much to perpetuate and to extend slavery"—and the various laws and technicalities surrounding servitude and slavery in England, Ireland, and Europe.[51]

Bishop England's proslavery interpretation of the encyclical offered an influential, if controversial, account of Christian history. And it proved particularly important given that abolitionists continued to appeal to *In Supremo*. In 1843, the Irish Catholic leader Daniel O'Connell used the pope's stance to castigate American Catholic priests for supporting slavery. Boston radicals William Lloyd Garrison and Wendell Phillips followed O'Connell's lead. At an abolitionist rally in Feneuil Hall, Phillips read from *In Supremo* before proposing "three cheers for the abolitionist Pope Gregory XVI!"[52]

Bishop England could not respond, as he had died in 1842, but other Catholics would not let the abolitionists go unanswered. The *U.S. Catholic Miscellany* reprinted sections of England's arguments, insisting that the late bishop's historical research proved that "in Catholic theology the question is a settled one, and no one would be recognized as a Catholic who would utter the expressions we have heard from the lips of American abolitionists."[53] In 1844, the eighteen letters were collected by England's friend William George Read, who published them in Baltimore. Read, a Catholic lawyer, believed that these "celebrated letters" would finally disarm O'Connell and "a certain portion of the American press, [which] would eagerly avail themselves of his misstatements, to justify new calumnies against the Church."[54] The letters were published once again in 1849 by Bishop Ignatius Reynolds, who reproduced them in volume 3 of the *Works of the Right Reverend John England.*[55]

The republication of England's letters placed the Christian past squarely in the center of arguments over slavery. Abolitionists skewered Bishop England's reading of the encyclical. "The Bishop of Charleston," the *National Anti-Slavery Standard* sneered, "repels with suitable sensibility the calumny that Catholic Christians ever thought of doing or teaching others to 'do as we would have them do to ourselves.'" The Boston periodical challenged Bishop England's translation of the Latin encyclical, providing its own reading that stressed "the important fact that Christianity did once abolish slavery." While Bishop England insisted the pope only condemned the slave trade, the review pointed out that his predecessors, including Pope Alexander III, clearly taught that every Christian was a freeman.[56] As the *National Anti-Slavery Standard* pointed out, this could hardly be squared with hereditary slavery as practiced in the South. Meanwhile, southern publications praised the bishop's proslavery argument: *De Bow's Review* praised the letters as "among the ablest papers ever written upon the subject," while the *New Orleans Bulletin* encouraged ministers to find in them "an armory of weapons to use against those at the North who would excommunicate them."[57]

After the pope's encyclical, competing accounts of church history frequently appeared in religious arguments over slavery and all the more as Protestant denominations splintered and split over the question. And, as the next chapter will show, rival interpretations of *In Supremo* continued through the 1840s and into the 1850s. Antislavery authors picked up the encyclical's narrative, arguing that Christianity's historical amelioration of slavery was to be fulfilled in present-day abolition. On the other hand, proslavery writers insisted that the pope's condemnation of the slave trade did not contradict the practice and teaching of the church throughout time.[58]

"Holy Men and Martyrs Held Slaves": History and the Splitting of Protestant Denominations

By the 1840s, the question of slavery threatened to divide the nation along sectional lines, as southern secessionists and radical northern abolitionists alike called for disunion, and the second party system began to fragment over the question of slavery's expansion into the west.[59] Political division was mirrored in the ecclesiastical world. By 1845, the three largest Protestant denominations—Presbyterians, Methodists, and Baptists—had split over slavery.[60] In the middle of these denominational schisms, Christianity's historic relationship to slaveholding became all the more controversial, and pro- and antislavery Presbyterians, Baptists, and Methodists turned to church history to justify their position to their intradenominational opponents.

Perhaps the most theologically thoughtful of these exchanges was the 1844 epistolary debate between Rhode Island Baptist Francis Wayland and his South Carolinian counterpart Richard Fuller. Wayland, moral philosopher and president of Brown University from 1826 to 1855, believed slavery to be evil but opposed radical abolitionism, while Fuller, who also opposed radical abolitionism, was a lawyer, nationally known Baptist minister, and slaveholder—and in the same year as this debate, helped to found the Southern Baptist Convention.[61] The two Baptists published their correspondence over the morality of slavery in Philadelphia's *Christian Reflector*. Notable for its irenic tone, the debate exemplified the difficulty that otherwise like-minded evangelical Protestants had in agreeing on the meaning of scripture.[62] Fuller's and Wayland's exchange was published as a book in 1845 and widely reprinted, going through five editions in its first two years.

In addition to debating biblical teaching on slavery, Wayland and Fuller argued over Christian tradition. In the seventh letter, Wayland brought history into the question after acknowledging that the New Testament gave no clear precept against slavery, which would have produced an insurrection. Instead, Christ intended to bring slavery to an end through the gradual influence of Christian morals. Then, citing Bela Bates Edwards's article, Wayland argued that this in fact was what occurred: "As the gospel spread from city to city, and began to exert an influence upon the public mind, the laws respecting slavery were gradually relaxed . . . until, throughout the whole empire, slavery was at last abolished." Wayland quoted Clement, Paulinus, Cyprian, Ambrose, and other church fathers to "illustrate the manner in which the early church interpreted the teaching of the gospel respecting slavery, and also the effect which this teaching had upon their practice." Christian principles "once abolished slavery," Wayland proclaimed, and "have almost done it for the second time."[63]

In response to Wayland's appeal to tradition, Fuller marshaled evidence from both patristic teaching and Christian precedent. Fuller picked up on John Chrysostom's commentary on 1 Corinthians 7, one of the scriptural references most contested in the antebellum debate: "Let every man abide in the same calling wherein he was called. Art thou called being a servant? Care not for it: but if thou mayest be made free, use it rather" (1 Corinthians 7:20–22). This passage appeared to enjoin slaves to be content while also affirming the superiority of freedom. According to the fourth-century bishop Chrysostom, however, Paul meant in this passage that "slavery is no harm but rather an advantage," as it helped the slave disregard "riches and wrath and all the other like passions."[64] Chrysostom's interpretation, unpopular with the Protestant reformers, was generally out of favor by the nineteenth century.[65] Further, Chrysostom's *Homilies* posed problems for slaveholders, as elsewhere in this work the bishop instructed Christians to educate their slaves and manumit them as soon as possible.[66] As nineteenth-century scholars recognized, Chrysostom's corpus by no means supported slavery.[67] Yet Fuller, and proslavery exegetes after him, quoted Chrysostom's commentary at length.[68]

Fuller also responded to Wayland with a proslavery reading of Christian history, countering that "during the apostolic periods, and for centuries after, the most holy men and martyrs held slaves." At no point did Christianity abolish slavery, Fuller insisted, but rather "infused its mild and benevolent spirit into the institution, making it quite a different thing."[69] Fuller's historical argument drew criticism and a lengthy rebuttal from a number of antislavery authors, including Albert Barnes, a New School Presbyterian and one of the era's bestselling biblical commentators. Barnes took umbrage with Fuller's claim that Christendom never abolished slavery.[70] He published a long rejoinder, *Scriptural Views on Slavery*, and in the final pages honed in on "an important inquiry" about Christianity on slavery. According to Barnes, much hinged on Fuller's claims about Christian history. "If all Christian ministers and churches should act now on what was understood by the early

Christians to be the proper way to act," he asked, "would the system be vindicated and perpetuated?" The question was answered emphatically in the negative. Drawing on B. B. Edwards, Gibbon, and patristic authors, Barnes concluded that Christianity effectively abolished slavery in Europe.[71] Six years later, Barnes's work would be quoted by Black abolitionist Frederick Douglass in his famous speech "What to the Slave Is the Fourth of July?"[72]

Baptists were not alone in arguing over the Christian past. Antislavery Presbyterians appealed to church history when they censured slaveholders or excluded them from holding ministerial office. The abolitionist John Gregg Fee refused to extend fellowship to slaveholders, a stance that ultimately led to his separation from the Presbyterian Synod of Kentucky in the 1840s. In 1848, Fee used Christian history to defend his position, arguing that early Christians had not tolerated slavery in the church and, drawing from B. B. Edwards's articles, citing a host of church fathers as evidence.[73] Proslavery Presbyterians, in turn, argued that such discipline not only disregarded the authority of scripture but also departed from Christian precedent. William Graham, a New School Presbyterian in Cincinnati, argued that abolitionists purported to judge the biblical authors, the church fathers, and the entire church throughout time.[74] Graham's antiabolitionist book led to his suspension by the New School Synod in Cincinnati; when he was reinstated after appealing, this in turn caused a backlash from the antislavery side of the New School, and one Presbytery broke away as a result.[75]

Christian history also featured significantly in the Methodist schism. At the 1844 Methodist General Conference, James Osgood Andrew, a Methodist bishop from Georgia, came under sharp criticism from northern Methodists for owning slaves. Over the protest of their southern counterparts, northerners passed a resolution suspending Bishop Andrew from exercising his position. In turn, southerners, led by Henry Bidleman Bascom, drew up a plan to form the Methodist Episcopal Church, South. In 1845, Bascom wrote a defense of the new denomination in which he argued that abolitionists set themselves in judgment over scripture and "the principal fathers and writers of the Church," who have "steadily and formally recognized the state and relations of slavery." Those early Christians who attempted to abolish slavery, according to Bascom, were "directly condemned by nearly all the principal early and later fathers. Ignatius, Chrysostom, and Jerome especially, denounce the practice as unchristian."[76]

Antislavery Methodists also recognized that Christian history was crucial for interpreting their denominational divide. In 1848, Dr. Charles Elliott, a

Methodist minister, was commissioned by the General Conference to write a history of the Southern Methodist secession. Elliott aimed at producing a definitive account that showed the error of southern Methodists. Along the way, he realized the need to discuss the moral and legal characteristics of southern slavery, and, in 1851, published *Sinfulness of American Slavery*. The book challenged southern readings of the Christian past: "Most Christians consider slavery as wrong. . . . Indeed, the most conscientious in all ages have viewed the system as one that is inconsistent with the principles of right, as well as contrary to the word of God." Elliott pointed out that "early Christians very generally deemed it repugnant to Christianity, for any Christian to hold another in slavery," and supported this with quotations from Constantine, Gregory the Great, and Aquinas.[77] When he finally produced the *History of the Great Secession from the Methodist Episcopal Church*—a mind-numbing eleven hundred pages—Elliott prefaced it with a pitch for his next work. What was needed to clear up the question of church discipline, he explained, was a complete history of Christianity and slavery, and one that made especially clear what the early church practiced. "The apostolic constitutions and the writings of the Greek and Latin fathers," Elliott wrote, "will supply very useful historical explanations of the moral discipline of the Church in regard to slavery; till at length slavery proper gradually perished under the antislavery discipline, spirit, and practice of Christianity."[78] This future work of Elliott's, *Bible and Slavery*, would appear in 1863.[79]

Not everyone believed that Christian history came down on one side of the argument. Alexander Campbell, for example, opposed slavery but refused to join the abolition movement and would not discipline proslavery ministers. In 1845, while other denominations were splitting, the Restorationist leader pointed out that B. B. Edwards's careful research did not necessitate supporting radical abolition. In fact, Campbell argued, what Edwards showed was that the primitive church only reformed, and did not abolish, slavery.[80] He concluded that there was good historical justification for taking a moderate, gradualist approach to ending the institution.

Similarly, the historian Robert Baird believed that abolitionism was unduly dividing the church. After studying with Samuel Miller at Princeton Theological Seminary, Baird went on to work for a number of evangelical organizations—first as an agent for the American Bible Society in 1827, then the American Sunday School Union in 1829, and eventually for the American and Foreign Christian Union from 1835.[81] In 1846, Baird helped launch the Evangelical Alliance, an organization that sought to promote transatlantic unity and missionary cooperation.[82] Over the course of his trips to Europe promoting "Protestant evangelicalism, Sunday School organization, Bible distribution, and temperance reform," Baird also addressed European audiences on the topic of American religious life.[83] He turned these lectures into *Religion in America*, one of the most enduring and influential accounts of American religious history.[84]

Baird was troubled by abuses in the slave system and considered the institution a "grave evil" that would eventually give way to Christian principles. Yet he also insisted on the inviolability of states' rights and argued that slavery would ultimately prove beneficial in Christianizing Africa—a position that reflected his belief in the superiority of Anglo-Saxon culture.[85] When, in the late 1840s, the Evangelical Alliance split over disagreements on slavery, Baird was heartbroken. In a passionate speech, he castigated zealous British abolitionists: "Must our American churches wait till their country be rid of slavery, before they shall be fit to cooperate with British Christians in spreading the Gospel throughout the world?" Baird found it shameful that the question of slavery prevented evangelicals from working together to "promot[e] religion . . . among the hundreds of thousands of poor Irish Romanists who are coming to us." He reminded listeners that both Britain and the United States might be overwhelmed by an incoming mass of unconverted foreigners.[86] In light of this, slavery ought to take a back seat to evangelical missions and the preservation of national Protestantism.[87]

Robert Baird's lament exemplifies one evangelical response to abolitionism. The splitting of Protestant denominations and international organizations like the Evangelical Alliance appeared a tragedy to those more concerned with maintaining unity for the sake of Christian mission. By contrast, for James Pennington, whose history opened this chapter, such unity could not be maintained by allowing slavery to persist. Pennington and other abolitionists drew on the history of Christianity to argue that the peculiar institution was destined to be defeated. Slavery was, for Pennington, an "institution of the *dark age!*"

If abolitionists were the first to make arguments from the Christian past, their proslavery counterparts made up for lost time with a strong response—especially after Pope Gregory's XVI encyclical appeared to suggest a historical consensus against slavery. By the late 1840s, the bitter arguments and schisms in American denominations had only encouraged historical entrenchment. When Baptists, Presbyterians, and Methodists failed to win over their ecclesiastical brethren through scripture, they insisted that tradition was on their side. Antislavery ministers argued that the teaching of the early church and the "spirit" of Christianity throughout history justified the use of church discipline against slaveholders; proslavery clergy countered that the very same church fathers accepted slavery and that it was the abolitionists who departed from the norms of traditional Christianity. Both were convinced they were on the right side of church history.

7

Fighting for the Past

Christian History during Crisis and War

Only two years after Robert E. Lee surrendered his army to Ulysses S. Grant, Robert Lewis Dabney was not done fighting. A Presbyterian theologian, erstwhile professor of systematic theology and church history at Union Theological Seminary, and one of the most influential scholars in Old School Presbyterianism, Dabney was also a patriotic Virginian. The recent defeat of the Confederacy smarted, but perhaps more infuriating was the moral superiority of the victorious North. And so, months after the Army of Virginia laid down its arms, Dabney took up his pen. He would defend the "lost cause" of the South, he wrote, against abolitionists' "perverted judgments," "fanaticism," and "anarchy and barbarism." In so doing Dabney believed he would "justify the history of our native States and . . . sustain the hearts of their sons in the hour of cruel reproach."[1]

Six years earlier, Dabney had been a professor at Union Seminary who watched nervously as southern states began seceding in the wake of Lincoln's election. Although an ardent defender of slavery, he did not support secession until Virginia joined the movement. Then his path seemed obvious. He served for several months as a chaplain in the Virginia Infantry, and after Thomas "Stonewall" Jackson heard him preach, the general asked the professor to become his chief of staff. Dabney only filled that role for four months before illness caused him to resign in August 1862. He would spend the rest of the war teaching at the seminary and, after Jackson's death in the spring of 1863, writing a two-volume biography of the late general at the request of Jackson's widow. Dabney's *Life and Campaigns of Lieut.-Gen. Thomas J. Jackson*, which celebrated the Christian piety of the Confederate general, remains in print today.[2]

Having defended his general as the war was being lost, now, on the other side of Appomattox, Dabney defended his state. He was prepared to double down on what he considered the central question of the southern cause: "the righteousness of African servitude."[3] Over several hundred pages in *Defense*

The Old Faith in a New Nation. Paul J. Gutacker, Oxford University Press. © Oxford University Press 2023.
DOI: 10.1093/oso/9780197639146.003.0008

of Virginia he upheld slavery as not only legally and morally justified, but also confirmed by Christian tradition. Aware of the long debate that had preceded him, Dabney cited and engaged a number of the most widely read theological treatments of slavery, including the Fuller-Wayland exchange from the mid-1840s.

Dabney insisted that the history of Christianity underscored the teaching of scripture on slavery. In fact, the Christian past only made more obvious that scripture condemned abolitionists. Dabney read St. Paul's injunction in 1 Timothy 6, which taught obedience to masters, as also instructing leaders to exclude from the church those who taught abolitionism. How strange, wrote Dabney, as "we have no evidence that, either in the primitive or mediaeval church, any marked disposition prevailed to assail the rights of masters over their slaves. . . . This denunciation of the apostle seems to have been sufficient to give the *quietus* to the spirit of abolition, so long as any reverence for inspiration remained." Dabney drew a bizarre conclusion: the apostle gave this order because divine providence "foresaw that though the primitive church stood in comparatively slight need of such admonitions, the century would come, after the lapse of eighteen ages, when the church would be invaded and defiled by the deadly spirit of modern abolitionism."[4] In other words, the long history of Christian affirmation of slavery showed that St. Paul, under divine inspiration, had ultimately written his rebuke to condemn nineteenth-century abolitionists.

The professor went on to narrate abolition as an unprecedented innovation of modernism: "Neither primitive, nor reformed, nor Romanist, nor modern divines taught the doctrine of the intrinsic sinfulness of slave-holding," he argued. "The church as a body never dreamed it." Who was to blame for this novelty? French Jacobins—and some fanatical and "erratic" teachers like John Wesley. Nineteenth-century abolitionists such as Francis Wayland, then, were forced to believe that Christ, in his inspired teaching and through the witness of his apostles, "deliberately chose a plan which consigned seventeen centuries of Christians to a sin, and as many of slaves to a wrong, which he all along abhorred."[5] This, to Dabney, was an absurdity.

Much had happened in the twenty years between Wayland's argument with Richard Fuller and Dabney's defense of the southern lost cause. After the country's largest Protestant denominations split over slavery, the nation would soon follow. And, just as Presbyterians, Methodists, and Baptists argued over the history of Christianity and slavery during the 1840s, the Christian past continued to be debated during the sectional crisis, secession, and subsequent war. In the 1850s, gradualists, abolitionists, and proslavery authors alike increasingly turned to the Christian past to justify their positions. In fact, Christian history proved central to several of the most important proslavery arguments put forward by legal scholars and social theorists. After the South seceded and the Civil War began, the meaning of the Christian past continued to matter for both North and South. For Confederates, church history contributed to the project of constructing white Christian nationalism, while, in the North, controversy and outrage followed a proslavery account of Christian history written by Episcopal bishop John Henry Hopkins.

Although antebellum Protestants are typically represented as uninterested in or overtly hostile toward church history, the Christian past played a significant role in how both North and South navigated the question of slavery during the sectional crisis and, indeed, during the war. To be sure, the Good Book—which by the Civil War enjoyed "an unprecedentedly large readership and influence" in America—took center stage in the argument over slavery.[6] Both northern and southern Protestants vigorously quarreled over the meaning of the Bible, and both readily used scriptural passages to endorse secession or union, going to war, and killing.[7] Given the cultural predominance and proliferation of the Bible and biblical texts, it is little wonder scholars portray the theological debate over slavery as starting and ending with the Bible.[8] Even as recent historiography modifies or nuances Mark Noll's thesis about the theological controversy, it continues to overlook the role of Christian history in the debate. Simply put, the Christian past does not appear in most recent works on religion and slavery.[9] Exceptions to this neglect only prove the rule.[10]

But for defenders of slavery, not merely the Bible but also Christian tradition supported their position, and these authors mined the past for arguments that slaveholding and Christianity had always been compatible. Conversely, Black and white antislavery authors used church history to argue for racial equality and the Christian imperative to emancipate slaves. In fact, in some of the works analyzed below—John Fletcher's *Studies on Slavery*, for example, and Thomas Cobb's *Inquiry into the Law of Negro Slavery*—relatively equal attention is given to both biblical and historical evidence. Further, as will be seen, several of the proslavery arguments that shaped southern jurisprudence and secession relied more on claims about Christian history than they did on appeals to the Bible. Far from irrelevant or esoteric, church history bore ramifications not only for theological or denominational disputes but also for the most important political question of the nineteenth century. The previously unnoticed historical dimensions of religious arguments over slavery prove central to understanding why these debates failed—and why reconstruction would also founder.

An Institution of the Dark Age: Historical Criticisms of Race-Based Slavery

Underneath arguments about the history of Christian slaveholding lay the often-implicit question of race. By the early 1850s, most religious defenses of southern slavery assumed innate racial differences and argued that the institution was paternalistic—that slavery benefited Africans by providing the opportunity for religious and cultural development.[11] John Fletcher's *Studies on Slavery* exemplified how this paternalism could draw on the Christian past. A northerner transplanted to New Orleans, Fletcher in 1852 published a defense of slavery that sought to respond to the leading moral and theological antislavery works, including Wayland and Barnes. Drawing on philosophy, scripture, and history, Fletcher's 630-page work offered "eight studies" of slavery designed to be read and studied by all "dispassionate seekers after truth, who may belong to different political sects."[12]

In the fourth of these studies, Fletcher turned to ecclesiastical history to demonstrate the perpetuity of Christian slaveholding. "In this investigation, we must apply to the records of the Catholic Church," Fletcher explained, "although . . . strong and bitter prejudice may exist against these records." The history of Christianity, according to Fletcher, showed that from the early church through the medieval era, slavery was never considered incompatible with the faith. He narrated this past over the course of several hundred pages, reproducing quotations from church fathers and councils that seemed to condone slavery. For much of this material, he relied heavily on Bishop England's writing: "In presenting the action and records of the church and early fathers, we have freely adopted the sentiments and facts digested by Bishop England, to whom, we take occasion here to say, we feel as much indebted."[13]

Fletcher also argued that racial slavery was benevolent, citing St. Augustine's claim that slaves enjoyed the protection of beneficent masters. But he went further. Against the general consensus of eighteenth-century historiography, Fletcher argued that early Christianity did not diminish the extent of

Greco-Roman slavery but rather transformed it—a useful historical narrative for those who wanted to see southern slavery not abolished but rather made more humane. Christian tradition, he concluded, supported the southern claim that "the institutions of slavery and Christianity can never be antagonistic."[14]

African American historians were quick to point out that church history demonstrated the contradictions in racial paternalism. The interpretation of early church tradition developed by Black historians in the early republic continued to proliferate in African American literature in the late 1840s and 1850s. African church fathers proved particularly useful, as Black nationalists frequently turned to Augustine, Cyprian, Tertullian, and other early theologians of the church to demonstrate the religious and intellectual capability of Africans.[15] Henry Highland Garnet, the Presbyterian abolitionist, educator, and minister, gave an address to a female benevolent society that celebrated the usual men who "indicate the ancient fame of our ancestors," including "Cyprian, Origen, and Augustine." As had earlier African American historians, Garnet blamed African enslavement on Charles V and that "Roman Catholic priest," Bartolomé de las Casas, condemning both "guilty priest and King" to perpetual infamy. In his concluding paragraphs, the minister turned to present-day reasons for hope: the "old doctrine of the natural inferiority of the colored race, propagated in America by Mr. Thomas Jefferson, has long since been refuted by . . . witness from among the slandered, both living and dead: Pushkin in Russia, Dumas in France, Toussaint in Hayti, Banaker, Theodore Sedgwick Wright, and a host in America, and a brilliant galaxy in Ancient History." For Garnet, modern-day champions of racial equality joined in a long line of able Africans that stretched back to early Christianity and beyond.[16]

Similar historical arguments were made by a fellow student of Garnet's, Samuel Ringgold Ward, in his *Autobiography of a Negro Fugitive* (1855). Enslaved in Maryland, as a three-year-old Ward escaped with his parents to New Jersey. By his twenties, Ward had become a highly regarded orator in abolitionist circles, and was invited to pastor a predominantly white Congregationalist church in western New York. In 1851, his participation in the rescue of a fugitive slave in Syracuse, New York caused him to flee to Canada to escape prosecution under the new Fugitive Slave Act. There, he was enlisted by the Anti-Slavery Society of Canada to fundraise in Britain. It was a successful trip, as Ward's speeches in London and elsewhere in Britain enabled the society to support slaves escaping across the northern border throughout the 1850s.

Ward's *Autobiography* told this story, and was a great success, selling well enough to secure his retirement to ministry in Jamaica. In the book, Ward showed his frustration with arguments that African Americans were morally or intellectually inferior:

> Nor could I degrade myself by arguing the equality of the Negro with the white; my private opinion is, that to say the Negro is equal morally to the white man, is to say but very little. As to his intellectual equality, Cyprian, Augustine, Tertullian, Euclid, and Terence, would pass for specimens of the ancient Negro, exhibiting intellect beyond the ordinary range of modern literati, before the present Anglo-Saxon race had even an origin.

Ward added that anyone acquainted with Henry Highland Garnett, Frederick Douglass, James W. C. Pennington, James McCune Smith, "and others of like high and distinguished attainments, might, perhaps, be deemed excusable, if he simply called the names of these gentlemen as sufficient to contradict any disparaging words concerning the modern Negro." For Ward, contemporary Black abolitionists and long-dead church fathers together proved the absurdity of the racial argument for slavery—and also showed the "cool impudence, and dastardly cowardice" showed by those who would shut Black men out of educational institutions, limit them to physical labor, and then insist they were "naturally, morally, intellectually, or socially, inferior to the white." This hypocrisy, he concluded, was uniquely insidious in the United States.[17]

Some white antislavery authors also distinguished between the history of slaveholding in Christendom and the more recent practice of race-based slavery.[18] Moses Stuart, Congregational minister and professor of biblical literature at Andover Theological Seminary, presented a nuanced account of Christianity and slavery in his 1850 work *Conscience and the Constitution*. Stuart, called "the father of Biblical Science in America" for his use of German philological and critical hermeneutical methods, conceded that the Bible permitted slavery, at least in the abstract.[19] In fact, Stuart sided with Chrysostom and Theophylact against abolitionist readings of 1 Corinthians 7—he believed that the Pauline text did not consider physical freedom preferable to slavery.

However, Stuart clarified, scripture did not allow for race-based slavery. If slavery in general was permitted by the Bible, slavery as practiced in the southern United States was not. Stuart argued that Christian doctrine and Christian history taught the equality of all races: "Were not such men as Origen, and Clement of Alexandria, and Cyprian, and Athanasius, and Arius, and Jerome, and Augustine, and others like them, Africans?" Sounding much like earlier African American historians, he concluded that "intellect springs up in nearly equal measures, wherever it is cultivated and called forth." Toward these ends, Stuart urged gradual abolition and African colonization.[20]

Stuart was not the only northerner to distinguish between claims that Christianity condemned slavery wholesale and the more specific argument that racial slavery in particular was at odds with Christian precedent. In his prize-winning legal treatise, *The Law of Freedom and Bondage* (1858), John Codman Hurd narrated the history of Christianity and slaveholding. A New York lawyer and legal scholar, Hurd relied on John Fletcher and Bishop John England for his historical material. Using these proslavery accounts of Christian history, Hurd concluded that the early church in no way abolished slavery. However, he clarified that over time Christendom did outlaw slavery of fellow Europeans, and noted the important change from Christian Europe only allowing slavery of infidels to the much later development of slavery based on racial distinctions.[21] Fletcher's legal treatise placed abolition outside the norms of Christian history, but also highlighted differences between ancient and modern slavery. In 1877, Hurd received an honorary doctor of laws from Yale University for his treatise.

Some abolitionists used church history to paint racial slavery not only as anti-American but also anti-Protestant. The Connecticut physician Edward Coit Rogers wrote *Letters on Slavery to Pro-Slavery Men* (1855) in response to Fletcher's *Studies on Slavery*, among other proslavery works. Rogers was not particularly careful with his citation of early Christian tradition—for example, he quoted Fletcher's description of Gnostic and Manichaean sects' opposition to slavery, but attributed this position to "Christians in Asia Minor at a very early period." But he insisted that the early church had been "wholly at war with slavery," a claim supported with quotations from Polycarp, Ignatius, Augustine, Gregory the Great, Ambrose, Cyprian, and others, concluding that "the purest of the church fathers labored against slavery."[22] He traced the history of Christian emancipation, citing ancient sources as well as recent historiography by August Neander and the English Catholic historian John Lingard to show "the divine influence of the Christian church in destroying slavery."

The development of modern slavery, Rogers went on, could be directly linked to the degradations of medieval Catholicism. As the purity of apostolic Christianity began to wane, Rogers explained, Christendom came to accept slavery through the papacy, which, "from a very early period, had been on the side of slavery." Racial slavery, he claimed, had been created by the papacy. He acknowledged the recent letter by Gregory XVI condemning the African slave trade, but disagreed that his predecessors had opposed African slavery—only slavery of Amerindians. The proslavery southerner, in other words, was on the side of Roman Catholicism: "You go to the bible, it is true, but not to support *negro* slavery. That knows no difference between the Etheopian [*sic*] and the Caucasian," Rogers concluded. "It is solely the authority of five despotic, corrupt popes, in the worst age of the church, that furnishes you specific rights to enslave the children of Africa." If Catholicism created modern slavery, the Reformation stood against it. "Protestantism," Rogers argued, "in denying the despotism of the popes, denounces negro slavery." According to Rogers, the reformers advocated the right of liberty and the equality of all. After quoting Luther, Calvin, and Zwingli, the abolitionist hammered the point home: "No man then, is a legitimate protestant who lends his sanction to this infamous system."[23]

Even as proslavery authors used patristic interpretation to support biblical endorsement of slavery, African American and white antislavery authors pointed out that the North African heritage of many patristic theologians belied a racial hierarchy. Even if scripture and tradition permitted slavery in certain forms, antislavery authors insisted that the historical church never endorsed the institution as it existed in the South. Black and white historians in the abolitionist camp distinguished between ancient and race-based slavery, arguing that the latter was the fruit of corrupt medieval Catholicism and out of line with the history of genuine Christianity.

"Subtle Heresies of an Early Period": History and the Rise of the Republican Party

Abolitionism gained momentum after the Fugitive Slave Act of 1850 and the Kansas-Nebraska Act in 1854, developments that proved the insidious influence of "slave power" to northerners.[24] As the sectional crisis came to a head, moderate antislavery authors used the Christian past to encourage northerners that history was on their side. In 1854, church historian Philip Schaff argued in his survey of church history that "the spirit and genius of Christianity . . . has in all ages, without any radical noise and revolution, or contempt for historically established legal rights and the principles of equity, urged towards the orderly constitutional abolition of slavery."[25] Schaff, who supported gradual emancipation, argued that this was the historic Christian position. He would repeat this gradualist argument in an article in 1858 titled "The Influence of the Early Church on the Institution of Slavery" and again in his 1861 book *Slavery in the Bible*.[26] For Schaff, and other gradual emancipationists, the "spirit" of Christianity ought to bolster confidence that slavery was headed toward extinction, despite evidence to the contrary.

Schaff was not the only scholar to treat slavery in this way. Lydia Maria Child had long considered the question of the history of Christianity and slavery. When she produced her magnum opus in 1855, the three-volume *Progress of Religious Ideas*, Child gave significant attention to the question. Child did not particularly care for patristic theology—she complained that "nearly all the writings of the Fathers consisted of sectarian controversy, Biblical interpretation employed in its service, and fervent exhortations to celibacy"—but admired the church fathers' teaching on social concern for the poor and slavery. She quoted Lactantius, Chrysostom, Basil, and monastics such as Isidore and Benedict, arguing that "it early began to be the feeling that one Christian ought not to hold another as a slave; the relation, even under the best circumstances, seeming inconsistent with Christian brotherhood." While bishops and emperors did not legally abolish slavery, Child observed throughout the patristic and early medieval era a "latent consciousness of wrong" reflected in Christian practices—especially the frequent practice of Christians freeing their slaves upon baptism or when nearing death. For Child, as for Schaff, it was the "spirit" of Christianity that opposed slavery through history.[27]

As antislavery sentiment heated up in the wake of the Kansas-Nebraska Act, proslavery authors continued to argue that abolition was outside the bounds of historic Christianity. Nathan Lord, a Congregationalist minister in Maine, and president of Dartmouth College from 1828 to 1863, provides a telling example of northern opposition to abolitionism. Lord was initially taken with antislavery arguments. He helped launch the American Anti-Slavery Society and served as vice president in 1833, but by the 1850s he had completely reversed his position. In 1854, he published *A Letter of Inquiry to Ministers of the Gospel of All Denominations, on Slavery*, seeking to raise questions about the morality of slavery "while these fitful and portentous blasts thicken, as they are likely to do, into a destructive storm."[28]

Lord was put off from his earlier antislavery views through the antiscripture statements of William Lloyd Garrison and, by the 1850s, had become convinced that the Bible endorsed the institution.[29] He concluded that "slavery is not, of itself, a moral evil," but rather "an ordinance of the God of Nature and Revelation." Now, the enemy was not slavery, but rather a divisive, heterodox abolitionism. Lord called fellow ministers to consider the origins of abolitionism, asking

> whether the fallacy did not originate far back in subtle heresies of an early period of Christianity, affecting injuriously the ethics and theology of that and succeeding periods, but more remarkably developed, at present, in a wide-spread humanitarian philosophy which has insinuated itself, almost imperceptibly, but very considerably into the church of God.[30]

Lord's conclusion was that American ministers must reject the fanaticism of abolition and seek to maintain Christian unity even as they differed on slavery. It was a popular argument. By 1860, his *Letter of Inquiry* would go into four editions. Eventually, Lord's position on slavery and the Civil War—a war that he attributed to radical abolition—produced enough controversy at Dartmouth that Lord was compelled to resign his presidency after serving for thirty-five years.

Similar arguments came from William Gannaway Brownlow, a Methodist preacher and newspaperman in Kentucky. Like Lord, Brownlow was embittered by the schisms of the 1840s and went from being an antislavery activist in the 1830s to an ardent defender of slavery by the 1850s, a shift largely due to his disillusionment with the contentious debates in the denomination.[31] Brownlow championed the Southern Methodist church, arguing in sermons and public debates that church discipline against slaveholders was unsustainable in light of Christian history. He cited Gibbon, Robertson, and Mosheim to make a case that "the gospel made considerable progress among the citizens of the Roman empire; and, as nearly every family owned slaves, it is certain that slaveholders were converted and admitted into the Church."[32] These sorts of historical arguments continued to emerge from proslavery authors, both northern and southern, throughout the 1850s.

The election year of 1856 also saw renewed attention to Catholic voters and thus to the decades-old arguments over the history of the Catholic church and slavery. That year, a Catholic in Kentucky reproduced material from

Bishop England's work to prove that when it came to slavery, Catholics would be loyal, law-abiding citizens. In response to charges made by an Alabamian Know-Nothing agitator, the anonymous Catholic wrote, "There is a positive and unchangeable law of the Church which would forbid any conscientious Catholic being an Abolitionist." Citing Augustine, Ambrose, Chrysostom, and other church fathers, the author concluded that "every Catholic is bound by a canon law to support the *fugitive slave law of* 1850, as well as the principles of the Kansas and Nebraska bill."[33]

At the same time, abolitionists maintained that they stood on the right side of church history. During the 1856 campaigns, supporters of the new Republican Party returned to Pope Gregory's account of the history of Catholic opposition to the slave trade. The *New York Independent* reproduced the papal bull on its front page, next to a piece that criticized Bishop England's reinterpretation of the letter and narrated a dialogue between a Catholic and his employee in which the former said, "No true Catholic can vote to support slavery."[34] Even as their nominee John C. Frémont distanced himself from abolitionists, the Republican Party was glad to appeal to Pope Gregory to gain support from Irish Catholics. The party printed forty thousand copies of a pamphlet that included the papal bull, writings from abolitionist Daniel O'Connell, and excerpts from the *Independent's* dialogue. The pamphlet's title page urged supporters of the party, "Read and circulate to Catholic citizens!"[35]

Also in the fall of 1856, Albert Barnes completed *The Church and Slavery*, an expansion of his earlier arguments from church history. The Presbyterian minister believed that the Union was in grave danger because of slavery, and that he had a duty to denounce the institution and call the church to side with abolition. He was especially critical of southern ministers who painted abolitionists as fanatics and misrepresented modern slavery as "of the same nature" as ancient slavery. "No one can estimate the actual influence of ministers of the gospel in sustaining slavery," he lamented. Barnes insisted these proslavery ministers denied the plain facts of Christian history:

> The general course of the Christian church has been against slavery. This was undeniably true in the early history of the church. I know not that it has ever been alleged that any of the prominent defenders of the Christian faith among the "fathers" were advocates of slavery, or that any decree of synods or councils can be adduced in favour of the system.

Barnes concluded that Christian principles ended slavery in both the Roman and British Empires.[36]

Frémont lost to James Buchanan, but some southerners believed that the Republican electoral success in the North boded ill for future elections. In the wake of the election, southern intellectuals in the late 1850s defended slavery with renewed vigor. The specter of abolition led some southerners to celebrate medieval social hierarchies over and against modern notions of equality and liberty.[37] At times, this produced significant departures from typical Protestant readings of church history, especially the narrative that the Protestant Reformation ended the era of Catholic tyranny and corruption. One of the most noteworthy reinterpretations came from George Fitzhugh, the South's leading social theorist. In his widely read *Cannibals All! Or, Slaves without Masters*, published in 1857, Fitzhugh made an extended case for the superiority of a hierarchical social order over the inequalities of laissez-faire capitalism.[38]

In *Cannibals All!* Fitzhugh also challenged the account of the Reformation in William Blackstone's *Commentaries on the Laws of England* (1765–69), still an authoritative legal history in the 1850s. Blackstone represented the English Reformation as a crucial step in establishing the liberty of Englishmen; Fitzhugh, in contrast, argued that the Reformation undermined proper social order in England, not least by dismantling the benevolent hierarchy of church and state. He explained: "In destroying the noblest charity fund in the world, the church lands, and abolishing a priesthood, the efficient and zealous friends of the poor, the Reformation tended to diminish the liberty of the mass of the people, and to impair their moral, social and physical wellbeing." The Reformation represented a step toward a capitalist society, which cloaked itself in the language of freedom and equality while reducing ordinary people to "slaves without masters."[39]

Fitzhugh's criticism of the Reformation resembled arguments made by contemporary American Roman Catholics.[40] As an Episcopalian, however, Fitzhugh distinguished the intent of the Reformation from its unfortunate legacy. "Like the American Revolution," Fitzhugh explained, the Reformation had been distorted into "the unwilling and unnatural parent of the largest and most hideous brood of ills." According to radical "modern philosophers," the Reformation birthed the ideals of equality and private judgment. Such distortion led directly to the "civil discord and domestic broils" of the 1850s, he argued. The disorder, violence, and anarchy that threatened the nation, he proclaimed, were due to New England ministers preaching the supposed "right of private judgment, liberty of speech, freedom of the press and of religion."[41] According to Fitzhugh, northern inequality could be blamed squarely on the Protestant Reformation. He was not the only southerner to make this move.[42] In their zeal to defend slavery, proslavery authors deviated from even the most cherished Protestant historical narratives.

"Is the Church Now More Holy?": History and the Sectional Crisis

By the late 1850s, Christian history became even more prominent in proslavery discourse, especially in the work of legal scholars.[43] Southern lawyers were keen to make the historical arguments that Christians throughout time had carefully distinguished between the spiritual freedom of all believers and the right to physical freedom. In *An Inquiry into the Law of Negro Slavery* (1858), the Georgian lawyer Thomas R. R. Cobb used the Christian past to support his argument for proslavery jurisprudence, while another southern lawyer, George Sawyer of New Orleans, made a similar argument from Christian history in his 1858 treatise, *Southern Institutes; or, An Inquiry into the Origin and Early Prevalence of Slavery and the Slave-Trade.*

An evangelical Presbyterian and accomplished legal scholar, Cobb helped codify Georgia law in the late 1850s before serving as a delegate to the state's secession convention. In *An Inquiry into the Law of Negro Slavery*, Cobb offered nearly six hundred pages of legal, historical, and philosophical arguments for slavery "at the most sophisticated levels of southern thought."[44] The first half of Cobb's treatise traced religious and historical arguments in favor of slavery and, beginning with the early church, narrated what Christian tradition had to say about the institution. "That the true 'heavenly freedom' was open to all, bond or free," Cobb argued, "was inculcated by all the Fathers." To underscore the point, Cobb multiplied quotations from Tertullian, Ignatius, Jerome, and Ambrose on the superiority of spiritual freedom, and Augustine, Chrysostom, and others on the need for Christian slaves to remain in their condition. Cobb acknowledged "the mild and humanizing influences of Christianity" on the condition of slaves but, following Bishop England, insisted that slaveholding persisted unchecked and unquestioned throughout the Middle Ages.[45] Cobb's account of the Christian past provided crucial backing for his discussion of legal history. The book's synthesis of southern proslavery thought proved widely influential, with several state supreme courts using its arguments in decisions on slavery-related cases in the late 1850s and early 1860s.[46]

Similarly, in *Southern Institutes*, George Sawyer argued that although some medieval Christians practiced manumission, they only did so with intellectually and morally equal races. The implication regarding Christian ownership of Africans was clear. According to Sawyer, the medieval church never encroached upon the "right" of the master to own a slave nor ever called it a sin. Quoting Constantine and Gregory the Great, Sawyer argued that church history showed "the most scrupulous observance of the right of property in the master to the service and the control of the person of the slave." With abolitionists in mind, the lawyer posed the question: "Is the Church now more holy than in the pristine days of the Apostles?"[47] By appealing to the early church, Sawyer played on the primitivist narratives of Christian history that predominated in antebellum theological discourse.

James W. C. Pennington, building on his prior work in the 1840s, offered a contrary argument in a series of articles in the *Anglo-African Magazine* in 1859. In this series, titled "A Review of Slavery and the Slave-Trade," Pennington summarized the history of slavery from ancient times through the present and argued that European slavery was not abolished because of the feudal system but rather as "the natural effects of *christianity.*" The Christian doctrines of human equality, divine impartiality, and eternal judgment made it inevitable that Christian Europe would free its slaves. Pennington then quoted a number of abolitionist charters as "positive proof that Christianity was the only cause of the suppression of slavery" and concluded that abolition must be the natural progression of Christianity in Europe and the United States.[48] Even as the political storm clouds grew darker, Pennington and other antislavery activists insisted that the Christian past demonstrated the inevitability of abolition. Church history was the story of Christian principles of freedom and equality slowly overcoming the political and economic forces of greed.[49]

As secession loomed, proslavery ministers insisted all the more that ecclesiastical history completely justified Christian slaveholding. Ebenezer Boyden, a northerner who served for half a century as an Episcopalian rector in Virginia, published a vigorous condemnation of abolitionism in 1860. Boyden pointed to patristic and medieval exegesis, arguing that "for eighteen centuries there was but one interpretation . . . that slavery is an allowable institution, not a hideous sin." Against antislavery readings of the Bible, Boyden insisted that "the Christian fathers" and even the "old Puritans" understood scripture to allow slavery. He charged abolitionists with effectively excom-municating "the whole Christian Church of the past, with the Hebrew and Patriarchal Churches [and] their own Puritan forefathers who, in fact, were pro-slavery, slave-owning, and slave-trading."[50] Boyden used church history to cast New England abolitionists as hypocritical moralists who denied their own past and threatened both Christian and national unity.

However, the most influential historical argument for Christian slave-holding came not from the South, but from John Henry Hopkins, bishop of the Episcopal Diocese of Vermont. In December 1860, several New York politicians wrote a letter asking Bishop Hopkins for his opinions on slavery. In January 1861, just after South Carolina voted to secede from the Union, Hopkins's answer was published in several New York papers and printed as the *Bible View of Slavery*. Twenty thousand copies of the latter were distrib-uted by the brand-new American Society for Promoting National Unity.[51]

In the *Bible View of Slavery* Hopkins argued that abolition had no basis in scripture. He himself was a proponent of gradual emancipation and coloni-zation, and considered himself personally opposed to slavery, but from the early 1850s had been a vocal critic of abolitionism. Slaveholding may be un-fortunate, but it was not sinful in principle. This view he defended by walking through scripture from the Old Testament through the New, arguing that slavery persisted in every era in biblical history.[52]

Initially, Hopkins's proslavery argument did not provoke a widespread re-action from abolitionists—that would come several years later. But he was answered by Leonard Marsh, professor of Greek and Latin at the University of Vermont, who in a scathing critique of *Bible View* argued that Hopkins had completely ignored the history of scriptural interpretation, which, by his lights, proved that the principles of scripture aimed toward abolition: "From the time of the Apostles, there has been, in the hearts of christians, a feeling, ever becoming deeper, and spreading wider, that slavery is incompatible with the spirit and principles of christianity." According to Marsh, abolition did not have its roots in eighteenth-century innovation—nor, as Hopkins had claimed, in early Christian heresies—but in properly orthodox doctrine. As evidence, Marsh pointed to early Christian and medieval customs of man-umitting slaves. He admitted that although Christians frequently owned slaves, "This inconsistency was felt, and . . . the christian heart acknowl-edged the incompatibility of slavery with Christianity." By the beginning of the Protestant Reformation, Marsh concluded, "Slavery was all but extinct in every part of Europe."[53] Marsh, and other northern ministers, directly challenged Hopkins's understanding of Christian history.[54] The argument with Hopkins, however, was only getting started.

"Antiquated Excuses": History during War

After the South seceded and the Civil War began, the meaning of the Christian past only took on greater urgency. For Confederates, church history proved useful in constructing white Christian nationalism, particularly in the best-selling *Cause and Contrast: An Essay on the American Crisis* (1862). Written by Irish Catholic immigrant T. W. MacMahon, *Cause and Contrast* provided a historical narrative that vindicated slavery in explicitly racist terms. MacMahon endeavored to use history to demonstrate both white supremacy and the antiquity of Christian slaveholding. He insisted that early Christians embraced Roman slave codes and customs and argued that "general enfranchisement was never contemplated by the greatest and wisest of Christian writers, philosophers, law-givers, and saints." MacMahon listed a number of patristic sources—including Athanasius, Augustine, Gregory the Great, and Basil—as having supported slavery.[55] His narrative provided a pedigree for emerging Confederate nationalism and was very well received upon its publication in 1862, selling three thousand copies in its first week of print.[56]

As the war progressed, northern ministers continued to justify their cause in historical terms. In May 1863, months after Lincoln's Emancipation Proclamation came into effect, Congregationalist minister Joseph Parrish Thompson published a fast-day sermon titled *Christianity and Emancipation*. To those who argued that freeing slaves went against the consensus of Christian history, Thompson replied that this confused genuine Christianity with Roman Catholicism. He explained that the early church was characterized by a "spirit of freedom and of equality" that was lost after Constantine and the establishment of Christianity. Medieval practices of slaveholding, he reasoned, should be understood as a symptom of the "apostasy of the middle ages." The Reformation, then, was a crucial step toward freeing the slaves. While the Protestant reformers had not focused on "philanthropic reform," Thompson argued that they recovered the "primitive" church's emphases on spiritual equality and freedom. Over time, this recovery produced emancipation.[57] Thompson's argument here reflected a typical northern outlook in which the American ideals of equality and liberty had their roots in the Reformation.[58]

Meanwhile, Hopkins's defense of slavery came back into view during the fractious Pennsylvania gubernatorial election in 1863. Pennsylvania Democrats sought to unseat the Republican incumbent, Governor Andrew G. Curtin, a close friend of Abraham Lincoln who had mustered the resources of the state into the war effort. In April 1863, Episcopalians in Philadelphia wrote to Bishop Hopkins asking for permission to reprint the *Bible View*: "We believe that false teachings on this subject have had a great deal to do with bringing on the unhappy strife between two sections of our common country, and that a lamentable degree of ignorance prevails in regard to it."[59] After the bishop agreed, the *Bible View* was disseminated across the state—and the Democratic Party reprinted it as part of its campaign literature, using Bishop Hopkins's arguments to bolster support for the party's candidate, Judge George Woodward, among Pennsylvanians sympathetic to the southern cause.

The reemergence of Hopkins's proslavery pamphlet in the middle of an election produced a strong backlash. Antislavery newspapers, such as the *National Anti-slavery Standard*, castigated Hopkins; several printed a satirical letter that reproduced Hopkins's argument with the word "slavery" replaced by "polygamy."[60] George M. Stroud, an abolitionist judge in Philadelphia, printed selections from Hopkins's work paired with the proslavery views of Judge Woodward and excerpts from a firsthand account of slavery in Georgia.[61] One hundred sixty-four Episcopalian clergy in Pennsylvania, including Bishop Alonzo Potter, put their names to a public protest that accused Hopkins of "strengthen[ing] the hands of the rebellion, and weaken[ing] the hands of the government in the pending struggle."[62]

Hopkins indignantly replied, expressing amazement that he was being attacked for something written two years prior, but also refusing to back down on his reading of scripture and, he added, church tradition: "I *know* that the doctrine of that Church was clear and unanimous on the *lawfulness* of slavery for eighteen centuries together; and on that point I regard your 'protest' and 'indignant reprobation' as the idle wind that passes by." Hopkins then mentioned his forthcoming book, in which he would provide a more extensive defense of the compatibility of Christianity and slavery. "I shall prove in that book, by the most unquestionable authorities, that slaves and slaveholders were in the Church from the beginning," he wrote, "that slavery was held to be consistent with Christian principles by the Fathers and Councils, and by all Protestant divines and commentators up to the very close of the last century; and that this fact was universal among all churches and sects throughout the Christian world." With no small degree of animus, Hopkins promised to include Bishop Potter's name in the opening of the book "so that if I cannot give you fame, I may, at least, do my part to give you notoriety." Two days before the gubernatorial election, this reply to Bishop Potter was printed in a Pennsylvania Copperhead newspaper, the *Philadelphia Mercury*.[63]

Hopkins lived up to his word and published an expanded argument in *A Scriptural, Ecclesiastical, and Historical View of Slavery* (1864). He doubled down on the proslavery reading of 1 Corinthians 7, insisting that the best scholarship on the Greek proved that "the old interpretation of St. Chrysostom is vindicated, in opposition to the majority of the modern expositors." Hopkins cited other ancient commentators to bolster his exegetical case before turning to various patristic and medieval theologians, including Augustine, whom he believed distinguished between spiritual and physical freedom. He insisted on the perpetuity of Christian slaveholding, reproducing selections from various church councils to show that slavery "was acknowledged by the Church for the first nine hundred years of the Christian era . . . while not one suggestion can be found imputing *sin* to the relation between the master and the slave." In fact, slaves belonged not only to ordinary Christians, but also to churches, monasteries, and clergy. Church history, according to Hopkins, proved the compatibility of Christianity and slaveholding.[64]

While Hopkins's book went into several editions, this argument was not well received in the North in 1864, as the war effort teetered on the brink. The *North American Review* lamented that "few books more saddening than this have been produced even by the party spirit of these agitated and reckless times." The review made sure to point out a number of historical errors made by Hopkins and concluded that the bishop's reading of church history displayed "a degree of ignorance which amounts to irresponsibility."[65] Fellow Episcopal bishop Mark Antony De Wolfe Howe published a rebuttal in 1864, castigating Hopkins for weaving "Patristic Dicta and Papal Bulls, and Conciliar Decrees, and Episcopal Pastorals" into a mantle of "antiquated excuses" to cover an enormous sin.[66]

The most extensive response to Hopkins's historical account was written in 1864 by Daniel R. Goodwin, Episcopal priest and provost of the University of Pennsylvania from 1860 to 1868. An ameliorist and proponent of African colonization, Goodwin criticized Hopkins for assuming "that the principles, the genius and spirit and practical influence of Christianity are not and have not always been against slavery." Goodwin set out to demonstrate the falsity of this assumption. He argued that before Constantine the church "was powerless to influence the government," and afterwards it was "rapidly corrupted in its moral sense by its contact with a slaveholding aristocracy." Yet the church still abolished slavery nearly completely throughout the Roman Empire. Each of Hopkins's quotations was reinterpreted by Goodwin, including Chrysostom's "over-refinement" of 1 Corinthians 7. Goodwin then offered his own selections, including Chrysostom's attribution of slavery to "insatiable avarice and envy," along with passages from Augustine, Gregory of Nyssa, Pope Gregory XVI, and the Protestant reformers. When it came to opposing slavery, "The clergy and the dignitaries of the church may often have lagged behind," Goodwin concluded, "but the spirit of Christianity has lived in the hearts of the Christian people."[67]

The controversy over Hopkins illuminates several features of the debate about historic Christian slaveholding, particularly the ways in which arguments over history mirrored the basic shape of the argument over scripture. Hopkins stressed that church tradition, like scripture, did not consider slavery a sin in the abstract, insisting on a straightforward—if rather selective—appropriation of the teaching and practice of the historic church. His opponents, by contrast, prioritized the trajectory of Christian history, which they claimed moved inexorably toward emancipation. Hopkins's critics gave greater weight to the "spirit" of the Christian past than to any formal condemnation or acceptance of it. As in exegetical arguments, the fault line formed between literalist and intuitive readings.[68]

Even though Bishop Hopkins's historical arguments invoked outrage throughout the North, he emerged relatively unscathed and went on to serve as the presiding bishop of the Episcopal Church from 1865 to 1868. In fact, Hopkins's leadership and antiabolitionist writings helped bring about postbellum reunification between northern and southern Episcopalians. As Hopkins's grandson wrote, the bishop's defense of slavery "increased his popularity in the South, [but] made for him many influential enemies . . . throughout the North."[69] In its own way, then, Hopkins's account of Christian history helped reunify the white Protestant nation.[70] On the other side of the bloody struggle, the legacy of slavery could be easily overlooked for the sake of national unity.[71]

For others, however, church history gave reason for not reunifying— for continuing the fight, if not with arms, in print. As the opening of this chapter described, Robert Dabney insisted in his *Defense of Virginia* (1867) that slavery had always been accepted by Christians. Dabney's conviction that abolition was a modern heresy went hand in hand with his racism—after the war, he publicly opposed extending the vote to freedpeople or offering free education to Black children. In 1867, Dabney gave a speech to the Virginia Synod against the ordination of Black ministers in the Presbyterian Church in the United States. Again, the history of Christianity featured in his argument. He argued that "the primitive Church . . . from the very days of the apostles onward, always refused to ordain slaves, although they freely admitted them to the Church."[72] In his role as moderator of the 1870 General Assembly, Dabney led the way in opposing reunification between northern and southern Presbyterians. The lost cause would at least be preserved in his church, if not in his country.

When the embittered Dabney insisted on the absurdity of Christ allowing his church to remain in "seventeen centuries of sin," he strained the logic of his Presbyterianism.[73] Dabney's incredulity fit rather poorly with Protestant historical convictions. But his consternation is also revealing of how the slavery arguments, like no other question or debate in this era, pushed Protestants to rethink long-standing assumptions about church history. With the exception of Schaff and a few others, virtually every Protestant subject in this book believed firmly in a general narrative of medieval decline from the pure apostolic church. This declension was more often assumed than argued—it rarely was challenged, and typically was taken for granted by American Protestants. But in their eagerness to challenge or defend slavery, some would depart from even this most enduring Protestant historical narrative.

This was only one of many ironies in the debates over slavery, which saw Catholics ignoring or reinterpreting papal decrees, Episcopalians celebrating early American Puritans, Presbyterians defending medieval society while criticizing the Reformation, Baptists treating patristic exegesis as authoritative, and anticlerical abolitionists praising the pope. Not all of this irony was lost on contemporaries. As has been discussed, African American historians, in particular, took pleasure in pointing out the hypocrisy of proslavery authors who cited North African church fathers in their arguments for white supremacy.

Perhaps most unexpected, given the typical depiction of American Protestants as disinterested in church history, is the sheer prevalence of the Christian past in the debate. From the 1830s through the Civil War, Christians across various Protestant denominations readily drew on patristic and medieval theology, argued about precedent, and even insisted on the importance of tradition. Dozens of published tracts, treatises, and sermons show that arguments over slavery were also debates about the meaning of the Christian past, and church history proliferated not only in the publications of theologians and ministers but also of lawyers, politicians, and statesmen. The popularity, frequency, and range of these historical arguments show that an era characterized as ahistorical and antitraditional in fact saw extensive engagement with the history of Christianity.

The widespread use of Christian history modifies our understanding of the antebellum "theological crisis," as Mark Noll describes it.[74] Certainly, American theologians failed to overcome their disagreements in part because of widely shared hermeneutical assumptions and a kind of biblicism. However, this biblicism was not in practice defined by disregard of tradition nor inattention to history. Put another way, the theological crisis foundered not because pro- and antislavery authors ignored the Christian past but precisely because they attended to and used that past to make conflicting arguments. The historical narratives reconstructed by each side of the debate only strengthened the conviction that theirs was a holy cause. Increasingly certain that the Bible endorsed their respective positions, pro- and antislavery Christians also believed that they were on the right side of church history. Rather than tradition and history providing resources for the resolution of the crisis, the remembered religious past only made the debate all the more intractable. Arguments over slavery show that history, much like theology, remained subservient to politics, culture, and race, illustrating both the plasticity and the limitations of historical memory. History did not bridge but instead deepened the divide between pro- and antislavery Christians.

Epilogue

On June 1, 2020, police in Washington, DC used tear gas to disperse protestors and clear a path for Donald Trump to walk to St. John's Episcopal Church. There the president posed for a photograph while holding up a Bible before walking back to the White House. The intended meaning was obvious: in a moment of widespread protest over racial injustice and police brutality, Trump, like his many evangelical supporters, stood for the Bible. The image encapsulated one of the bizarre aspects of the story of Trump's rise from laughable candidacy to electoral victor: namely, how a vulgar, impious reality TV star won over some voters with his awkward, at times unbelievable, appeals to evangelical values. Even allowing for some skepticism about the exit polls that showed Trump receiving the vote of 81 percent of self-identified white evangelicals, he won the presidency in part because of strong support among evangelicals. Four years later, Trump posed with a Bible to remind these voters that he was still their man.

As a public relations stunt, Trump's Bible photo might seem unserious, but the president certainly understood the importance of Christian scripture to a significant voting bloc. Evangelicals are biblicists, and the extent to which American religiosity has been dominated by evangelical Protestantism correlates to the degree to which American culture has been shaped by the Bible. For this all one needs is to read the titles of recent scholarly works: *An American Bible: A History of the Good Book in the United States*; *Sacred Scripture, Sacred War: The Bible and the American Revolution*; *The Bible in American Life*; *The Bible in American Law and Politics*; *American Zion: The Old Testament as a Political Text from the Revolution to the Civil War*; *In the Beginning was the Word: The Bible in American Public Life*. The list could go on.

And even if the Bible's influence in 2020 is not what it was in 1820, it nonetheless holds its place among a significant demographic. Sacred scripture remains authoritative for evangelicals, who demonstrate their biblicism in the quantity of words spent on what the Bible means: from convention halls, to social media, to the blogosphere, evangelicals argue over the Bible's teaching

The Old Faith in a New Nation. Paul J. Gutacker, Oxford University Press. © Oxford University Press 2023.
DOI: 10.1093/oso/9780197639146.003.0009

on reproductive ethics, sexuality, environmental care, women's ordination, and much more. What does it mean to embody "biblical womanhood"? Does the present-day notion of "social justice" fit with or contradict "biblical justice"? What does a "biblical worldview" say about economics?[1] If importance could be quantified by the proliferation of arguments over what is "biblical," then the Christian scriptures have never enjoyed a higher status among evangelicals and the churches they attend.

But even as intraevangelical arguments center on the Bible, they are never only about the Bible. Especially on the most contested questions, when evangelicals differ about what the Bible means, they quickly turn to the practices and interpretations of Christians before them: clergy dispute the history of the female diaconate, theologians contest the gendered implications of fourth-century Trinitarian theology, bloggers spar over the relationship between orthodox doctrine and sexual norms, while others recover the history of the church's political and economic activism. In part because of these and other contemporary controversies, Christian history matters not only to scholars, but also to pundits, pastors, and ordinary laypeople. The Christian past, remembered in various ways and toward various ends, continues to shape the evangelical world.

This is nothing new. American Protestants have always been interested in Christian history. Even as they claimed to rely on the Bible alone, nineteenth-century Protestants concerned themselves with the theology and practices of past Christians; cited saints, scholars, and councils from throughout the tradition; engaged patristic, medieval, and Reformational exegesis; and worked hard to locate themselves within the broad history of Christianity. While the Bible held preeminent authority for these Protestants, it wielded this authority within and alongside other religious texts and traditions. Frequently, these other sources were employed to underscore, clarify, and adjudicate the authority of scripture. Only by paying attention to the ways in which the Christian past was remembered can we understand what evangelical biblicism did and did not mean.

Further, the story of Protestant historical memory implies a hermeneutical point: namely, that there is no way to avoid tradition. Put another way, there is no tradition-less reading of the Bible. Various Protestants give different relative weight to scripture and tradition, and even those evangelicals who want to avoid the so-called *nuda scriptura* (bare scripture) hermeneutic still rank scripture above and apart from any postbiblical teaching of the church. It makes sense to call these evangelicals biblicists. But in every Christian community, including those who position themselves against tradition, are implicit narratives of how they fit within or against the history of Christianity writ large. These historical assumptions shape a church's or denomination's self-understanding and guide their interpretation of the Bible. In short, the story of American Protestants and the Christian past invites religious communities, especially those who are biblicist, not to think they have avoided the problems of history or tradition, but rather to pay attention to the stories and traditions they have inherited.

On the other hand, churches and denominations who prioritize tradition in their theology and praxis—especially those who appeal to tradition as authoritative—may also find a cautionary tale in this book. Some may want to believe that the mistakes made in nineteenth-century American theology might have been avoided if Protestants had given any attention to the past. But it is now clear that they did. Instead of solving things, historical memory—by which I mean appropriation of the most widely read historiography of the day—arguably made the weaknesses of American Protestantism more acute. Much like scripture, tradition proved pliable, easily bent to one's own ends. The story of American religious memory invites traditionalist denominations to reflect on how they receive and remember history, precedent and tradition, and the ways in which this can go wrong.

Identifying our own historical biases and blind spots is difficult, if not impossible, work; far easier to criticize the historical assumptions that were influential two centuries ago. From a safe distance, we can interrogate historical narratives that shaped American religious and political life. This valuable work is beyond the scope of this book, but one example is worth highlighting: the Spanish Inquisition. Nineteenth-century anti-Catholicism was fed by quite high estimations of the violence of the Inquisition, most vividly exemplified by William Craig Brownlee's claim that it "cost Spain in all TWO MILLIONS OF LIVES!"[2] While not reaching Brownlee's hyperbole, twentieth-century histories and encyclopedias numbered the Inquisition's executions between 30,000 and 120,000.[3] Yet archival work in the 1990s showed that these figures were vastly overinflated—in fact, death rates in Inquisition courts compare favorably to secular courts of the day.[4] In other words, historians have significantly revised a narrative that played a significant role in the establishment of American religious freedom and the construction of Protestant nationalism—a narrative that persists to a remarkable degree today. Other influential myths also invite reevaluation: the memory of medieval Christendom as the "Dark Ages,"[5] the decline narrative of the church's "Constantinian fall,"[6] or the dismissal of Christian orthodoxy as "Hellenized" by alien Greek philosophy.[7] More work can and should be done on the legacy of these flawed narratives—notably, all reflecting anti-Catholic and antimedieval biases—in American history.

Yet even as we use historical tools to reevaluate these and other outdated myths, the story told in this book ought to mitigate too much optimism. The sobering lesson of American engagement with Christian history is that there is rarely a clean line between past and present. Contemporary debates over theology, ethics, and politics will require more, not less, attention to the ways in which the past, and especially the religious past, is remembered, debated, and memorialized. At the same time, those of us who teach and write history need a healthy dose of realism about the limited usefulness of historical memory. The implications of the past for present-day concerns are rarely clear and always provisional. Historical memory can be used or misused, can illuminate or obscure, can disarm or reinforce prejudice. We need to read history, but never history alone.

Notes

Introduction

1. Biblicism is one of David Bebbington's four characteristics of evangelicalism. He describes biblicism as evangelicals' "devotion to the Bible, . . . the result of their belief that all spiritual truth is to be found in its pages," and quotes John Wesley's desire to be "*homo unius libri* [a man of one book]." David Bebbington, *Evangelicalism in Modern Britain: A History from the 1730s to the 1980s* (London: Routledge, 1993), 12.

2. Philip Schaff, *History of the Christian Church*, 2nd ed. (Edinburgh: T&T Clark, 1883), I:50.

3. Nathan Hatch argued that post-Revolution Christians grew increasingly optimistic that religion would make progress once unencumbered by tradition and old authorities. Nathan O. Hatch, *The Democratization of American Christianity* (New Haven, CT: Yale University Press, 1989), 9–11. As Hatch puts it, American Christianity took shape "in a culture that mounted a frontal assault upon tradition." Ibid., 182. Mark Noll argues that American Christianity became characterized by an antitraditional approach to theology and scripture. Mark A. Noll, *America's God: From Jonathan Edwards to Abraham Lincoln* (Oxford: Oxford University Press, 2002). Likewise, E. Brooks Holifield argues that Revolutionary ideology led to a theological populism that frequently rejected Protestant precedent and Christian tradition at large. E. Brooks Holifield, *Theology in America: Christian Thought from the Age of the Puritans to the Civil War* (New Haven, CT: Yale University Press, 2003), 18–19.

4. Mark A. Noll, *The Civil War as a Theological Crisis* (Chapel Hill: University of North Carolina Press, 2006), 22.

5. Hatch, *Democratization*, 169.

6. Noll, *The Civil War*, chap. 3. Contra Noll, Fox-Genovese and Genovese argue that an antislavery biblical argument required departing from Protestant orthodoxy, not just the common-sense hermeneutic. See Elizabeth Fox-Genovese and Eugene D. Genovese, *The Mind of the Master Class: History and Faith in the Southern Slaveholders' Worldview* (Cambridge: Cambridge University Press, 2005), 527.

7. For example, see George C. Rable, *God's Almost Chosen Peoples: A Religious History of the American Civil War* (Chapel Hill: University of North Carolina Press, 2010), 14; Molly Oshatz, *Slavery and Sin: The Fight against Slavery and the Rise of Liberal Protestantism* (Oxford: Oxford University Press, 2012), 10, 58; John Patrick Daly, *When Slavery Was Called Freedom: Evangelicalism, Proslavery, and the Causes of the Civil War* (Lexington: University Press of Kentucky, 2015), 31ff.

8. Jan Assmann, *Moses the Egyptian: The Memory of Egypt in Western Monotheism* (Cambridge, MA: Harvard University Press, 1997), 9.

9. For example, Seth Perry recently argued that biblicism in early nineteenth-century America was less a reality than a rhetorical construct. Scripture wielded its authority, Perry shows, through lived experience and relationships, belying early American claims to rely on "the Bible alone." Perry pushes back on accounts of American Protestantism as democratizing and innovative, while inviting new questions about what biblicism did and did not mean. Seth Perry, *Bible Culture and Authority in the Early United States* (Princeton, NJ: Princeton University Press, 2018), 2, 5–8.

10. In Beth Barton Schweiger's masterful study of southern reading, she finds several evidence of ordinary people reading religious historiography, including a North Carolinian farmer who read Reformation history in the 1850s, and, nearby, the Speer women, who read histories of the Reformation and the Middle Ages. See Beth Barton Schweiger, *A Literate South: Reading before Emancipation* (New Haven, CT: Yale University Press, 2019), 16, 29.

11. See Richard Beale Davis, *A Colonial Southern Bookshelf: Reading in the Eighteenth Century* (Athens: University of Georgia Press, 1979), 39–40. For the history of John Foxe in America, see Adrian Chastain Weimer, *Martyrs' Mirror: Persecution and Holiness in Early New England* (Oxford: Oxford University Press, 2011) and Heike Jablonski, *John Foxe in America: Discourses of Martyrdom in the Eighteenth- and Nineteenth-Century United States* (Paderborn: Ferdinand Schöningh, 2017).

12. As Lewis Spitz argues, Mosheim's application of source criticism to church history, together with his intention to write an impartial account, made him an earlier pioneer of modern historical writing. Lewis Spitz, "Johann Lorenz Mosheim's Philosophy of History," *Concordia Theological Monthly* 20, no. 5 (May 1949): 338–39. See Euan Cameron's discussion of Mosheim's reputation. Euan Cameron, *Interpreting Christian History* (New York: Wiley & Sons, 2008), 149.

13. For example, Francis McFarland's notes from his study at Princeton Theological Seminary (1819–20) show that historical material, and references to Mosheim and other historians, appear in a number of courses: lectures by Archibald Alexander on church history, lectures by Alexander on polemical theology, lectures by Samuel Miller on church governance, and more. See Box 3, Folder 5, Francis McFarland Papers, RG 459, Presbyterian Historical Society, Philadelphia, PA.

14. See Schweiger, *A Literate South*, 10–11.

15. Johannes Laurentius a Mosheim, *An Ecclesiastical History, Antient And Modern, From The Birth Of Christ, To The Beginning Of The Present Century* (London: A. Millar, 1765), I:xxvii, xxi.

16. See Cameron, *Interpreting Christian History*, 149–50.

17. As Peter Messer argues, Hume and Robertson were widely considered "the most important historians of the era." Peter C. Messer, *Stories of Independence: Identity, Ideology, and History in Eighteenth-Century America* (DeKalb: Northern Illinois University Press, 2005), 7, 11.

18. Joseph Milner, *The History of the Church of Christ* (York: G. Peacock, 1794), I:ix–xi.

19. Most devastating of these critiques was S. R. Maitland, *A Letter to the Rev. H. J. Rose with Strictures on Milner's Church History* (London: J. G. & F. Rivington, 1834), 10. Maitland published criticisms of Milner in 1834, 1835, and 1836. For Milner's

reception and adaptation in America, see Paul Gutacker, "Joseph Milner and His Editors: Eighteenth- and Nineteenth-Century Evangelicals and the Christian Past," *Journal of Ecclesiastical History* 69, no. 1 (January 2018): 86–104.

20. The English educator John Walker's history, for example, devoted a number of pages to lamenting the "rude manners" of the Middle Ages and the "mistaken zeal" of the Crusades. John Walker, *Elements of Geography and of Natural and Civil History*, 3rd ed. (Dublin: T. M. Bates, 1797), 316–20. The Scottish historian Alexander Tytler also wrote an introductory history that was republished in America: Alexander Fraser Tytler, *Elements of General History, Ancient & Modern*, 3rd ed. (Edinburgh: Creech, 1805), 241–46. Thomas Gisborne, Anglican priest and member of the Clapham Sect, wrote a survey of Christian faith that went into several printings in America. Thomas Gisborne, *A Familiar Survey of the Christian Religion: And of History*, 2nd ed. (London: A. Strahan, 1799).

21. According to the Congregationalist periodical *The Independent*, Buck's *Dictionary*, along with Mosheim, remained the primary source of church history for most Congregational ministers in 1855. See "Church History," *The Independent* (New York), July 5, 1855, America's Historical Newspapers. Charles Buck's entries on medieval Catholic persecution, as Matthew Bowman documents, were among his most popular, and these were often reprinted in pamphlet form. Matthew Bowman and Samuel Brown, "Reverend Buck's Theological Dictionary and the Struggle to Define American Evangelicalism, 1802–1851," *Journal of the Early Republic* 29, no. 3 (2009): 458.

22. For examples of periodicals extracting Milner, see *Weekly Record* (Chillicothe, OH), April 27, 1815, May 24, 1815, May 31, 1815, April 10, 1816, and *North Star* (Danville, VT), August 1, 1822, March 30, 1824, April 13, 1824, April 20, 1824. America's Historical Newspapers.

Chapter 1

1. For this dispute, see Peter E. Gilmore, "Rebels and Revivals: Ulster Immigrants, Western Pennsylvania Presbyterianism and the Formation of Scotch-Irish Identity, 1780–1830," PhD diss., Carnegie Mellon University, 2009, 534–39; Robert Emery, "Church and State in the Early Republic: The Covenanters' Radical Critique," *Journal of Law and Religion* 25, no. 2 (2009): 487–501; Steven Wedgeworth, "'The Two Sons of Oil' and the Limits of American Religious Dissent," *Journal of Law and Religion* 27, no. 1 (2011): 141–61; Joseph S. Moore, *Founding Sins: How a Group of Antislavery Radicals Fought to Put Christ into the Constitution* (Oxford: Oxford University Press, 2016).

2. Covenanters took their name from the Covenant of 1643, which had established Reformed religion in Scotland, and, they believed, was akin to the Old Testament covenants between Israel and God. After the Glorious Revolution brought about the abandonment of the 1643 covenant, Covenanters dissented from the established church. See Gilmore, "Rebels and Revivals," 125–26.

3. Rodger C. Henderson, "Findley, William (1742–1821), Member of the U.S. House of Representatives," in *American National Biography Online*, February 2000. http://www.anb.org/articles/03/03-00170.html.

4. Gordon S. Wood, *Empire of Liberty: A History of the Early Republic, 1789–1815* (Oxford: Oxford University Press, 2009), 223.

5. William Findley, *Observations on "The Two Sons of Oil": Containing a Vindication of the American Constitutions, and Defending the Blessings of Religious Liberty and Toleration* (Pittsburgh, PA: Patterson & Hopkins, 1812), 84–87.

6. Ibid., 52, 86, 103, 110. The emphasis is Findley's.

7. Ibid., 107, 125.

8. Historians writing on Revolutionary-era arguments for freedom neglect how antiestablishment narratives grew from widespread assumptions about the history of Christianity. See J. G. A. Pocock, *The Machiavellian Moment: Florentine Political Thought and the Atlantic Republican Tradition* (Princeton, NJ: Princeton University Press, 1974), chap. 15; Peter C. Messer, *Stories of Independence: Identity, Ideology, and History in Eighteenth-Century America* (DeKalb: Northern Illinois University Press, 2005), 5; H. Trevor Colbourn, *The Lamp of Experience: Whig History and the Intellectual Origins of the American Revolution* (Chapel Hill: University of North Carolina Press, 1965). Others acknowledge the historical understandings of religious dissenters, but do not notice how this was grounded in, and encouraged by, leading accounts of Christian history. See Edwin S. Gaustad, *Neither King nor Prelate: Religion and the New Nation, 1776–1826* (Grand Rapids, MI: Eerdmans, 1993); John Witte Jr., "'A Most Mild and Equitable Establishment of Religion': John Adams and the Massachusetts Experiment," in *Religion and the New Republic: Faith in the Founding of America*, ed. James H. Hutson (New York: Rowman & Littlefield, 2000), 1–31; John Witte and Joel A. Nichols, *Religion and the American Constitutional Experiment*, 4th ed. (Oxford: Oxford University Press, 2016), 8–9. On history and dissent, see J. C. D. Clark, *The Language of Liberty, 1660–1832: Political Discourse and Social Dynamics in the Anglo-American World* (Cambridge: Cambridge University Press, 1994); Karen O'Brien, *Narratives of Enlightenment: Cosmopolitan History from Voltaire to Gibbon* (Cambridge: Cambridge University Press, 1997), 205–6, 210; Christopher S. Grenda, "Faith, Reason, and Enlightenment: The Cultural Sources of Toleration in Early America," in *The First Prejudice: Religious Tolerance and Intolerance in Early America*, ed. Chris Beneke and Christopher S. Grenda (Philadelphia: University of Pennsylvania Press, 2011), 23–52; Carl H. Esbeck and Jonathan J. Den Hartog, eds., *Disestablishment and Religious Dissent: Church-State Relations in the New American States, 1776–1833* (Columbia: University of Missouri Press, 2019). For the most part, the literature gives the impression that memory of the Christian past had nothing to do with how early national Americans negotiated the question of church and state. One exception is a study of John Foxe that connects martyrology to arguments for religious toleration. See Jablonski, *John Foxe in America*, chap. 3. Another analyzes church history in earlier American discourse on religious liberty: Hans R. Guggisberg, "Religious Freedom and the History of the Christian World in Roger Williams' Thought," *Early American Literature* 12, no. 1 (1977): 36–48. In

his work, Thomas Curry notes references to Constantine and medieval corruption, but not the works that undergirded these historical allusions. Thomas J. Curry, *The First Freedoms: Church and State in America to the Passage of the First Amendment* (Oxford: Oxford University Press, 1987), 17, 116, 130–31, 144. In a later work, Curry shows that dissenters believed that disestablishment of state churches would undo the great error of Christendom, but does not explore the historiography that led dissenters to locate their efforts within Christian history. Thomas J. Curry, *Farewell to Christendom: The Future of Church and State in America* (Oxford: Oxford University Press, 2001), 7–11, 28–30, 37.

9. Johannes Laurentius a Mosheim, *An Ecclesiastical History, Ancient and Modern, From the Birth of Christ to the Beginning of the Present Century* (London: A. Millar, 1765), I:xxv–xxvi. For Mosheim's achievements, see Lewis Spitz, "Johann Lorenz Mosheim's Philosophy of History," *Concordia Theological Monthly* 20, no. 5 (May 1949): 338–39; Euan Cameron, *Interpreting Christian History* (New York: Wiley & Sons, 2008), 149. While he affirmed Trinitarian doctrine, the Lutheran worried that fourth-century credal formulations were too speculative.

10. Mosheim, *An Ecclesiastical History*, I: xxv–xxvi, 45, 61, 86, 88, 98–99. E. P. Meijering, "Mosheim on the Philosophy of the Church Fathers," in *Nederlands Archief Voor Kerkgeschiednis, 56* (Leiden: Brill, 1976), 380; E. P. Meijering, "Mosheim on the Difference between Christianity and Platonism: A Contribution to the Discussion about Methodology," *Vigiliae Christianae* 31, no. 1 (March 1977): 73.

11. So argues Cameron in Cameron, *Interpreting Christian History*, 151.

12. However, Protestant churches were not immune from excess, and Mosheim pointed to the Anabaptists and Quakers as proof. Mosheim, *An Ecclesiastical History*, I:671, 682, II:ii, 151.

13. See Michael Printy, "The Reformation of the Enlightenment: German Histories in the Eighteenth Century," in *Politics and Reformations: Histories and Reformations: Essays in Honor of Thomas A. Brady, Jr*, ed. Christopher Ocker and Thomas A. Brady (Boston: Brill, 2007), 140–41. Maclaine's appendix intended to rebut David Hume and cast private judgment and "liberty of conscience" as fundamental principles of the Reformation, arguing that the Reformers promoted "the rights of human nature . . . and the exercise of religious liberty." Mosheim, *An Ecclesiastical History*, Appendix 1, pp. 2, 7.

14. Edward Gibbon, *The History of the Decline and Fall of the Roman Empire* (London: W. Strahan and T. Cadell, 1776), I:483–85, 488, 491–92, 550–552.

15. See S. P. Foster, *Melancholy Duty: The Hume-Gibbon Attack on Christianity* (Dordrecht: Springer Science & Business Media, 1997), 16–19.

16. Jean-Jacques Rousseau, *"The Social Contract" & Discourses*, trans. George D. H. Cole (London: J.M. Dent & Sons, 1913), 130.

17. David Hume, *The History of England, from the Invasion of Julius Caesar to the Revolution in 1688* (London: A. Millar, 1762), II:439–40. Hume's *History* went into fifty editions during its first fifty years of publication. See Nicholas T. Phillipson, *David Hume: The Philosopher as Historian* (New Haven, CT: Yale University Press, 2012), 131.

18. William Robertson, "View of the State of Society in the Middle Ages," in *The History of the Reign of the Emperor Charles V.*, vol. I (London: W. and W. Strahan, 1769). See also John Bennett Black, *The Art of History: A Study of Four Great Historians of the Eighteenth Century* (New York: Russell & Russell, 1965), 121, 129; H. E. Barnes, *A History of Historical Writing* (New York: Dover Publications, 1963), 157–58.

19. For a helpful introduction to Priestley's narrative of corruption, see Karen O'Brien, "English Enlightenment Histories, 1750–c.1815," in *The Oxford History of Historical Writing*, ed. Axel Schneider, vol. III (Oxford: Oxford University Press, 2011), 529.

20. Hume and Robertson disagreed on the Reformation. See David Hume, "Of Superstition and Enthusiasm," in *Essays, Moral, Political and Literary* (Basil: J.J. Tourneisen, 1793), 70; Mary Fearnley-Sander, "Philosophical History and the Scottish Reformation: William Robertson and the Knoxian Tradition," *Historical Journal* 33, no. 2 (1990): 323–38. Priestley, meanwhile, challenged Gibbon's disparagement of Christianity's growth, arguing instead that primitive Christianity succeeded because of its divine power. Joseph Priestley, *An History of the Corruptions of Christianity* (Birmingham: Piercy & Jones, 1782), II:444. For Priestley on Catholic despotism, see II:139–40. See also Alison Kennedy, "Historical Perspectives in the Mind of Joseph Priestley," in *Joseph Priestley, Scientist, Philosopher, and Theologian*, ed. Isabel Rivers and David L. Wykes (Oxford: Oxford University Press, 2008), 189.

21. See Black, *The Art of History*, 50; Leonard Krieger, "The Heavenly City of the Eighteenth-Century Historians," *Church History* 47, no. 3 (1978): 288–89. Hugh Trevor-Roper argues that the point of this historiography was to show that Catholicism ended the civility of the Antonine Age and brought about the "Dark Ages." Hugh Trevor-Roper, *History and the Enlightenment* (New Haven, CT: Yale University Press, 2010), 138.

22. Joseph Milner, *The History of the Church of Christ* (Cambridge: J. Burgess, 1797), III:iv.

23. See ibid., III:161, 187, II:323. A. G. Dickens and John Tonkin overstate Milner's anti-Catholicism, while S. J. Barnett wrongly argues that Milner wrote a history of "proto-Protestants" who opposed the papacy. A. G. Dickens, John Tonkin, and Kenneth Powell, *The Reformation in Historical Thought* (Cambridge, MA: Harvard University Press, 1985), 190; S. J. Barnett, "Where Was Your Church before Luther? Claims for the Antiquity of Protestantism Examined," *Church History* 68 (1999): 35.

24. For his treatment of Pope Eugenius III (1088–1153), see Milner, *History of the Church*, III:366. For Pope Celestine (1215–96), see Joseph Milner, *The History of the Church of Christ, Volume the Fourth, Part I. Containing the Remainder of the Thirteenth Century; Also the Fourteenth, Fifteenth, and Part of the Sixteenth, Centuries*, ed. Isaac Milner (Cambridge: Cambridge University Press, 1803), 36–37.

25. Even while acknowledging that these men supported the papacy, Milner represented them as genuine believers, repristinated long quotations from their writings, and encouraged readers to imitate their piety. For Gregory, see Milner, *History of the Church*, III:77. Anselm and Boniface are treated at III:332 and III:200–201. For Bernard, see III:443. Milner opposed Mosheim's criticisms of Cyprian and

disparagement of Augustine's theological writings. See I:487–89, II:502. At the same time, Milner was much less willing than Mosheim or Gottfried Arnold (1666–1714) to celebrate medieval "proto-Protestants" who were persecuted by the papacy. Unlike Mosheim, Milner refused to call the twelfth-century dissenter Arnold of Brescia a true Christian, and mitigated Mosheim's praise for the Beguines and the Paulicians. For Arnold, see III:504; for other persecuted sects see III:230, 407.

26. So argues Darren Schmidt: "Milner's decidedly optimistic coterie of medieval Catholic figures elevated as godly representatives was a striking revision of Protestant historiography." Darren W. Schmidt, "Reviving the Past: Eighteenth-Century Evangelical Interpretations of Church History," PhD diss., University of St Andrews, 2009, 30–31. For anti-Catholic historiography, see Barnett, "Where Was Your Church," 41.

27. Milner, instead, traced the start of doctrinal decay to the 270s, arguing that the decade before Diocletian's persecution was marked by laxity and loss of doctrine. Milner, *History of the Church*, II:29–30.

28. Ibid., III:9, 128, 154, 295.

29. A leading Unitarian publication lambasted Milner for his praise of medieval "hermits, and monks" and his portrayal of the "dark ages" as virtuous. *Christian Disciple and Theological Review* 4, no. 22 (1822): 307–9.

30. "Milner's Church History," *Episcopal Recorder* 13, no. 44 (1836): 175; "Ecclesiastical History," *Christian Review* 1, no. 3 (1836): 428.

31. "On Some Uses of Ecclesiastical History," *Evangelical and Literary Magazine* 11, no. 3 (1823): 113.

32. As chapter 3 explains, Milner's favorite medieval Catholics all appeared in a much more negative light in the adaptation published by the American Sunday School Union, as well as another by textbook author Susannah Rowson. For more on the American and British reception of Milner, see Paul Gutacker, "Joseph Milner and His Editors: Eighteenth- and Nineteenth-Century Evangelicals and the Christian Past," *Journal of Ecclesiastical History* 69, no. 1 (January 2018): 86–104.

33. On Hume's history, one review noted "almost every reader condemns many of its author's principles, and yet recommends it to general perusal," and concluded the work deserved a standing among "European performances of merit." "The History of England," *American Monthly Review* 3, no. 1 (September 1795): 29.

34. "Parallel between Hume, Robertson and Gibbon," *Monthly Magazine, and American Review* 1, no. 2 (May 1799): 90–92, 95. For Brown's interest in the Christian past, see Mark Kamrath, *The Historicism of Charles Brockden Brown: Radical History and the Early Republic* (Kent, OH: Kent State University Press, 2010), 109, 120.

35. Early state constitutions often guaranteed religious liberty even as they continued various kinds of state support for specific churches. See Witte and Nichols, *Religion*, 98ff. For this timeline, see Carl H. Esbeck, "Dissent and Disestablishment: The Church-State Settlement in the Early American Republic," *Brigham Young University Law Review*, no. 4 (2004): 1457ff. See also Thomas E. Buckley, *Church and State in Revolutionary Virginia, 1776–1787* (Charlottesville: University of Virginia Press, 1977).

36. Jewel L. Spangler, *Virginians Reborn: Anglican Monopoly, Evangelical Dissent, and the Rise of the Baptists in the Late Eighteenth Century* (Charlottesville: University of Virginia Press, 2008), 3.

37. For this alliance, see Thomas S. Kidd, *God of Liberty: A Religious History of the American Revolution* (New York: Basic Books, 2012), 185. For a legal account of the emergence of religious freedom, see Michael I. Meyerson, *Endowed by Our Creator: The Birth of Religious Freedom in America* (New Haven, CT: Yale University Press, 2012). Andrew Murphy argues that religious dissent has often been overshadowed by religious skeptics or moderates, and highlights the role religious radicals in the seventeenth-century development of religious toleration. See Andrew R. Murphy, *Conscience and Community: Revisiting Toleration and Religious Dissent in Early Modern England and America* (University Park: Pennsylvania State University Press, 2001), 12–13.

38. William Tennent and Newton B. Jones, "Writings of the Reverend William Tennent, 1740–1777 (Continued)," *South Carolina Historical Magazine* 61, no. 4 (1960): 198, 205.

39. See Thomas S. Kidd and Barry Hankins, *Baptists in America: A History* (Oxford: Oxford University Press, 2015), ix, 22, 44–45. Virginia's religious landscape was more diverse and less intolerant than previously understood. See Paul Rasor and Richard E. Bond, eds., *From Jamestown to Jefferson: The Evolution of Religious Freedom in Virginia* (Charlottesville: University of Virginia Press, 2011).

40. Kidd and Hankins, *Baptists in America*, 49.

41. Isaac Backus, *An Appeal to the Public for Religious Liberty, against the Oppressions of the Present Day* (Boston: John Boyle, 1773), 14–15.

42. Ibid., 24.

43. Kidd and Hankins, *Baptists in America*, 49–50.

44. For Leland's biography, see Ellis Sandoz, ed., *Political Sermons of the American Founding Era: 1730–1805*, 2nd ed., vol. II (Indianapolis, IN: Liberty Fund, 1998), 1080. Leland has been called "the leading religious figure during the founding period to champion the philosophy of universal religious freedom." See Meyerson, *Endowed by Our Creator*, 8.

45. Sandoz, *Political Sermons*, II:1080, 1088–89.

46. Ibid., II:1096–97.

47. John Leland, *The Writings of the Late Elder John Leland: Including Some Events in His Life*, ed. L. F. Greene (New York: G.W. Wood, 1845), 357.

48. Ibid.

49. Ibid., 278.

50. Ibid., 442.

51. For the constitutional revision, see ibid., 476. For the dedication, see ibid., 553. Other examples from Leland's corpus can be found in ibid., 567, 579–80, 686–87.

52. See, for example, the historical treatise by Pennsylvania Baptist minister David Jones. State churches, Jones argued, "have laid a foundation for persecution and bloodshed, wherever they have prevailed," and should be considered anti-Christian. David Jones,

Peter Edwards's *Candid Reasons Examined, and Answered* (Philadelphia: Dennis Heartt, 1811), 174.

53. Roger Williams, *The Bloudy Tenent of Persecution for Cause of Conscience*, ed. Richard Groves (Macon, GA: Mercer University Press, 2001), 81. Curry contrasts Williams's view of Christian history with that of John Cotton in Curry, *The First Freedoms*, 17. For more on Williams's rhetorical use of church history, see Hans R. Guggisberg, "Religious Freedom and the History of the Christian World in Roger Williams' Thought," *Early American Literature* 12, no. 1 (1977): 36–48.

54. Roger Williams, *The Bloody Tenent yet more Bloody* (London: Giles Calvert, 1652; Ann Arbor: Text Creation Partnership, 2011), 244, http://name.umdl.umich.edu/A96610.0001.001.

55. Wetmore's speech did not call for disestablishment, but rather for politicians to recognize that the state was less significant than the church. For Wetmore, the former served the latter, rather than the other way around. See Christopher Grasso, *A Speaking Aristocracy: Transforming Public Discourse in Eighteenth-Century Connecticut* (Chapel Hill: University of North Carolina Press, 2012), 75–76.

56. Izrahiah Wetmore, *A Sermon Preached before the General Assembly* (New London, CT: n.p., 1773), 30.

57. Kidd and Hankins, *Baptists in America*, 62.

58. See Philip Hamburger, *Separation of Church and State* (Cambridge, MA: Harvard University Press, 2002), 156; Mark S. Scarberry, "John Leland and James Madison: Religious Influence on the Ratification of the Constitution and on the Proposal of the Bill of Rights," *Penn State Law Review* 113, no. 3 (2009): 733–800.

59. As J. C. D. Clark has shown, an antiestablishment view of history undergirded the political discourse of Revolutionary leaders. Clark, *The Language of Liberty*, chap. 15.

60. "Report on Books for Congress," in *The Papers of James Madison Digital Edition*, ed. J. C. A. Stagg (Charlottesville: University of Virginia Press, Rotunda, 2010), http://rotunda.upress.virginia.edu/founders/JSMN-01-06-02-0031 (accessed March 2, 2019). Hereafter *The Papers of James Madison Digital Edition* will be referred to as *PJMDE*.

61. "Letter From William F. Gray," in *PJMDE*.

62. "Letter to Thomas Jefferson," in *PJMDE*.

63. As Matthew Crow notes, Jefferson read Eusebius, Bede, Origen, and Jerome, as well as quite a few histories of Christianity, including Mosheim and Gibbon. Crow discusses the influence of Mosheim's account of the early church on Jefferson's historical understanding. Matthew Crow, *Thomas Jefferson, Legal History, and the Art of Recollection* (Cambridge: Cambridge University Press, 2017), 252–53. Robert Louis Wilken points out the affinity Jefferson had for Tertullian: Robert Louis Wilken, *Liberty in the Things of God: The Christian Origins of Religious Freedom* (New Haven, CT: Yale University Press, 2019), 189–91.

64. "To Peter Carr, with Enclosure," in *The Papers of Thomas Jefferson Digital Edition*, ed. James P. McClure and J. Jefferson Looney (Charlottesville: University of Virginia Press, Rotunda, 2008–19, http://rotunda.upress.virginia.edu/founders/TSJN-01-12-02-0021 (accessed March 2, 2019). Hereafter *The Papers of Thomas Jefferson Digital*

Edition will be referred to as *PTJDE*. See also "Supplemental List of Recommended Books," in *PTJDE*.

65. Thomas Jefferson, Catalog of books for the University of Virginia Library, 1825, Accession #38-747, Special Collections, University of Virginia Library, Charlottesville, VA; University of Virginia Library and William (William Harwood) Peden, *1828 Catalogue of the Library of the University of Virginia* (Charlottesville: Printed for the Alderman Library of the University of Virginia, 1945), 86.

66. Jefferson wrote this in August 1813: "To John Adams," in *PTJDE*.

67. Jefferson drew on Eusebius, Milton's antiepiscopal works, and various church fathers. See "III. Jefferson's Outline of Argument," in *PTJDE*; "VII. Notes on Episcopacy," in *PTJDE*; "VIII. Notes on Heresy," in *PTJDE*.

68. "82. A Bill for Establishing Religious Freedom, 18 June 1779," *Founders Online*, National Archives, version of January 18, 2019, https://founders.archives.gov/documents/Jefferson/01-02-02-0132-0004-0082.

69. Thomas Jefferson, "Query 17," in *Notes on the State of Virginia*, ed. William Peden (Chapel Hill: University of North Carolina Press, 1954), 157–61.

70. Jefferson called his orthodox opponents "barbarians" who sought to return to "the times of Vandalism, when ignorance put every thing into the hands of power & priestcraft." "To Joseph Priestley," in *PTJDE*. In an 1801 letter, Jefferson criticized Massachusetts clergy who failed to hold the "original purity and simplicity" of Christianity "divested of the rags in which they have inveloped it." "To Moses Robinson," *PTJDE*.

71. According to Curry, Henry's proposal "produced one of the most important and decisive Church-State debates ever to take place in America." Curry, *Farewell to Christendom*, 29.

72. James Madison, "Memorial and Remonstrance against Religious Assessments," in *PJMDE*.

73. This petition is in Curry, *Farewell to Christendom*, 123–24 n. 7. For the influence of this compared to Madison's, see ibid., 29.

74. These include Martin Marty, Jon Butler, and William Lee Miller. See Mark David Hall, "Madison's Memorial and Remonstrance, Jefferson's Statute for Religious Liberty, and the Creation of the First Amendment," *American Political Thought* 3, no. 1 (2014): 32–63. While Hall has recently questioned this view, he concedes that the *Memorial* and the Virginia Statute had a significant "influence on American views of church-state relations," and continue to be cited in juridical decisions on religious freedom in the twenty-first century. Ibid., 36.

75. As Schofield puts it, Priestley's earlier historical writings took a number of controversial positions: "insistence that the early Christian church had been unitarian, denial of the virgin birth of Christ, and supporting Nazareth as his birthplace." Robert E. Schofield, "Priestley, Joseph (1733–1804), Theologian and Natural Philosopher," in *Oxford Dictionary of National Biography*, online ed. (2004; Oxford University Press, 2013), https://doi.org/10.1093/ref:odnb/22788.

76. For the *General History's* narrative, see Robert E. Schofield, *The Enlightened Joseph Priestley: A Study of His Life and Work from 1773 to 1804* (University Park: Pennsylvania State University Press, 2009), 389ff.

77. J. D. Bowers, *Joseph Priestley and English Unitarianism in America* (University Park: Pennsylvania State University Press, 2010), 135. See also Leonard Smith, *The Unitarians: A Short History* (Cumbria: Lensden Publishing, 2006); Kennedy, "Historical Perspectives"; John McLachlan, "Joseph Priestley and the Study of History," *Transactions of the Unitarian Historical Society* 19, no. 4 (April 1990): 252-63.

78. Joseph Priestley, *A General History of the Christian Church, from the Fall of the Western Empire to the Present Time* (Northumberland, PA: A. Kennedy, 1802), v-vi. The emphasis is Priestley's.

79. In Priestley's telling, the Protestant Reformation was no golden era, as the Reformers could not do much more than "correct the more prominent abuses" of popish practice and doctrine. Priestley, *A General History*, xvii-iii. He pointed out that "dark and ignorant as we esteem the middle ages to have been," the medieval era saw some serious intellectual work. Further, it was not only theology that suffered in this era, but all sciences—including medicine and chemistry—which were in "the same low and imperfect state." Ibid., xxiv-xxvi. See also xxx-xxxi, 86.

80. For Adams's legacy, see Nina Baym, *American Women Writers and the Work of History, 1790-1860* (New Brunswick, NJ: Rutgers University Press, 1995); Linda K. Kerber, *Women of the Republic: Intellect and Ideology in Revolutionary America* (Chapel Hill: University of North Carolina Press, 1980); Ronald Hoffman and Peter J. Albert, eds., *Women in the Age of the American Revolution* (Charlottesville: University of Virginia Press, 1989).

81. Carol Berkin, "Adams, Hannah (1755-1831), Historian of Religions and Writer," *American National Biography Online*, February 2000, https://doi.org/10.1093/anb/9780198606697.article.1400008. According to Cott, Adams was the first woman writer to live off her publishing. Nancy F. Cott, *The Bonds of Womanhood: "Woman's Sphere" in New England, 1780-1835* (New Haven, CT: Yale University Press, 1977), 7.

82. As one of the rules she was guided by, Adams would omit any pejoratives—including "Heretics, Schismatics, Enthusiasts, Fanatics"—and providing, whenever possible, "a few of the arguments of the principal sects, from their own authors." Hannah Adams, *An Alphabetical Compendium of the Various Sects* (Boston: Manning & Loring, 1801), vii.

83. Thomas A. Tweed, "An American Pioneer in the Study of Religion: Hannah Adams (1755-1831) and Her Dictionary of All Religions," *Journal of the American Academy of Religion* 60, no. 3 (1992): 437.

84. For example, her account of Arminianism detailed the arguments against Calvinistic doctrines and then, in its last several paragraphs, declared, "It is an article in the Christian faith, that God will render rewards and punishments to men for their actions in this life." Her description of Calvinism, in contrast, simply reproduced the formulations given by Calvinist thinkers. Adams, *An Alphabetical Compendium*, 53-58, 85-89. Discussion of Trinitarian arguments took three pages compared to ten for various kinds of Unitarians and seventeen on Universalists. See ibid., 272-74, 278-87,

287–303. A measure of Protestant bias is also evident, particularly in dealing with Roman Catholicism under the heading of "Papists": "Papists, so called by Protestants, from their adhering to the Pope. *Roman Catholics* is the title, which they apply to themselves." In the entry on Catholicism, Adams was unable to avoid a critique of papal authority: "This denomination supposes, that the bishops of Rome are the descendants of St. Peter." While other articles typically do not include criticisms of a particular sect's doctrines, Adams inserted Protestant counterarguments to the Catholic view of the papacy. Ibid., 209.

85. Ibid., x, xi, xii. In an aside reminiscent of Gibbon, Adams noted that "the Augustan was the most learned and polite age the world ever saw." Ibid., xii, note. Adams closely followed Mosheim's account of the interaction with pagan philosophy, arguing along with the German historian that the Alexandrian Christians "imagine[d] that a coalition might, with great advantage, be formed between its system and that of Christianity." In the wake of a number of philosophers converting to the Christian faith, Adams laments, "Pagan ideas and opinions were by degrees mixed with the pure and simple doctrines of the gospel." Ibid., xxxiii–iv. For her take on pagan philosophy, see ibid., xxxv.

86. Ibid., 361, 448, 470.

87. Ibid., 448, 454, 459, 464–65.

88. "About Us," WallBuilders.com, https://wallbuilders.com/about-us/ (accessed August 14, 2020).

89. David Barton, *Original Intent: The Courts, the Constitution, and Religion* (Aledo, TX: Wallbuilder Press, 2013), chap. 11; Stephen K. McDowell, *Building Godly Nations* (Charlottesville, VA: Providence Foundation, 2004), chap. 11.

90. As Catherine Brekus traces in her recent article, the historiography of early American religion was characterized for over a century by a "valorization of Protestants as essentially democratic and tolerant," among other emphases. See Catherine A. Brekus, "Contested Words: History, America, Religion," *William and Mary Quarterly* 75, no. 1 (February 6, 2018): 10.

Chapter 2

1. Daniel Merrill, *The Mode and Subjects of Baptism Examined, in Seven Sermons. To Which Is Added, A Brief History of the Baptists* (Salem, MA: Joshua Cushing, 1804).

2. Thomas S. Kidd and Barry Hankins, *Baptists in America: A History* (Oxford: Oxford University Press, 2015), 78.

3. See Joshua Millett, *A History of the Baptists in Maine* (Portland, ME: C. Day, 1845), 263–68.

4. Merrill, *The Mode and Subjects*, 134–35.

5. Methodists increased from 5,000 adherents in 1776 to nearly 65,000 in 1800 and 130,000 by 1806; Baptists numbered 35,000 in 1784, 65,000 in 1790, and, by 1810, a staggering 173,000. Roger Finke and Rodney Stark, *The Churching of America,*

1776–1990: Winners and Losers in Our Religious Economy (New Brunswick, NJ: Rutgers University Press, 1992), 59. The Stone-Campbellites, or Restorationists, emerged at the start of the century and by 1860 represented the nation's fifth largest Protestant group at some 200,000. William E. Tucker and Lester G. McAllister, *Journey in Faith: A History of the Christian Church* (Atlanta, GA: Chalice Press, 1975), 154–55.

6. In 1776, Congregationalists made up 20.4 percent of religious adherents, Episcopalians 15.7 percent, and Presbyterians 19 percent, while Baptists only made up 16.9 percent and Methodists 2.5 percent. By 1850, Baptists made up 20.5 percent and Methodists 34.2 percent, while Congregationalists, Episcopalians, and Presbyterians combined to a mere 18.1 percent of market share. See Finke and Stark, *The Churching of America*, 55–57.

7. Nathan O. Hatch, *The Democratization of American Christianity* (New Haven, CT: Yale University Press, 1989), 9–11, 169, 182.

8. Noll argues that the new nation was Christianized through the theological synthesis of evangelical religion, Common Sense moral philosophy, and republican ideology. American Christianity, according to Noll, became characterized by an antitradition approach to theology and scripture. See Mark A. Noll, *America's God: From Jonathan Edwards to Abraham Lincoln* (Oxford: Oxford University Press, 2002). As Holifield puts it, Revolutionary ideology led to an increased wiliness to throw off "any remnants of deference to the educated and powerful, including the educated theologians." What emerged was an egalitarian and anticlerical "theology of the common people," a theological populism that frequently rejected Protestant precedent and Christian tradition at large. E. Brooks Holifield, *Theology in America: Christian Thought from the Age of the Puritans to the Civil War* (New Haven, CT: Yale University Press, 2003), 18–19. For an earlier argument about American Protestants departing from the corruptions of history, see C. C. Goen, *Broken Churches, Broken Nation: Denominational Schisms and the Coming of the American Civil War* (Macon, GA: Mercer University Press, 1985), 25.

9. Quoted in Heather A. Haveman, *Magazines and the Making of America: Modernization, Community, and Print Culture, 1741–1860* (Princeton, NJ: Princeton University Press, 2015), 150.

10. Haveman explains the rise of religious magazines as a symptom of post-disestablishment competition. Ibid., 148–50. In the decades following the American Revolution, new popular periodicals and newspapers outpaced population growth, and religious publications especially: while only 12 religious periodicals were printed in America prior to 1789, 578 religious newspapers and magazines appeared over the forty years to follow. See ibid., 26–27, 160–61. Candy Brown argues that the expansion of religious print and increasing denominational competition mutually reinforced each other. Candy Gunther Brown, *The Word in the World: Evangelical Writing, Publishing, and Reading in America, 1789–1880* (Chapel Hill: University of North Carolina Press, 2004), 12–13, 37, 58–59. See also Haveman, *Magazines*, 176; Gaylord P. Albaugh, *History and Annotated Bibliography of American Religious Periodicals*

and *Newspapers Established from 1730 through 1830* (Worcester, MA: American Antiquarian Society, 1994).

11. The Waldensians, followers of Peter Waldo (c.1140—c.1205), emphasized vernacular reading of scripture, lay preaching, and voluntary poverty. They were excommunicated in 1184 and denounced as heretics at the Fourth Lateran Council (1215). While some medieval Waldensians baptized by immersion, others continued to baptize infants, and scholars generally disagree with the Baptist successionist view advocated by Merrill. See Euan Cameron, *Waldenses: Rejections of Holy Church in Medieval Europe* (Hoboken, NJ: Wiley, 2001). The Petrobrussians were short-lived followers of Peter of Bruys (d. c.1131), the French heresiarch who rejected infant baptism and other Catholic practices. See Jeffrey Burton Russell, *Dissent and Reform in the Early Middle Ages* (Eugene, OR: Wipf and Stock, 2005), 74–75. The Wickliffites, or Lollards, came to reject the necessity of baptism for salvation, although John Wycliffe (d. 1384) remained a dissenting Roman Catholic priest who never rejected infant baptism. While the extent of Lollardy is debated, it continued from the mid-fourteenth century through the English Reformation. See Eamon Duffy, *The Stripping of the Altars: Traditional Religion in England, c.1400–c.1580* (New Haven, CT: Yale University Press, 2005). The Hussites followed Czech reformer Jan Hus (c. 1369–1415). While Hus was burned as a heretic for his teachings on the church, the Eucharist, and other Catholic practices, his followers continued to baptize infants. A majority of Czech lands remained Hussite by the early sixteenth century. See John Klassen, "Hus, the Hussites and Bohemia," in *The New Cambridge Medieval History*, ed. Christopher Allmand (Cambridge: Cambridge University Press, 1998), 367–91.

12. Merrill, *The Mode and Subjects*, 125, 127–28, 131, 134–36.

13. Ibid., 134–36.

14. Samuel Hopkins, for whom "Hopkinsian" Calvinism is named, frequently cited Mosheim's history. See *The Works of Samuel Hopkins*, ed. Sewall Harding (Boston: Doctrinal Tract and Book Society, 1852), 53. For "New Light" revivalism, see Robert W. Caldwell, *Theologies of the American Revivalists: From Whitefield to Finney* (Westmont, IL: InterVarsity Press, 2017).

15. Samuel Worcester, *Two Discourses, on God's Gracious Covenant* (Salem, MA: Haven Pool, 1805), 62.

16. Daniel Merrill, *Twelve Letters, Addressed to Rev. Samuel Austin* (Boston: Manning & Loring, 1806), 94–95.

17. Daniel Merrill, *Letters Occasioned by Rev. Samuel Worcester's Two Discourses* (Boston: Manning & Loring, 1807), 66–67.

18. Thomas Baldwin, *The Baptism of Believers Only* (Boston: Manning & Loring, 1806), 323–24.

19. Samuel Worcester, *Serious and Candid Letters to the Rev. Thomas Baldwin* (Salem, MA: Haven Pool, 1807), 101–10, 137. See also Thomas Baldwin, *A Series of Letters* (Boston: Manning & Loring, 1810).

20. Samuel Austin, *A View of the Economy of the Church of God, as It Existed Primitively* (Worcester, MA: Thomas & Sturtevant, 1807), 263–65; Merrill, *Twelve Letters*.

21. For the first installment, see "Brief Survey of Ecclesiastical History, in A Series of Letters," *Massachusetts Missionary Magazine* 5, no. 2 (July 1807): 47–56.

22. Joseph Field, *Strictures on Seven Sermons* (Northampton, MA: T. M. Pomroy, 1806), 75, 80.

23. Jabez Chadwick, *Four Sermons, on the Mode and Subjects of Christian Baptism* (Utica, NY: Seward and Williams, 1811), iii–vi, 75–86. Chadwick's theological evolution was not complete, however, as in 1831 he once again renounced infant baptism and formed his own church. See James Harvey Hotchkin, *A History of the Purchase and Settlement of Western New York, and of the Rise, Progress, and Present State of the Presbyterian Church in That Section* (New York: M. W. Dodd, 1848), 359.

24. For example, one Congregationalist used church history to show that Baptists had always been contentious and divisive. See Clark Brown, *The Covenant of God's Mercy* (Keene, NH: John Prentiss, 1814), 54–60.

25. Daniel Merrill, *A Miniature History of the Baptists* (New Haven, CT: J. Barber, 1815).

26. In 1819, Baptist minister Asa Wilcox reproduced Merrill's arguments in an extensive defense of believer's baptism. A detailed historical rebuttal to Wilcox came from Congregational minister Hubbel Loomis: Hubbel Loomis, *Defence of Letters on Christian Baptism* (Hartford, CT: Peter B. Gleason, 1819), 16–19.

27. For reprints and abridgements of the history, see the website Worldcat.org. For Benedict's importance and legacy, see H. Leon McBeth, *The Baptist Heritage* (Nashville, TN: B & H Publishing Group, 1987), 56–57.

28. The Reformed Baptist Roger Williams, for example, was guilty only of the "heresies" of "religious liberty, and national justice." David Benedict, *A General History of the Baptist Denomination in America: And Other Parts of the World* (Boston: Lincoln & Edmands, 1813), 13–14, 29–31, 384, 454.

29. Ibid., 381, 451. For the many references to religious liberty, see ibid., 96, 133, 147, 156, 159, 269, 361, 396, 399–400, 408, 440, 451, 454–55, 460, 475–77, 513, 516, 561.

30. For an example, see a July 4 sermon by Baptist minister Robert Howell, who cites the history of persecution and the Inquisition in arguing for religious freedom: "The true relations between religion and civil government," by Robert Boyte Crawford Howell, July 4, 1845, AR595, Box 2, Volume 3, Robert Boyte Crawford Howell Collection, Southern Baptist Historical Library and Archives, Nashville, TN.

31. James A. Rogers, *Richard Furman: Life and Legacy* (Macon, GA: Mercer University Press, 2001), 295.

32. For each of these, see Glenn T. Miller, *Piety and Intellect: The Aims and Purposes of Antebellum Theological Education* (Atlanta, GA: Scholars Press, 1990), 311, 327, 332. James P. Boyce, founder of SBTS, believed that the seminary needed to commit itself to serious scholarship. He urged Baptist educators to counter the historiographical distortions regarding their own denominational history and Christian history generally. John Albert Broadus, *Memoir of James Petigru Boyce, D.D., LL.D.: Late President of the Southern Baptist Theological Seminary* (New York: A. C. Armstrong and Son, 1893), 136–37.

33. James Davis Knowles, *Importance of Theological Institutions* (Boston: Lincoln & Edmands, 1832), 11. The seminary initially only employed professors for biblical literature and biblical theology. Ibid., 18.

34. Ibid., 11–13.

35. In 1838, Irah Chase (1793–1864), professor of biblical theology at Newton since 1825, moved to the ecclesiastical history chair upon the hiring of Horatio Hackett as a fourth professor. Margaret Lamberts Bendroth, *A School of the Church: Andover Newton across Two Centuries* (Grand Rapids, MI: Eerdmans, 2008), 32–33. Chase published a critical treatment of the *Apostolic Constitutions*, discussions on baptism in Basil the Great, Origen, and Irenaeus, a historical dismissal of infant baptism, and an article on Neander. Heman Lincoln Chase, *A Tribute of Affection to the Memory of Professor Irah Chase* (Boston: G.C. Rand & Avery, 1865), 99–100.

36. Hamilton formed in 1823 as a merger between the Baptist Education Society of the State of New York and Baptist Theological Seminary at New York City. It was later renamed Madison University and finally Colgate University. By 1831 it had eighty students. Knowles, *Importance*, 18.

37. George W. Lasher, *George W. Eaton, D.D., LL.D: A Memorial* (Hamilton, NY: Colgate University, 1913), 40. Eaton became Professor of Systematic Theology in 1850, president of Madison University from 1857, and later president of Madison Seminary. His teaching of church history received the highest praise from his son-in-law George Lasher, who wrote that "his pupils became enthusiastic in the study of Church History." Ibid., 40, 42.

38. George W. Eaton, *Claims of Civil and Ecclesiastical History as Indispensable Branches of Ministerial Education* (Utica, NY: Bennett, Backus, & Hawley, 1841), 8, 11, 12.

39. Eaton was skeptical of the claim that all medieval dissenters had been Baptists. He believed some Baptist principles had been held by the Petrobrussians, Waldenses, and Anabaptists, yet "he did not adopt the theory that a succession of churches, each deriving its life from some other, had come down from the apostles to the present day." Lasher, *George W. Eaton*, 16–17; 40–42.

40. Eaton, *Claims of Civil*, 15, 17, 19–20. Eaton ended his address with an appeal for donations of $1,000–$2,000 to acquire more historical books for the seminary library. Ibid., 28, 32.

41. Lorenzo Dow, *History of Cosmopolite: Or the Four Volumes of Lorenzo Dow's Journal*, 4th ed. (Washington, OH: Joshua Martin, 1848), 538, 544, 565–67.

42. While itinerating in 1810, Asbury read Milner's *History*, which he found informative but rather "too unctuous." Francis Asbury, *The Journal and Letters of Francis Asbury*, ed. Elmer T. Clark (Nashville, TN: Abingdon Press, 1958), III:434. For Asbury's appeals to history, see ibid., III:475, 491–92.

43. For these statements, see Gary Holloway and Douglas A. Foster, *Renewing the World: A Concise Global History of the Stone-Campbell Movement* (Abilene, TX: Abilene Christian University Press, 2015), chap. 2.

44. For the importance of Guirey and this *History*, see Richard Thomas Hughes and R. L. Roberts, *The Churches of Christ* (Westport, CT: Greenwood Publishing Group, 2001), 223.

45. William Guirey, *The History of Episcopacy* (Raleigh, NC: Joseph Gales, 1799), 16, 39.

46. The Republican Methodists united with similarly minded New Englanders to form the United Church of Christ. Guirey and O'Kelly disagreed over baptism, and Guirey left to found the Virginian Christian Conference. The two factions would reunite after the Civil War. See Michael R. McCoy, "O'Kelly, James (1735?–16 October 1826), Methodist Preacher and Schismatic," *American National Biography Online*, February 2000, http://www.anb.org/articles/01/01-00678.html.

47. O'Kelly blamed the rise of episcopacy for "producing the divisions, the corruptions, where the demon of intolerance was begotten by the devil, nursed by the nursing fathers, even kings and bishops, until blood touched blood. See the fruits; crowded prisons, tortured criminals, garments stained with brother's blood; new tortures invented, until the inquisition came out, and its severity increased, after the emperor professed Christianity I refer you to history, sacred and profane." James O'Kelly, *The Author's Apology for Protesting against the Methodist Episcopal Government* (Hillsborough, NC: Dennis Heartt, 1829), 52.

48. See Finke and Stark, *The Churching of America*, 165.

49. See John Gross, *The Beginnings of American Methodism* (Nashville, TN: Abingdon Press, 1961), 21–24.

50. David Sherman, *History of the Wesleyan Academy, in Wilbraham, Mass. 1817–1890* (Boston: McDonald & Gill, 1893), 51. Ruter's students included Isaac Goodnow (1814–1894), founder of Kansas State University, and two Methodist bishops, Osman Baker (1812–1871) and John Keener (1819–1906).

51. From its beginnings, Wilbraham Wesleyan Academy included courses on ecclesiastical history. See Gross, *Beginnings of American Methodism*, 21. Likewise, Allegheny College required ecclesiastical history. Ernest A. Smith, *Allegheny—a Century of Education* (Meadville, PA: Allegheny College History, 1916), 24.

52. Gross, *Beginnings of American Methodism*, 23.

53. Two works produced in this time were *A History of Martyrs* and a *Sketch of Calvin's Life and Doctrine*.

54. George Gregory, *An History of the Christian Church, from the Earliest Periods to the Present Time*, vol. I (London: G. Kearsley, 1790), v–vi.

55. Martin Ruter, *A Concise History of the Christian Church* (Pittsburgh, PA: B. Waugh and T. Mason, 1834), preface.

56. Ibid., 96–97, 100–104, 258ff.

57. Robert D. Clark, *The Life of Matthew Simpson of the Methodist Episcopal Church* (New York: Macmillan, 1956), 43.

58. Several of these arguments were published in the *Pittsburgh Conference Journal*. See ibid., 43–44.

59. *Journals of the General Conference of the Methodist Episcopal Church* (New York: Carlton & Porter, 1856), II:170.

60. Gross, *Beginnings of American Methodism*, 26; Smith, *Allegheny*, 72.

61. Dr. Charles Kittredge True, professor at Wesleyan University, republished it with exam questions included. Martin Ruter, *A Concise History of the Christian Church, from Its*

First Establishment to the Nineteenth Century, ed. Charles K True (New York: Carlton & Lanahan, 1865), 445ff.

62. Finke and Stark, *The Churching of America,* 165.

63. William C. Hunt, "Part II: Separate Denominations: History, Description, and Statistics," in *Bureau of the Census Special Reports: Religious Bodies* (Washington, DC: U.S. Government Printing Office, 1910), 431.

64. Paul K. Conkin, *American Originals: Homemade Varieties of Christianity* (Chapel Hill: University of North Carolina Press, 2000), chap. 1. See also James L. Gorman, *Among the Early Evangelicals: The Transatlantic Origins of the Stone-Campbell Movement* (Abilene, TX: Abilene Christian University Press, 2017).

65. The editors of a recent global history of Restorationism note that Campbell believed the Churches of Christ to belong to the "line of persecuted, often invisible New Testament Christians who had resisted apostate Roman Catholicism." However, they do not explain which religious histories would have supported this historical interpretation. D. Newell Williams, Douglas A. Foster, and Paul M. Blowers, eds., *The Stone-Campbell Movement: A Global History* (Atlanta, GA: Chalice Press, 2013), 2. Greater attention has been given to the influence of John Locke and Scottish Common Sense philosophy on Alexander Campbell and less on his historical study. For example, see Richard T. Hughes, "Historical Models of Restoration," in *The Encyclopedia of the Stone-Campbell Movement,* ed. Douglas A. Foster (Grand Rapids, MI: Eerdmans, 2004), 635–38.

66. In their work on the history of the Churches of Christ, Allen and Hughes describe primitivism as an antihistorical mindset in which studying the past is considered unimportant. The clear implication is that early Restorationists neither read nor used church history. See Crawford Leonard Allen and Richard T. Hughes, *Discovering Our Roots: The Ancestry of Churches of Christ* (Abilene, TX: Abilene Christian University Press, 1988), 2–3. In his recent book, Richard Hughes looks more closely at Alexander Campbell's understanding of Christian history, explaining his understanding of the "Grand Apostasy," Christendom, and the Reformation. But he does not explore where Alexander derived these narratives. See Richard T. Hughes, *Reviving the Ancient Faith: The Story of Churches of Christ in America.* 2nd ed. (Abilene, TX: Abilene Christian University Press, 2008), 22–23, 26–28. One biography of Campbell helpfully notes his reading of religious historiography: Eva Jean Wrather, *Alexander Campbell: Adventurer in Freedom: A Literary Biography,* ed. D. Duane Cummins (Fort Worth, TX: TCU Press, 2005), 45–49, 67, 120, 190, 193. Likewise, the introduction to the *Encyclopedia of the Stone-Campbell Movement* points to Campbell's 1837 discussion on the difficulty of writing an objective history of Christianity, but does not deal with his treatment of historiographic sources, nor his argument about that history. Douglas A. Foster, "Stone-Campbell History over Three Centuries: A Survey and Analysis," in *The Encyclopedia of the Stone-Campbell Movement,* ed. Douglas A. Foster (Grand Rapids, MI: Eerdmans, 2004), xxi–xxii.

67. See John B. Boles, *The Great Revival: Beginnings of the Bible Belt* (Lexington: University Press of Kentucky, 1996), 152.

68. Presbytery of Springfield, *An Apology for Renouncing the Jurisdiction of the Synod of Kentucky* (Lexington, KY: John Weaver, 1804), 39, 37.

69. Presbytery of Springfield, *An Apology for Renouncing*, 41–42.

70. Thomas Campbell, *Declaration and Address of the Christian Association of Washington*, Centennial Edition (Pittsburgh, PA: Christian Association of Washington, 1908), 4, 16, 18–19.

71. Ibid., 38, 41, 45.

72. For example, in an 1822 circular letter to the Redstone Baptist Association, Thomas instructed pastors on scriptural reading and teaching, noting, "In Mosheim, and other historians, there is frequent mention of the simplicity of teaching in the first and second centuries, corresponding with what we have written." *Minutes of the Redstone Baptist Association, Held at Washington, Washington County, PA*, http://www.sidne yrigdon.com/Reds1819.htm#1822-01 (accessed October 12, 2018).

73. Wrather and Cummins point this out, but do not explain what church histories Campbell read, nor how these shaped his theological conclusions. Wrather, *Alexander Campbell*, 45–49, 67, 120, 190, 193. For more on Campbell's intellectual formation, see Douglas A. Foster, *A Life of Alexander Campbell* (Grand Rapids, MI: Eerdmans, 2020).

74. Alexander Campbell, *Strictures on Three Letters Respecting the Debate at Mount Pleasant* (Pittsburgh, PA: Eichbaum and Johnston, 1822), 264–78.

75. Alexander Campbell, *A Debate on Christian Baptism: Between the Rev. W. L. MacCalla, a Presbyterian Teacher, and Alexander Campbell* (Buffaloe, VA: Campbell & Sala, 1824), 378–79.

76. These debates, as Eric Schlereth argues, were more about "establishing the public legitimacy of a religious interpretation" than about resolving the question at hand. Eric R. Schlereth, *An Age of Infidels: The Politics of Religious Controversy in the Early United States* (Philadelphia: University of Pennsylvania Press, 2013), 150.

77. Haveman, *Magazines*, 174.

78. Thomas Haweis disliked Joseph Milner's portrait of various schismatics and heretics in the church's past. He wrote a three-volume history of the church in 1800 that was largely a rebuttal of Milner's account. See Arthur Skevington Wood, *Thomas Haweis, 1734–1820* (London: S.P.C.K., 1957), 221.

79. Alexander Campbell, ed., *The Christian Baptist* (Cincinnati, OH: D.S. Burnet, 1835), I:9.

80. Ibid., I:27.

81. Ibid., VI:544.

82. Ibid., III:189–91.

83. Alexander quoted Mosheim on primitive church governance, on the Protestant Reformation, in articles condemning creeds and confessions, and in the disputes over baptism. Ibid., VI:497; Alexander Campbell, ed., *The Millennial Harbinger*, vol. II (Bethany, VA: W.K. Pendleton, 1731), 65, 160–61, 220. In one article he wished "that the Quakers, Regular Baptists, and the Weslyan Methodists, would read twice, if not three times, the following extract from Mosheim." *The Millennial Harbinger*, II:492.

84. In an 1834 reading plan, Alexander recommended Gibbon, Milner, Robertson's various histories, and Hume's *History*. *The Millennial Harbinger*, II:491–92. He borrowed the reading plan from Thomas Smith Grimké, *Reflections on the Character and Objects of All Science and Literature* (New Haven, CT: Hezekiah Howe, 1831).

85. In 1833 the Campbellites merged with the Stoneites. By 1860, their combined movement would be the fifth largest Protestant denomination, numbering over two hundred thousand. Tucker and McAllister, *Journey in Faith*, 154–55. For Campbell on schools, see Hughes, *Reviving the Ancient Faith*, 34–35.

86. Citing a host of historians, Campbell argued that the true, invisible church continued in the Novatians, the fourth-century Donatists, the twelfth-century Waldenses, and the sixteenth-century Reformers. Alexander Campbell and John Baptist Purcell, *A Debate on the Roman Catholic Religion* (Cincinnati, OH: J.A. James, 1837), 66–68, 80–81, 100–101, 192.

87. Alexander Campbell, "Notes of Apostacy," *Millennial Harbinger* 1, no. 1 (January 1837): 15–16.

88. Ibid., 17–18.

89. Ibid., 15–16, 17–18. Campbell was a Jacksonian Democrat in 1820, but by 1840 became a Whig. See Harold Lunger, *The Political Ethics of Alexander Campbell* (Eugene, OR: Wipf and Stock, 2012), 139.

90. By the late 1830s, Campbell was shifting his emphasis from recovering primitive Christianity to uniting Americans in defense of the Protestant nation. See Richard T. Hughes and Crawford Leonard Allen, *Illusions of Innocence: Protestant Primitivism in America, 1630–1875* (Chicago: University of Chicago Press, 1988), 170–72.

91. Elias Smith, founder of the New England Christian Church, engaged with church history in a six-part series titled "History of the Clergy" in *Christian's Magazine*. "Where shall the origin of the clergy be found?" Smith asked, and gave his own answer: "In the history of the church of *Rome, Constantinople* and *England*. The *clergy* are an order of men which belong to the church of Anti-christ, and no other." Smith walked through the history of clerical corruption, drawing chiefly from Mosheim's history. Elias Smith, "History," *Christian's Magazine, Reviewer, and Religious Intelligencer* 1, no. 2 (January 2, 1805): 39.

92. As Allen and Hughes explain, primitivism had a special appeal in the religious free market "because it promised the assurance of being right amid the welter of claims and counter-claims of the competing denominations." Allen and Hughes, *Discovering Our Roots*, 93.

93. James Graham, *Reasons for Renouncing Infant Baptism* (Charleston, SC: J. Hoff, 1810), 68; David Jones, *Peter Edwards's Candid Reasons Examined, and Answered* (Philadelphia: Dennis Heartt, 1811), 174; John P. Campbell, *A Sermon, Preached in Stoner-Mouth Meeting House* (Lexington, KY: Thomas Smith, 1811), 110–32.

94. Lutheran historian Mosheim had described the early church as baptizing with immersion, an historical aside seized on by several Baptist ministers in their sermons. William White, *Christian Baptism: Exhibiting Various Proofs* (Burlington, NJ: S.C. Ustick, 1808), 216–17; James G. Ogilvie, *A Sermon, Delivered in the Baptist Meeting House* (Hudson, NY: William L. Stone, 1816), 19; George Witherell, *A Sermon, on*

the *Subjects and Mode of Baptism* (Plattsburgh, NY: A.C. Flagg, 1817), 13; Stephen Chapin, *A Series of Letters on the Mode and Subjects of Baptism* (Boston: Lincoln & Edmands, 1819), 24. Conversely, Presbyterians and Congregationalists quoted Mosheim's disparaging account of early Baptists. Nathaniel Scudder Prime, *A Familiar Illustration of Christian Baptism* (Salem, NY: Dodd & Stevenson, 1818), 192–95; Brown, *Covenant of God's Mercy*, preface, 54–60.

95. E.g., the website of Eggemoggin Baptist Church in Merrill's own town, Sedgewick, ME. "History," *Eggemoggin Baptist Church*, http://ebctest.downeastit.com/history/ (accessed October 12, 2018).

96. Hatch, *Democratization of American Christianity*, 169.

97. The founding theological treatise of the Shakers includes hundreds of citations from Mosheim, and dozens of references to other eighteenth-century historians. Benjamin S. Youngs, *The Testimony of Christ's Second Appearing.* (Lebanon, OH: John M'Clean, 1808). See Stephen J. Stein, *The Shaker Experience in America: A History of the United Society of Believers* (New Haven, CT: Yale University Press, 1994), 69–72. Charles Finney used church history to attack his critics and justify his innovations. See Charles G. Finney, *Lectures on Revivals of Religion* (New York: Leavitt, Lord & Co., 1835), 187, 249.

Chapter 3

1. John Bowden, *Observations, by a Protestant, on a Profession of Catholic Faith* (New York: Clayton & Kingsland, 1816), 3–4.

2. The Jesuits were suppressed by Pope Clement XIV in response to rivalry within the Roman Catholic hierarchy and anti-Jesuit sentiment in several Catholic countries in Europe. John W. O'Malley, SJ, *The Jesuits: A History from Ignatius to the Present* (Lanham, MD: Rowman & Littlefield, 2014), 115–16.

3. Bowden, *Observations*, 3–4.

4. Ibid., 4, 7.

5. Bowden cited Milner, Cave, Eusebius, and, especially, Mosheim. Ibid., 11, 47–48, 77–89, 120. For his use of primitivist discourse see ibid., 9, 19–20, 54, 86, 103, 112.

6. Ibid., 131. This supports Tisa Wenger's argument that religious freedom was the grounds for limiting the religious practice of Catholics. Tisa Wenger, *Religious Freedom: The Contested History of an American Ideal* (Chapel Hill: University of North Carolina Press, 2017).

7. Gordon S. Wood, *Empire of Liberty: A History of the Early Republic, 1789–1815* (Oxford: Oxford University Press, 2009), chap. 10. For an account of postwar optimism and patriotism, see Wood, chaps. 18–19; Daniel Walker Howe, *What Hath God Wrought: The Transformation of America, 1815–1848* (Oxford: Oxford University Press, 2007), chap. 1.

8. For an optimistic account of the expansion of democracy during these years, see Sean Wilentz, *The Rise of American Democracy: Jefferson to Lincoln* (New York: Norton,

2005). Howe disagrees with Wilentz on the progressive bent of Jacksonian democracy. See Howe, *What Hath God Wrought*, 2007, 4.

9. See Martin E. Marty, *Righteous Empire: The Protestant Experience in America* (New York: Dial Press, 1970).

10. John D. Wilsey, *American Exceptionalism and Civil Religion: Reassessing the History of an Idea* (Downers Grove, IL: InterVarsity Press, 2015), chap. 1.

11. Each of these organizations contributed significantly to the growth of religious publishing and literacy. See John Fea, *The Bible Cause: A History of the American Bible Society* (Oxford: Oxford University Press, 2016); Anne M. Boylan, *Sunday School: The Formation of an American Institution, 1790–1880* (New Haven, CT: Yale University Press, 1988).

12. Haselby argues Protestant nationalism emerged from competition between the northeastern Protestant establishment, which desired to shape the character of the nation, and frontier revivalism, which resented this missionary enterprise as elitist, paternalistic, and greedy. The conflict between these two competing kinds of evangelicalism was ultimately resolved into religious nationalism. Sam Haselby, *The Origins of American Religious Nationalism* (Oxford: Oxford University Press, 2015), 3.

13. For race and citizenship, see Robert G. Parkinson, "Enemies of the People: The Revolutionary War and Race in the New American Nation," PhD diss., University of Virginia, 2005; Douglas Bradburn, *The Citizenship Revolution: Politics and the Creation of the American Union, 1774–1804* (Charlottesville: University of Virginia Press, 2009); George William Van Cleve, *A Slaveholders' Union: Slavery, Politics, and the Constitution in the Early American Republic* (Chicago: University of Chicago Press, 2010); Bruce Dain, *A Hideous Monster of the Mind: American Race Theory in the Early Republic* (Cambridge, MA: Harvard University Press, 2002).

14. For this, see Gary B. Nash, *Forging Freedom: The Formation of Philadelphia's Black Community, 1720–1840* (Cambridge, MA: Harvard University Press, 1988). Historians debate the extent to which Revolutionary ideals opened up possibilities for African American political participation. Ira Berlin argues that Revolutionary ideals pushed in various directions for slaves. Ira Berlin, *Many Thousands Gone: The First Two Centuries of Slavery in North America* (Cambridge, MA: Harvard University Press, 1998). Rothman argues that these ideals were unable to overcome political and market forces. Adam Rothman, *Slave Country: American Expansion and the Origins of the Deep South* (Cambridge, MA: Harvard University Press, 2005), xi. In contrast, Onuf argues that the founding "was predicated on a conception of whiteness." Peter S. Onuf, "American Exceptionalism and National Identity," *American Political Thought* 1, no. 1 (May 1, 2012): 77–100.

15. See Bill Ong Hing, *Defining America through Immigration Policy* (Philadelphia: Temple University Press, 2004), 278ff. For the colonial roots of American anti-Catholicism, see Thomas S. Kidd, *The Protestant Interest: New England after Puritanism* (New Haven, CT: Yale University Press, 2004).

16. "An anti-Catholic petition from New York Nativists, 1837," from the National Archives and reproduced in Charles C. Haynes, *Religion in American History: What*

to Teach and How (Alexandria, VA: Association for Supervision and Curriculum Development, 1990), 79.

17. Typically, American nationalism is portrayed as disconnected from history, as early Americans deliberately distanced themselves from European traditions and norms. David Waldstreicher calls this a "nationalism that rejected the past." David Waldstreicher, *In the Midst of Perpetual Fetes: The Making of American Nationalism, 1776–1820* (Chapel Hill: University of North Carolina Press, 1997), 51. Daniel Walker Howe begins his history of America from 1815 to 1848 with a prologue, "The Defeat of the Past." See Howe, *What Hath God Wrought*, 8. If history appears in the genealogies of American nationalism, it is classical history or histories of the Revolution, and not the history of Christianity. On classical history, see Eran Shalev, *Rome Reborn on Western Shores: Historical Imagination and the Creation of the American Republic* (Charlottesville: University of Virginia Press, 2009), 2; Caroline Winterer, *The Culture of Classicism: Ancient Greece and Rome in American Intellectual Life, 1780–1910* (Baltimore: Johns Hopkins University Press, 2002). For Revolutionary histories, see Peter C. Messer, *Stories of Independence: Identity, Ideology, and History in Eighteenth-Century America* (DeKalb: Northern Illinois University Press, 2005), 7.

18. For the rise of American exceptionalism, see Joyce Oldham Appleby, *Inheriting the Revolution: The First Generation of Americans* (Cambridge, MA: Harvard University Press, 2009). As Henry May puts it, Americans thoroughly embraced the Enlightenment ideal that "the present age (the eighteenth century) is more enlightened than the past." The Enlightenment mindset that undergirded the forming of the new nation rejected tradition as a reliable guide. Henry F. May, *The Enlightenment in America* (Oxford: Oxford University Press, 1978), xiv. Jack Greene argues that exceptionalism was grounded on the proposition that America was exempt from the problems of history. Jack P. Greene, *The Intellectual Construction of America: Exceptionalism and Identity from 1492 to 1800* (Chapel Hill: University of North Carolina Press, 1993), 201–2. Greater attention has been given to the importance of theological readings of history—millennialist eschatology, for example, or Hebraic republicanism—in shaping American exceptionalism. See Ruth H. Bloch, *Visionary Republic: Millennial Themes in American Thought, 1756–1800* (Cambridge: Cambridge University Press, 1988), 83. For the Hebrew Bible's role in shaping the sense that America was a divinely chosen nation, see Eran Shalev, *American Zion: The Old Testament as a Political Text from the Revolution to the Civil War* (New Haven, CT: Yale University Press, 2013). Nicholas Guyatt argues that the belief that America had a unique place in divine history "played a leading role in the invention of an American national identity before 1865." Nicholas Guyatt, *Providence and the Invention of the United States, 1607–1876* (Cambridge: Cambridge University Press, 2007), 3, 218. Yet these accounts neglect where history and religion most clearly meet: religious historiography.

19. Daniel Walker Howe explains: " 'Manifest destiny' served as both a label and a justification for policies that might otherwise have simply been called American expansionism or imperialism. The assumption of white supremacy permeated these policies." Howe, *What Hath God Wrought*, 703.

20. For Rowson's publishing career, see Edward T. James et al., eds., *Notable American Women, 1607–1950: A Biographical Dictionary*, vol. III (Cambridge, MA: Belknap Press, 1971), 202–4.

21. See the list of historians recommended in Susanna Rowson, *An Abridgment of Universal Geography: Together with Sketches of History, Designed for the Use of Schools and Academies in the United States* (Boston: John West & Co., 1806), 105, 127.

22. "Republican motherhood," coined by historian Linda Kerber, describes the role women played in educating their sons to be virtuous citizens of the republic. See Linda K. Kerber, *Women of the Republic: Intellect and Ideology in Revolutionary America* (Chapel Hill: University of North Carolina Press, 1980), 12.

23. Ibid., 91, 286.

24. Rowson's textbook was advertised as an adaptation of these two historians. See "Literary Notice," *New England Galaxy and Masonic Magazine* 1, no. 49 (September 18, 1818): 2.

25. Susanna Rowson, *Biblical Dialogues Between a Father and His Family*, vol. II (Boston: Richardson and Lord, 1822), 375–76, 380. By the Middle Ages, "The clergy governed every nation with despotic sway." Rowson, II:381. Contrast her and Milner on Gregory the Great, whom she called the first pope and "at once pious, superstitious and ambitious." Rowson, II:377–80.

26. Ibid., II:377, 379, 386.

27. See Boylan, *Sunday School*, 60ff. See also David Paul Nord, *Faith in Reading: Religious Publishing and the Birth of Mass Media in America* (Oxford: Oxford University Press, 2004), 123.

28. See American Sunday-School Union, *First Report* (Philadelphia: ASSU, 1824), 18; American Sunday-School Union, *Ninth Report* (Philadelphia: ASSU, 1833), 20.

29. See Boylan, *Sunday School*, 168. See also K. Elise Leal, "'All Our Children May Be Taught of God': Sunday Schools and the Roles of Childhood and Youth in Creating Evangelical Benevolence," *Church History* 87, no. 4 (December 2018): 1056–90.

30. American Sunday-School Union, *Fourth Report* (Philadelphia: ASSU, 1828), 10.

31. See Boylan, *Sunday School*, 116–17.

32. The pedagogical tone was often explicit in reminders to keep the Sabbath, to attend to daily prayers, or not to neglect scripture reading. See ASSU Committee of Publication, ed., *Letters on Ecclesiastical History* (Philadelphia: American Sunday-School Union, 1832), I:21. For example, Gregory the Great's care for the poor offered Mrs. Lyman the opportunity to exhort her sons to fair business practices and honest bargaining in "their intercourse with one another." ASSU, *Letters*, I:168.

33. Ibid., I:21, 77, 168.

34. Ibid., I:95–96, 68.

35. Milner had argued that men who had supported the papacy or misunderstood justification by faith might still be genuine Christians—this disappeared in the ASSU adaptation. Instead, medieval developments were explicitly connected to the decline of the "true spirit of Christianity." Ibid., I:81.

36. Ibid., I:251.

37. For more on the revisions of Milner's history, and what this reveals about rising anti-Catholicism, see Paul Gutacker, "Joseph Milner and His Editors: Eighteenth- and Nineteenth-Century Evangelicals and the Christian Past," *Journal of Ecclesiastical History* 69, no. 1 (January 2018), 86–104.

38. For this controversy and Rowson's argument, see Eve Kornfeld, "Women in Post-Revolutionary American Culture: Susanna Haswell Rowson's American Career," *Journal of American Culture* 6 (Winter 1983): 62 n. 19. Marion Rust argues that Rowson's understanding of womanhood, as intellectual equals but limited in their roles, helped negotiate societal and economic boundaries. See Marion Rust, *Prodigal Daughters: Susanna Rowson's Early American Women* (Chapel Hill: University of North Carolina Press, 2008).

39. Susanna Rowson, *A Present for Young Ladies* (Boston: John West & Co., 1811), 52–54. Baym argues that the reformist impulse "kept history central to women even as female ideology modulated from an Enlightenment belief in intellectual equality to Victorian ideas of spiritual superiority." Nina Baym, *American Women Writers and the Work of History, 1790–1860* (New Brunswick, NJ: Rutgers University Press, 1995), 8.

40. Quoted in Lucia McMahon, "'Memorials of Exemplary Women Are Peculiarly Interesting': Female Biography in Early National America," *Legacy: A Journal of American Women Writers* 31, no. 1 (June 4, 2014): 62.

41. See ibid., 25.

42. Baym, *American Women Writers*, 5.

43. This is Mary Kelley's count. See Mary Kelley, *Learning to Stand and Speak: Women, Education, and Public Life in America's Republic* (Chapel Hill: University of North Carolina Press, 2012), 193.

44. In a list of "illustrious names" of British authors, Rowson named "Hume, Gibbon, Robinson, and Mrs. M'Cauley," while the "learned and pious men" of Germany included Mosheim. Rowson, *Abridgment of Universal Geography*, 105, 127.

45. Mrs. Lincoln Phelps, *The Female Student: or, Lectures to Young Ladies on Female Education. For the Use of Mothers, Teachers, and Pupils* (New York: Leavitt, Lord & Company, 1836), 183, 189. Phelps's own anti-Catholicism was displayed in her recommendation of Condillac on the Middle Ages, as the French historian showed "the causes which retarded the progress of science during that dark period, when almost all the learning was in the hands of superstitious monks." Ibid., 190.

46. "Editors' Table," *Godey's Magazine and Lady's Book* 34 (1847): 220, 269, 315.

47. Rebecca Eaton, *An Abridgment of Milner's Church History, for the Use of Schools and Private Families* (Andover, MA: Flagg and Gould, 1817), iii, 297.

48. By 1840, as Margaret Nash documents, "literally hundreds of institutions existed" for the education of women. Margaret Nash, *Women's Education in the United States, 1780–1840* (New York: Palgrave Macmillan, 2007), 5.

49. See Kelley, *Learning to Stand*, 72.

50. See Emily Conroy-Krutz, "No Acknowledged Standard: The Female Seminary Curriculum of the Early Nineteenth Century," in *Inequity in Education: A Historical*

Perspective, ed. Debra Meyers and Burke Miller (New York: Rowman & Littlefield, 2009), 75 n. 36.

51. *Twenty-Second Annual Catalogue of the Mount Holyoke Female Seminary* (Northampton, MA: Bridgman & Childs, 1859), 12; *Thirty-Third Annual Catalogue of the Mount Holyoke Female Seminary* (Northampton, MA: Bridgman & Childs, 1870), 20.

52. Mary Lyon, "The Character of Young Ladies," in *American Educational Thought: Essays from 1640–1940*, ed. Andrew J. Milson et al. (Charlotte, NC: Information Age Publishing, 2010), 108–9. See John Marsh, *An Epitome of General Ecclesiastical History*, 4th ed. (New York: W. E. Dean, 1834), 1.

53. Clarence P. Mcclelland, "The Education of Females in Early Illinois," *Journal of the Illinois State Historical Society* 36, no. 4 (December 1943): 378–407.

54. See Daniel H. Calhoun, "Eyes for the Jacksonian World: William C. Woodbridge and Emma Willard," *Journal of the Early Republic* 4, no. 1 (1984): 1–26.

55. For Willard's innovations in geography and history writing, see Susan Schulten, "Emma Willard and the Graphic Foundations of American History," *Journal of Historical Geography* 33, no. 3 (July 2007): 542–64; W. D. Walters, "Emma Willard's Geographies," *Pennsylvania Geographer* 37, no. 1 (1999): 118–38; Susan Grigg, "Willard, Emma Hart (1787–1870), Educator and Historian," *American National Biography Online*, February 2000, https://doi.org/10.1093/anb/9780198606697.article.0900806.

56. Nina Baym, "Women and the Republic: Emma Willard's Rhetoric of History," *American Quarterly* 43, no. 1 (1991): 5–6. Among other popular universal histories were those written by Sarah Pierce (four volumes published 1811–18) and Elizabeth Peabody (1859).

57. She came home, according to her student and future women's rights activist Elizabeth Cady Stanton, with a new sense of "profound self-respect" and "a dignity truly regal." Quoted in Alma Lutz, *Emma Willard: Daughter of Democracy* (Boston: Houghton Mifflin, 1929), 173.

58. Baym, "Women and the Republic," 4.

59. Willard held an affection for all things Greek. In 1833 Willard actively promoted the cause of Greek independence and founded the Troy Society for the Advancement of Education in Greece. See Anne Firor Scott, "What, Then, Is the American: This New Woman?," *Journal of American History* 65, no. 3 (1978): 693. The historian must "exhibit history in its proper relative proportions," Willard explained. "Thus tower Greece and Rome, amid the dimness of antiquity, and thus sink the dark ages, though nearer to the foreground." Emma Willard, *A System of Universal History, in Perspective* (Hartford, CT: F. J. Huntington, 1835), iii. Gibbon's influence on Willard's thematic scheme is obvious; she also cites the eighteenth-century historian several times. See Willard, *System of Universal History*, 114, 119, 132.

60. For Constantine and Theodosius, see Willard, *System of Universal History*, 103, 123, 129–30. She noted with chagrin how St. Ambrose, bishop of Milan, freely denounced the Arian empress Justina and reproached Theodosius, examples of "ecclesiastical power manifest[ing] itself as already superior to the civil." For other criticisms

of church leadership, see ibid., 130, 143, 153–54, 156, 167, 170, 184–85. As clerical power grew, Willard explained, "the most atrocious crimes were often committed by them with impunity." Ibid., 189. However, Willard also acknowledged that some popes were pious, and that the medieval church had made real contributions to peace and the good of society. Ibid., 236–37.

61. Ann Douglas suggests that Willard, Sarah Hale, and Lydia Sigourney were all attracted to Episcopalianism in part because it was upper class and prestigious. Ann Douglas, *The Feminization of American Culture* (London: Macmillan, 1977), 94.

62. For example, Willard descried the tenth-century "spirit of fanaticism (the prevailing spirit of the age)." Willard, *System of Universal History*, 163. She blamed the crusades on pilgrimage, "as the spiritual worship of the early Christians was exchanged for the frivolous rites and idle ceremonies of later days." Ibid., 172, 178, 180, 186. For religious extremism and intolerance, see ibid., 154, 202, 226–27, 237, 256. Protestants could also be intolerant—Willard criticized the "bigot" John Knox. Ibid., 245–46.

63. Ibid., 227–28, 256.

64. Ibid., 240.

65. Schulten argues that Willard "'mapped' history in order to create a national past that would translate the fact of the country as a territorial entity into the much more powerful idea of the country as a nation." Schulten, "Emma Willard," 543.

66. Jacob Oson, *A Search for Truth; or, An Inquiry for the Origin of the African Nation* (New York: Christopher Rush, 1817), 7. For Oson, see Randall K. Burkett, "The Reverend Harry Croswell and Black Episcopalians in New Haven, 1820–1860," *North Star* 7, no. 1 (Fall 2003): 1–20; Stephen G. Hall, "'A Search for Truth': Jacob Oson and the Beginnings of African American Historiography," *William and Mary Quarterly* 64, no. 1 (2007): 139–48.

67. For example, see African Americans' use of republican ideology to argue for their political belonging, analyzed in Paul J. Polgar, "'To Raise Them to an Equal Participation': Early National Abolitionism, Gradual Emancipation, and the Promise of African American Citizenship," *Journal of the Early Republic* 31, no. 2 (April 21, 2011): 229–58, https://doi.org/10.1353/jer.2011.0023.

68. Eric Burin, *Slavery and the Peculiar Solution: A History of the American Colonization Society* (Gainesville: University Press of Florida. 2005).

69. Liam Riordan, *Many Identities, One Nation: The Revolution and Its Legacy in the Mid-Atlantic* (Philadelphia: University of Pennsylvania Press, 2007), 272.

70. So argues John Ernest in *Liberation Historiography: African American Writers and the Challenge of History, 1794–1861* (Chapel Hill: University of North Carolina Press, 2004), 53. For the role of Anglo-Saxon history in creating the idea of white superiority, see Reginald Horsman, *Race and Manifest Destiny* (Cambridge, MA: Harvard University Press, 1986), 9.

71. This historiography, Ernest argues, was shaped both "by the pressures of a developing white American historiography that threatened to alienate African Americans from a historically informed understanding of individual and collective identity." Ernest, *Liberation Historiography*, 15, 255.

72. So explains Stephen G. Hall, *A Faithful Account of the Race: African American Historical Writing in Nineteenth-Century America* (Chapel Hill: University of North Carolina Press, 2009), 21–22. See also Laurie F. Maffly-Kipp, *Setting Down the Sacred Past: African-American Race Histories* (Cambridge, MA: Harvard University Press, 2010).

73. John Saillant describes Haynes's historiography: "This sense of belonging to Christian history and identifying with others who had been delivered from bondage fostered a great optimism among the first Black abolitionists that the slave trade and slavery would soon end." John Saillant, *Black Puritan, Black Republican: The Life and Thought of Lemuel Haynes, 1753–1833* (Oxford: Oxford University Press, 2003), 18–19.

74. Ernest quotes David Tracy's argument that African American theology insists that "Christendom could not and cannot survive any true experiment with authentic Christianity." *Liberation Historiography*, 100; David Tracy, "African American Thought: The Discovery of Fragments," in *Black Faith and Public Talk: Critical Essays on James H. Cone's Black Theology and Black Power*, ed. Dwight N. Hopkins (Waco, TX: Baylor University Press, 1999), 32.

75. Margaret Malamud notes that antislavery writers often used Volney. Margaret Malamud, "Black Minerva: Antiquity in Antebellum African American History," in *African Athena: New Agendas*, ed. Daniel Orrells, Gurminder K. Bhambra, and Tessa Roynon (Oxford: Oxford University Press, 2011), 77–78. For Walker, see Peter P. Hinks, *To Awaken My Afflicted Brethren: David Walker and the Problem of Antebellum Slave Resistance* (University Park: Pennsylvania State University Press, 1997), 181–82 n. 22.

76. Malamud, "Black Minerva," 73.

77. See Hall, *Faithful Account of the Race*, 24. For Marrant's conversion under the preaching of Whitefield, see James Sidbury, *Becoming African in America: Race and Nation in the Early Black Atlantic* (New York: Oxford University Press, 2007), 69.

78. [John] Marrant, *A Sermon Preached on the 24th Day of June 1789...* (Boston: Bible and Hart, [1798], Evans Early American Imprint Collection Text Creation Partnership), 20, 20n, http://name.umdl.umich.edu/N17016.0001.001. Several of these church fathers listed by Marrant were in fact from Cappadocia, not North Africa.

79. See Maffly-Kipp, *Setting Down*, 35.

80. Julie Winch, *A Gentleman of Color: The Life of James Forten* (Oxford: Oxford University Press, 2003).

81. Ibid., 212.

82. This is noted in Jared Hickman, "The Recanonization of Saint Cyprian," in *Sainthood and Race: Marked Flesh, Holy Flesh*, ed. Molly H. Bassett and Vincent W. Lloyd (New York: Routledge, 2014), 75ff.

83. Ibid., 75ff.

84. "Devoted to the Improvement of the Coloured Population," *Freedom's Journal* (New York), no. 2, April 4, 1828, America's Historical Newspapers.

85. See Floyd J. Miller, "'The Father of Black Nationalism': Another Contender," *Civil War History* 17, no. 4 (December 1971): 310–19. For Woodson's letters signed

"Augustine," see Byron W. Woodson, *A President in the Family: Thomas Jefferson, Sally Hemings, and Thomas Woodson* (Santa Barbara, CA: Praeger, 2001), 115.

86. "For the Freedom's Journal."

87. Readers of Edward Gibbon, Russwurm noted, already knew that "that the gospel was first received in the burning sands of Africa with great eagerness." He went on to quote from Gibbon's *Decline and Fall*: "African Christians soon formed one of the principal members of the primitive Church. During the course of the 3d century, they were animated by the zeal of Tertullian, directed by the abilities of Cyprian and Origen, and adorned by the eloquence of Laetautius." "Mutability of Human Affairs," *Freedom's Journal* (New York), April 20, 1827, America's Historical Newspapers.

88. James Oliver Horton and Lois E. Horton, *In Hope of Liberty: Culture, Community, and Protest among Northern Free Blacks, 1700–1860* (Oxford: Oxford University Press, 1997); Donald M. Jacobs, ed., *Antebellum Black Newspapers* (Westport, CT: Greenwood Press, 1976).

89. Quoted in Michael R. Frontani, "Alternative Press," in *Encyclopedia of American Journalism*, ed. Stephen L. Vaughn (New York: Routledge, 2008), 14.

90. "Facts for Colored Americans," *Colored American* (New York), May 6, 1837, America's Historical Newspapers.

91. For example, Frederick Dalcho (1770–1836), a medical doctor and Episcopalian deacon, used the "curse of Ham" argument to defend southern slavery. As evidence, he quoted from Augustine's writings, which he thought proved the Canaanite genealogy. Frederick Dalcho, *Practical Considerations Founded on the Scriptures: Relative to the Slave Population of South-Carolina* (Charleston, SC: A.E. Miller, 1823), 13. For the long history of this interpretation, see David M. Whitford, *The Curse of Ham in the Early Modern Era: The Bible and the Justifications for Slavery* (New York: Routledge, 2017).

92. "Prejudice Against Color in the Light of History," *Colored American* (New York), March 18, 1837, America's Historical Newspapers. This is a noteworthy example of what Manisha Sinha points out: that from the eighteenth century on, Black authors shaped abolition through a sophisticated critique of white American hypocrisy. Manisha Sinha, *The Slave's Cause: A History of Abolition* (New Haven, CT: Yale University Press, 2016).

93. See Mark Stephen Massa, *Anti-Catholicism in America: The Last Acceptable Prejudice* (New York: Crossroad Publishers, 2003), 23; Jon Gjerde, *Catholicism and the Shaping of 19th Century America* (Cambridge: Cambridge University Press, 2012), 4–5.

94. For gendered anti-Catholicism, see Marie Anne Pagliarini, "The Pure American Woman and the Wicked Catholic Priest: An Analysis of Anti-Catholic Literature in Antebellum America," *Religion and American Culture* 9, no. 1 (1999): 97–128; Cassandra L. Yacovazzi, *Escaped Nuns: True Womanhood and the Campaign against Convents in Antebellum America* (Oxford: Oxford University Press, 2018).

95. Marie Caskey Morgan, "Beecher, Lyman (1775–1863)," *American National Biography Online*, February 2000, http://www.anb.org/articles/08/08-00113.html.

96. M. Edmund, Hussey, "Fenwick, Edward Dominic (1768–1832), First Bishop of Cincinnati and Founder of the Order of Dominican Friars in the United States,"

American National Biography Online, February 2000, https://doi.org/10.1093/anb/9780198606697.article.0800464.

97. Jenny Franchot, *Roads to Rome: The Antebellum Protestant Encounter with Catholicism* (Berkeley: University of California Press, 1994), 138.

98. Lyman Beecher, *A Plea for the West*, 2nd ed. (Cincinnati: Truman & Smith, 1836), 62, 88, 134, 151–53.

99. Literature on anti-Catholicism has not fully explained the historical narratives that undergirded this construction. The influence and extent of those narratives primed Americans to perceive Catholic immigration as a threat and to consider nativism a historically justified approach. For this literature, see Massa, *Anti-Catholicism in America*; Jody M. Roy, "Nineteenth-Century American Anti-Catholicism and the Catholic Response," PhD diss., Indiana University, 1997; Gjerde, *Catholicism*; Franchot, *Roads to Rome*; Susan M. Griffin, *Anti-Catholicism and Nineteenth-Century Fiction* (Cambridge: Cambridge University Press, 2004); Maura Jane Farrelly, *Anti-Catholicism in America, 1620–1860* (Cambridge: Cambridge University Press, 2017).

100. Farrelly stresses that anti-Catholicism waned in the early republic, an emphasis contributes to her overall argument that this prejudice has not had a lasting influence in American politics and society today. However, the implicit anti-Catholicism in American religious and political life throughout this era suggests a more profound, and potentially lasting, importance of this bias. Farrelly, *Anti-Catholicism*, chap. 4.

Chapter 4

1. David R. Kerr, *Church History—What It Is—How It Should Be Studied—And for What Ends* (Pittsburgh, PA: W.S. Haven, 1855), 11–12, 19–20.

2. Quoted in John Albert Broadus, *Memoir of James Petigru Boyce, D.D., LL.D.: Late President of the Southern Baptist Theological Seminary* (New York: A. C. Armstrong and Son, 1893), 135–37.

3. See Glenn T. Miller, *Piety and Intellect: The Aims and Purposes of Antebellum Theological Education* (Atlanta, GA: Scholars Press, 1990), 332.

4. Roger Finke and Rodney Stark, *The Churching of America, 1776–1990: Winners and Losers in Our Religious Economy* (New Brunswick, NJ: Rutgers University Press, 1992), 77.

5. Roger L. Geiger, *The History of American Higher Education: Learning and Culture from the Founding to World War II* (Princeton, NJ: Princeton University Press, 2014), 145ff.

6. This count does not include Unitarian Harvard or Roman Catholic institutions. Robert Baird, *Religion in the United States of America*, 1st British Edition (Edinburgh: Blackie and Son, 1844), 371.

7. Finke and Stark, *The Churching of America*, 77.

8. See *The American Almanac and Repository of Useful Knowledge for the Year*, vol. XXXII, 4th series, vol. II (Boston: Gray and Bowen, 1861), 236; Finke and Stark, *The Churching of America*, 77. Methodists, the most suspicious of seminary education, finally established a seminary in 1847, yet they founded over two hundred educational institutions between 1830 and 1860. As John Wigger puts it, "[Francis] Asbury's successors obviously shared little of his fear about the corrupting potential of these institutions." John H. Wigger, *Taking Heaven by Storm: Methodism and the Rise of Popular Christianity in America* (Oxford: Oxford University Press, 1998), 176.

9. Andover included Priestley, George Gregory's *History*, and Mosheim and Milner. See *Catalogue of the Library*, 19; James Davis Knowles, *Importance of Theological Institutions* (Boston: Lincoln & Edmands, 1832), Appendix, Note C, 10. Yale's library featured George Campbell, Hume, Gibbon, Robertson, and Priestley, and Milner. See *Catalogue of Books*. Brown University's collection included these and more recent works such as Johann Karl Ludwig Gieseler (1792–1854) and Henry Hart Milman (1791–1868). See *Catalogue of the Library Belonging to the Theological Institution in Andover* (Andover, MA: Flagg and Gould, 1819).

10. In the 1804 "Course of Ecclesiastical Studies," the standard for Episcopalian seminaries for almost a century, the General Convention selected Mosheim as an essential work for future ministers. *Journal of the Proceedings of the Bishops, Clergy, and Laity, of the Protestant Episcopal Church* (New York: T. & J. Swords, 1804), 26–27. For the long tenure of this course of study, see Powel M. Dawley, *The Story of the General Theological Seminary: A Sesquicentennial History, 1817–1967* (Oxford: Oxford University Press, 1969), 19–21. Mosheim was recommended by Baptist educator Jonathan Maxcy in his 1816 "Course of Historical and Miscellaneous Reading." Maxcy also recommended Priestley, Gibbon, and Campbell. Maxcy, *A Course of Historical & Miscellaneous Reading, Drawn up for the Use of the Students of the South-Carolina College* (Columbia, SC: Telescope Office, 1816), 19. Likewise, Matthew L. R. Perrine, professor of church history from 1821 to 1836 at the Presbyterian Auburn Theological Seminary, encouraged young ministers with limited resources to acquire Mosheim and Milner. Matthew Perrine, "Catalogue of Books for a Young Minister on Different Subjects," n.d., The Matthew LaRue Perrine Manuscript Collection, Special Collections, Princeton Theological Seminary Library.

11. For Quaker criticisms, see John Drinker, *A Vindication of the Religious Society Called Quakers: Addressed to the Editors of the American Edition of Mosheim's Ecclesiastical History* (Mount Holly, NJ: S. C. Ustick, 1800), 3, 4; *A Refutation of Some of the Misrepresentations and Aspersions, of the Society of Friends, in Mosheim's Ecclesiastical History* (Charleston, MA: S. Etheridge, 1812), i–ii. For Episcopalians, see William White, "An Essay, Noticing Some Errors in the Ecclesiastical History of Dr. Lawrence Mosheim," *Christian Journal, and Literary Register* 2, no. 8 (April 2, 1818): 121; John Bowden, *The Apostolic Origin of Episcopacy Asserted: In a Series of Letters, Addressed to the Rev. Dr. Miller*, vol. II (New York: T.& J. Swords, 1808), 202. For Restorationists, see Alexander Campbell, *A Debate on Christian Baptism: Between the Rev. W. L. MacCalla, a Presbyterian Teacher, and Alexander Campbell* (Buffaloe, VA: Campbell & Sala, 1824), 378–79.

12. Philip Schaff, *History of the Christian Church*, 2nd ed. (Edinburgh: T&T Clark, 1883), I:50.

13. It seems that Americans disregarded church history until the last quarter of the nineteenth century, when, in large part because of Schaff, the scholarly discipline of "critical" church history emerged. Thus, Henry Bowden characterizes the time before 1876 as an era that neglected church history: Henry Warner Bowden, *Church History in the Age of Science: Historiographical Patterns in the United States, 1876–1918* (Carbondale, IL: Southern Illinois University, 1991), 32–42. Those who do note church history in nineteenth-century seminary curriculum, such as Glenn Miller, tend to only do so with denominations that clearly prioritized tradition. Miller, *Piety and Intellect*, 25, 28. Elizabeth Clark's superb study of church history focuses on the emergence of the discipline of religious studies, and considers only those institutions most important to her narrative—Princeton, Harvard, Yale, and Union. Further, by setting Methodists and Baptists outside of her purview, Clark misses the historical approaches shared by these denominations and their more established counterparts. Elizabeth A. Clark, *Founding the Fathers: Early Church History and Protestant Professors in Nineteenth-Century America* (Philadelphia: University of Pennsylvania Press, 2011). Other recent works that trace German influence on American higher education, with an eye toward religious history, include Thomas A. Howard, *Protestant Theology and the Making of the Modern German University* (Oxford: Oxford University Press, 2006); James Turner, *Religion Enters the Academy: The Origins of the Scholarly Study of Religion in America* (Athens: University of Georgia Press, 2011); Annette G. Aubert, "Henry Boynton Smith and Church History in Nineteenth-Century America," *Church History* 85, no. 2 (June 2016): 302–27.

14. Others could be included. For church history at Yale and Harvard, see Clark, *Founding the Fathers*, 1. For Episcopalian seminaries and church history—which is largely a story of encounter and response to the Oxford Movement—see both Diana Butler, *Standing against the Whirlwind: Evangelical Episcopalians in Nineteenth-Century America* (Oxford: Oxford University Press, 1995), chap. 4, and Miller, *Piety and Intellect*, 248ff.

15. Miller praised Hume for his "excellence of historical style," notwithstanding his "glaring partiality" and "spirit of hostility to religion." Robertson, Miller declared, "deserves a place among the greatest historians of the age," and even exceeded Hume in "purity, dignity, and elegance of diction." Gibbon fared far less well in Miller's evaluation: "The insidious and malignant zeal to discredit religion so often manifested in this work, is well known." Gibbon's structure, style, and evaluation of religion were all criticized by Miller, who recommended that readers familiarize themselves with Whitaker's multivolume rebuttal to Gibbon's narration of Christian history. Samuel Miller, *A Brief Retrospect of the Eighteenth Century*, vol. II (New York: T. and J. Swords, 1803), 130, 132–33, 135–36, 138.

16. So argues Mark Noll in Mark A. Noll, *Princeton and the Republic, 1768–1822: The Search for a Christian Enlightenment in the Era of Samuel Stanhope Smith* (Princeton,

NJ: Princeton University Press, 1989); Mark A. Noll, *America's God: From Jonathan Edwards to Abraham Lincoln* (Oxford: Oxford University Press, 2002), 129.

17. This is Clark's point in Clark, *Founding the Fathers*, 35–36.

18. John Henry Hobart, ed., *A Collection of the Essays on the Subject of Episcopacy, Which Originally Appeared in the Albany Centinel* (New York: T & J Swords, 1806).

19. Samuel Miller, *Letters Concerning the Constitution and Order of the Christian Ministry: As Deduced from Scripture and Primitive Usage* (New York: Hopkins and Seymour, 1807), 310–15. Miller explained the rise of episcopal power as due to general human corruption, increasing wealth, and "Jewish prejudices, pagan habits, and clerical ambition." Ibid., 328.

20. Clark notes that "his teaching of church history focused strongly on polity: he aimed to show that the Presbyterian form of church government was in place at Christianity's inception." Clark, *Founding the Fathers*, 36.

21. Ibid., 56–57. Reformed Theological Seminary, founded in Newburgh, New York, in 1801 by the Associate Presbyterian Church, mandated two years of church history. See Miller, *Piety and Intellect*, 100.

22. "The Life of Samuel Miller," *Biblical Repertory and Princeton Review* 42, no. 1 (January 1870): 37–38.

23. Samuel Miller, *An Essay on the Warrant, Nature, and Duties of the Office of the Ruling Elder, in the Presbyterian Church* (Philadelphia: Presbyterian Board of Publication, 1832), 107.

24. Miller gave this lecture several times between 1815 and 1839. Samuel Miller, "Third Introductory Lecture on Ecclesiastical History," March 2, 1815, Box 2, Folder 9, 16–17, The Samuel Miller Manuscript Collection, Special Collections, Princeton Theological Seminary Library, 9–10.

25. Miller criticized Mosheim but concluded he "furnishes the best plan—the best skeleton of a work of this kind," especially by providing the context so badly lacking in Milner's evangelical history. Samuel Miller, "Notes on Mosheim," July 2, 1831, Box 5, Folder 1, The Samuel Miller Manuscript Collection. Special Collections, Princeton Theological Seminary Library, 1, 3–4. On the other hand, he believed Mosheim failed to convey the spiritual significance of church history. Mosheim defined the church as "a society subjected to a lawful dominion, and governed by certain laws and institutions." Johannes Laurentius a Mosheim, *An Ecclesiastical History, Antient And Modern, From The Birth Of Christ, To The Beginning Of The Present Century* (London: A. Millar, 1765), I:xxi. As Lewis Spitz notes, this definition, while not in conflict with orthodoxy, is secular in emphasis—more "an association of humans" than a divine Kingdom. Lewis Spitz, "Johann Lorenz Mosheim's Philosophy of History," *Concordia Theological Monthly* 20, no. 5 (May 1949): 334. For Miller on Milner, see Miller, "Notes on Mosheim," 3, 5–8. Student notes from Miller's class taken in 1821 show him revising these historians. For example, he disagreed with Milner's account of Gregory the Great, who was "too ambitious" and "excessively superstitious," and preferred Gibbon's portrayal of the Paulicians above Mosheim's, which he called "extremely erroneous." James W. Douglas, "Notes on Church History and Church

Government," 1821, Box 25, Folder 4, The Samuel Miller Manuscript Collection, Special Collections, Princeton Theological Seminary Library, 18, 22.

26. This description of Miller's pedagogy comes from Clark, *Founding the Fathers*, 56–57.

27. These lines are from lectures Miller gave in 1821 and 1829, extracted in *The Life of Samuel Miller* (Philadelphia: Claxton, Remsen and Haffelfinger, 1869), 144.

28. Samuel Miller, *The Importance of Mature Preparatory Study for the Ministry* (Princeton, NJ: Princeton Press, 1829), 9–10. Miller also argued that the importance of an educated ministry was evidenced by church history, in the influence of "those in whom eminent piety, zeal, talents and learning were remarkably united . . . Augustine, of Ambrose of Milan, of Venerable Bede, of Wickliffe, of Huss, of Luther, of Calvin, of Knox, of Rivet, of Owen, of Baxter, of Doddridge." See ibid., 38.

29. Miller, "Third Introductory Lecture," 6, 8. The miraculous triumph of the early church, he argued, could only be established on biblical and ecclesiastical history. "The better our acquaintance is with these facts, the richer the materials we have in our minds, for a strong and lively faith." Ibid. preface.

30. Miller praised Augustine as "the most profound, correct, instructive writer from the time of the apostles to Luther." Ibid., 16.

31. Douglas, "Notes on Church History," 15, 18, 22.

32. Knowles, *Importance*, 18.

33. Ibid. In addition to the names already mentioned, Miller taught a number of influential authors, including Frederick Augustus Muhlenberg and William Swan Plumer; founders of educational institutions, including John Finley Crowe (Hanover College), George Washington Gale (Knox College), Basil Manly Jr. (Southern Baptist Theological Seminary), and Samuel Simon Schmucker (Gettysburg Seminary); and university presidents John Maclean Jr. (Princeton University) and John Monteith (University of Michigan).

34. See Clark, *Founding the Fathers*, 367 n. 5.

35. Miller, *Piety and Intellect*, 68.

36. Knowles, *Importance*, 18.

37. Luther Rice (1783–1836), a pioneer of Baptist missionary work, only encountered church history during his years at Andover Seminary by reading lectures by the Scottish Enlightenment figure George Campbell (1719–1796). See "Class Lecture Notes and Account Book, 1810," AR87, Box 1, Folder 2, Luther Rice Collection, Southern Baptist Historical Library and Archives, Nashville, TN. George Campbell's lectures, given during a course on theology at Marischal College in Aberdeen, Scotland, consisted of a series of arguments generally focused on the expansion of hierarchical power in the church.

38. J. Earl Thompson, "Church History Comes to Andover: The Persecution of James Murdock," *Andover Newton Quarterly* 15, no. 4 (March 1975): 213–15.

39. Miller documents the controversy, arguing that Murdock "was among the first American scholars to qualify as a professional church historian." Miller, *Piety and Intellect*, 72–73. Miller incorrectly dates Murdock's translation of Mosheim as prior to the controversy—it was published in 1832.

40. Nathaniel S. Richardson, "The Rev. James Murdock," *Church Review* 9, no. 4 (January 1857): 502. This is Thompson's description of the pedagogy in Thompson, "Church History Comes to Andover," 222.

41. See Thompson, "Church History Comes to Andover," 216, 219–20.

42. Richardson, "The Rev. James Murdock," 512–13, 519.

43. Ibid., 516. In 1847, J. A. Alexander called Münscher's work "the first formal Dogmengeschichte [or History of Doctrine] which has still maintained a place in public estimation." J. A. Alexander, "Art. VI.—What Is Church History?," *Biblical Repertory and Princeton Review* 19, no. 1 (January 1847): 98–99.

44. Leonard Woods, *History of the Andover Theological Seminary* (Boston: J. R. Osgood, 1885), 188.

45. Quoted in Thompson, "Church History Comes to Andover," 223.

46. Richardson, "The Rev. James Murdock," 509.

47. Thompson, "Church History Comes to Andover," 224–25.

48. In 1829 Andover replaced Murdock with Ralph Emerson, who taught there for twenty-five years. Among his students was Henry Boynton Smith, who attended Andover for a year after his conversion from Unitarianism to Congregationalism in 1834. Illness cut short Smith's studies at Andover. See Henry Boynton Smith, *Henry Boynton Smith: His Life and Work*, ed. Elizabeth L. Smith (New York: A. C. Armstrong & Son, 1881), 20.

49. Richardson, "The Rev. James Murdock," 516.

50. Murdock criticized Maclaine for occasionally revising or paraphrasing the text, and inserting his own opinions. Murdock provided a more literal translation, while adding details from Neander, Du Pin, and Milner in footnotes on various church fathers and medieval theologians. Johann Lorenz Mosheim, *Institutes of Ecclesiastical History, Ancient and Modern*, trans. James Murdock (New Haven, CT: A.H. Maltby, 1832), Preface, 3, 5.

51. *The Christian Examiner* praised Murdock "for the service he has rendered to the cause of theological learning in our country." "Review: Institutes of Ecclesiastical History, Ancient and Modern," *Christian Examiner* 54, no. 24 (1833): 282–84. In 1842, *The Dial*, edited by Ralph Waldo Emerson and Margaret Fuller, praised Murdock's efforts. Ralph Waldo Emerson, Margaret Fuller, and George Ripley, eds., "Review: Institutes of Ecclesiastical History, Ancient and Modern," *The Dial: A Magazine for Literature, Philosophy, and Religion* 2, no. 4 (April 1842): 533. The *Biblical Repertory and Princeton Review* served notice in 1869 of a new abridgement of Murdock's Mosheim, noting that "no historical, parochial, or clergyman's library is properly furnished without this work." Charles Hodge and Lyman Hotchkiss Atwater, eds., "Review: Institutes of Ecclesiastical History, Ancient and Modern," *Biblical Repertory and Princeton Review* 41, no. 4 (October 1869): 632.

52. Philip Schaff, *The Principle of Protestantism as Related to the Present State of the Church*, trans. John Williamson Nevin (Chambersburg, PA: Publication Office of the German Reformed Church, 1845), 107. This account of church history grew from the historical philosophy Schaff imbibed from August Neander and F. C. Baur and the dialectical principles of G. W. F. Hegel. See David R. Bains and Theodore Louis Trost,

"Philip Schaff: The Flow of Church History and the Development of Protestantism," *Theology Today* 71, no. 4 (January 1, 2015): 420.

53. Schaff, *The Principle of Protestantism*, 49, 187. He believed that the Oxford Movement reimposed authority and denied organic development. Ibid., 124. As Bains puts it, this address pointed to a "an American Protestantism that would be historically grounded." Bains and Trost, "Philip Schaff," 422.

54. Schaff, *What Is Church History?*, 4–5, 10.

55. Ibid., 5.

56. See student notes in Charles R. Gillett, "Notes by Gillett, C.R." 1877, UTS1: Philip Schaff Papers, 1838–1896, Series 3, Box 1, Folder 10, The Burke Library at Union Theological Seminary, Columbia University in the City of New York, 47.

57. Schaff, *What Is Church History?*, 122.

58. Student notes reflect Schaff's conviction that church history should be both scientific and Christian: "A subjective history must be based in objective history," Schaff taught. "It must be the witness to the true life." Gillett, "Notes by Gillett, C.R.," 47. The historian "must be a master of the facts, must digest it and must be in sympathy with the truth of Christianity" to grasp the "organic unity" of church history. Ibid., 50.

59. Clark, *Founding the Fathers*, 64–65.

60. Students celebrated him in *The Semi-Centennial of Philip Schaff* (New York: n.p., 1893).

61. Quoted in George H. Shriver, "Philip Schaff as a Teacher of Church History," *Journal of Presbyterian History* 47 (March 1969), 77–78. Schaff wrote in his 1893 resignation letter: "Teaching has been my life for more than fifty years." Quoted in Clark, *Founding the Fathers*, 45.

62. Clark, *Founding the Fathers*, 56.

63. Schaff, *What Is Church History?*, 4–5.

64. Shriver, "Philip Schaff as a Teacher, " 79.

65. James E Bradley, *Church History: An Introduction to Research, Reference Works, and Methods* (Grand Rapids, MI: Eerdmans, 1995), 16. For more on Neander's influence in the United States, see Joshua Bennett, "August Neander and the Religion of History in the Nineteenth-Century 'Priesthood of Letters,'" *Historical Journal* 63, no. 3 (2020): 633–59.

66. Schaff, *What Is Church History?*, 25–26.

67. Schaff wrote that Neander had "the most thorough study of authorities, an uncommon religious amiability and goodness, and a peculiar method of grasping and setting forth his subject." Ibid., 18.

68. August Neander, *History of the Planting and Training of the Christian Church by the Apostles*, trans. J. E. Ryland (Philadelphia: J. M. Campbell & Co., 1844), 217; August Neander, *General History of the Christian Religion and Church*, 2nd American Edition, vol. II (Boston: Crocker & Brewster, 1849), 226–27.

69. Schaff, *What Is Church History?*, 79.

70. In 1877, student notes from Schaff's class show him recommending Neander as the "father of modern church history," while also pointing to Mosheim, Geiseler, Milman, Gibbon, and others. Gillett, "Notes by Gillett," 50.

71. Clark, *Founding the Fathers*, 174, 176. Clark may overplay the contrast between Neander and Joseph Milner, however. Milner explicitly aimed at highlighting genuine piety in every age, including the medieval era. He celebrated almost 150 medieval figures as paragons of the faith. See Paul Gutacker, "Joseph Milner and His Editors: Eighteenth- and Nineteenth-Century Evangelicals and the Christian Past," *Journal of Ecclesiastical History* 69, no. 1 (January 2018), 86–104. This concern to find genuine Christianity in every age was why Samuel Miller believed Milner was an important supplement to Mosheim. Miller, "Notes on Mosheim," 5.

72. Kenneth Stewart mistakenly argues that Schaff's *Principle of Protestantism* made the case "that evangelical Protestantism is a fuller expression of the power and genius latent in the Christian gospel." Kenneth J. Stewart, *In Search of Ancient Roots: The Christian Past and the Evangelical Identity Crisis* (Downers Grove, IL: InterVarsity Press Academic, 2017), 35. In this work Schaff insisted that Protestantism, like Catholicism before it, was "one-sided and incomplete," and argued that in the next era of church history the "truth of both [would] be actualized as the power of one and the same life." See Philip Schaff, *The Development of the Church: "The Principle of Protestantism" and Other Historical Writings of Philip Schaff*, ed. David R. Bains and Theodore Louis Trost (Eugene, OR: Wipf and Stock, 2017), 189–90.

73. For these reviews and the heresy trial, see Schaff, *Development of the Church*, 209–10.

74. Janeway expanded the initial publication into *Antidote to the Poison of Popery*, a lengthy critique of Schaff's historical theories. The book reproduced "numerous quotations from Mosheim and Edgar, Fox and Quick," which offered "an accurate and pretty full acquaintance with the history of the Papacy or the Romish Church." Jacob J. Janeway, *Antidote to the Poison of Popery in the Writings and Conduct of Professors Nevin & Schaff* (New Brunswick, NJ: J. Terhune, 1856), iii. He hoped the work would "awaken the attention of Protestants" and "to excite them to search for the testimonies of credible historians in regard to the fatal errors, the gross ignorance, shameful licentiousness, and heathenish idolatry" of Rome. Ibid., 15. The book earned praise from a coterie of Reformed theological journals, including *Presbyterian Magazine*, *The Biblical Repertory*, *The Christian Intelligencer* and *The Theological and Literary Journal*. For these reviews, see ibid., iv–vii.

75. Clark, *Founding the Fathers*, 245.

76. Nevin first taught at the Presbyterian institution in Allegheny, Western Theological Seminary, but eventually rejected Presbyterian theology, largely through the influence of reading Neander. He left Western to teach at Mercersburg in 1840. See Richard E. Wentz, "Nevin, John Williamson (1803–1886), religious thinker and educator." *American National Biography Online*, February 2000. https://doi.org/10.1093/anb/9780198606697.article.0801082.

77. Hodge's discussion is given in Schaff, *The Development of the Church*, 215–18, 220–22.

78. Alexander, "What Is Church History?," 104–5, 109–10.

79. Charles Hodge, "History of the Apostolic Church," *Biblical Repertory and Princeton Review* 26, no. 1 (January 1854): 149–50, 157, 190, 192.

80. "Schaff's Church History," *Bibliotheca Sacra* 16, no. 62 (April 1859): 454–56.

81. Henry Boynton Smith, "Schaff's Church History," *American Theological Review* 1, no. 2 (May 1859): 318, 322–23.

82. Broadus, *Memoir*, 135. He believed recent historiography posed a serious threat to Baptist identity. He criticized historians like Schaff who spread "false theories as to church power, and the development and growth of the truth and principles of Scripture, that by all, save their most discerning readers, our pretensions to an early origin and a continuous existence have been rejected." Ibid., 136.

83. While church history was not as important as biblical studies, Kerr acknowledged, it provided "indispensable" knowledge for those leading the church. Kerr, *Church History*, 5–6, 8, 19–20. Among its benefits were that students saw the church "overcoming the combined influence of ignorance, superstition, prejudice, education, habit, priestcraft, and the bitterest persecutions." Ibid., 14.

84. These include a more nuanced view of the development of the papacy, and a moderation of the narrative of decline from a pristine apostolic church into medieval corruption. See Clark, *Founding the Fathers*.

85. John Wolffe argues that these years saw anti-Catholicism become more central to evangelical identity, both in Britain and in the United States. See John Wolffe, "Anti-Catholicism and Evangelical Identity in Britain and the United States, 1830–1860," in *Evangelicalism: Comparative Studies of Popular Protestantism in North America, the British Isles, and beyond 1700–1900*, ed. Mark A. Noll, David Bebbington, and George A. Rawlyk (Oxford: Oxford University Press, 1994).

86. Samuel Miller, ed., *A History of Popery: Including Its Origin, Progress, Doctrines, Practice, Institutions, and Fruits, to the Commencement of the Nineteenth Century* (New York: J.B. Haven, 1834), 3, 5.

87. Baird, *Religion in America*, 261–62.

88. Robert Baird, *The Life of Ramon Monsalvatge, a Converted Spanish Monk, of the Order of the Capuchins* (New York: J.F. Trow & Co., 1845), vii, xiii, xxvii, xxx.

89. Bernard S. Finn, "Morse, Samuel Finley Breese (1791–1872)," *American National Biography Online*, February 2000, http://www.anb.org/articles/13/13-01183.html.

90. Samuel Finley Breese Morse, *Foreign Conspiracy Against the Liberties of the United States* (New York: Leavitt, Lord & Co., 1835), 52.

91. Ibid., 99, 140, 166–68.

92. Ibid., 3.

93. William Craig Brownlee, *Popery, an Enemy to Civil and Religious Liberty; and Dangerous to Our Republic* (New York: Bowne & Wisner, 1836), 4.

94. Brownlee also wrote an anti-Quaker historical work. In response to Quakers who insisted that they had been unfairly represented by Protestant historians, particularly Mosheim, Brownlee argued that Mosheim's account was accurate. The publication won him an honorary doctorate from the University of Glasgow. William Craig Brownlee, *A Careful and Free Inquiry Into the True Nature and Tendency of the Religious Principles of the Society of Friends, Commonly Called Quakers* (Philadelphia: J. Mortimer, 1824), 84, 96.

95. Brownlee, *Popery*, 44, 55, 60, 63–64, 99, 106, 115.

96. "The Importance of American Freedom to Christianity," *Christian Review* 1, no. 2 (June 1836): 201–2, 14.

97. See Hasia Diner, *Erin's Daughters in America: Irish Immigrant Women in the Nineteenth Century* (Baltimore: Johns Hopkins University Press, 1983); Dale T. Knobel, *Paddy and the Republic: Ethnicity and Nationality in Antebellum America* (Middletown, CT: Wesleyan University Press, 1986).

98. For the importance of sermons in nineteenth-century American religious life, see Sacvan Bercovitch, *The American Jeremiad*, 2nd ed. (Madison: University of Wisconsin Press, 2012); section 3 of Nathan O. Hatch, *The Democratization of American Christianity* (New Haven, CT: Yale University Press, 1989); Catherine A. Brekus, *Strangers and Pilgrims: Female Preaching in America, 1740–1845* (Chapel Hill: University of North Carolina Press, 1999); Dawn Coleman, *Preaching and the Rise of the American Novel* (Columbus: Ohio State University Press, 2013); Robert H. Ellison, ed., *A New History of the Sermon: The Nineteenth Century* (Boston: Brill, 2010). In particular, Dawn Coleman argues that attention to sermons as "lived religion" works to destabilize "sharp distinctions between the clergy and laity." Her study of the *Annals of the American Pulpit* puts greater weight on "the extent to which ministerial discourse shaped the experience of the laity. That is, people learned how to experience preaching—how to approach it, respond to it, evaluate it—through language that ministers themselves provided." See Dawn Coleman, "The Antebellum American Sermon as Lived Religion," in *A New History of the Sermon: The Nineteenth Century*, ed. Robert H. Ellison (Boston, Brill: 2010), 526–27.

Chapter 5

1. Following quotations are taken from the second edition. See Sarah Josepha Buell Hale, *Woman's Record, or, Sketches of All Distinguished Women: From the Creation to A.D. 1854* (New York: Harper, 1855), xlvii. See Baym's treatment of this in Nina Baym, "Onward Christian Women: Sarah J. Hale's History of the World," *New England Quarterly* 63, no. 2 (1990): 256–57.

2. Hale, *Woman's Record*, 66.

3. Ann Douglas, *The Feminization of American Culture* (London: Macmillan, 1977), 47. See also Patricia Okker, *Our Sister Editors: Sarah J. Hale and the Tradition of Nineteenth-Century American Women Editors* (Athens: University of Georgia Press, 1995), 44–45. Hale argued that the Bible did not teach sexual equality, but provided the only "guarantee of woman's rights." Hale, *Woman's Record*, viii, xxxvii.

4. Joyce W. Warren, "Hale, Sarah Josepha Buell (1788–1879), Magazine Editor," *American National Biography Online*, February 2000, http://www.anb.org/articles/16/16-00686.html.

5. She recalled that reading David Ramsay's *History of the American Revolution* (1789) as a ten-year-old "made me a patriot for life." Quoted in Okker, *Our Sister Editors*, 40.

6. "Editors' Table," *Godey's Magazine and Lady's Book* 34 (1847): 220, 269, 315.

7. Hale, *Woman's Record*, vii–viii.

8. Hale explains this in Kantian categories in her prefatory argument: "Woman has a quicker capacity for comprehending moral truth or sentiment than man, but she cannot explain this truth, nor expose error to *his comprehension*, unless her intellect has been, in some measure, trained like his. Men have little sympathy with intuitive knowledge, or feeling—'pure Reason'—in the doctrine of Kant: hence they must have the truth set before them its relation with 'practical Reason.'" Hale, *Woman's Record*, viii–ix, xlvii. Baym helpfully sums up Hale's vision of historical progress: "Without Christianity, women are underestimated, degraded, enslaved; without women, Christianity is misunderstood, devalued, corrupted." Baym, "Onward Christian Women," 253. For Hale's Kantian categories, see Baym, 256–57.

9. See Warren, "Hale, Sarah Josepha Buell." "The Roman Catholic church degraded women," Hale argued, "when it degraded marriage by making the celibacy of the priests a condition of greater holiness than married life." *Woman's Record*, 152. *Woman's Record* reflected a degree of anti-Catholicism, as well as the antimedieval condescension of Gibbon, Hume, and Robertson, who all served as sources for Hale. Yet Baym is not quite accurate in concluding that Hale "virtually dismisses Catholicism as a Christian religion because of its attitude toward women." Baym, "Onward Christian Women," 253. Her desire to show women's role in Christian progress, paired with her High Church leanings, inclined Hale to be somewhat charitable toward the Catholic past. Hale was not above praising women who enjoyed prominence in the Roman Catholic calendar: Helena, Catherine of Siena, Monica, and other Catholic women. Hale, *Woman's Record*, 133, 135, 138, 108, 91.

10. Hale, *Woman's Record*, 152.

11. Historians have debated the extent to which Hale's gender ideology sequestered women to a private domestic sphere. In the 1970s, historians such as Susan Conrad and Ann Douglas represented Hale as antifeminist and a primary contributor to nineteenth-century sentimental and consumerist feminine culture. Susan Phinney Conrad, *Perish the Thought: Intellectual Women in Romantic America, 1830–1860* (Oxford: Oxford University Press, 1976); Douglas, *Feminization of American Culture*. Patricia Okker, however, sees Hale using gender conventions "to raise the status of women's work within the home and to encourage women's participation in public events." Okker argues that Hale "advocated a separate—and essential—public space for women." Okker, *Our Sister Editors*, 60.

12. Little scholarship has been done on how nineteenth-century authors, both male and female, treated women in Christian history. More attention has been given to American authors' use of women from Greek and Roman history. Caroline Winterer mentions no Christians in late antiquity, such as Augustine of Hippo or his mother Monica, both of whom pervaded nineteenth-century literature. Caroline Winterer, *The Mirror of Antiquity: American Women and the Classical Tradition, 1750–1900* (Ithaca, NY: Cornell University Press, 2009). While Mary Kelley analyzes classical figures in Hale and Child, she gives almost no attention to their engagement with Christian women prior to the 1500s. Kelley, *Learning to Stand*, 192, 203–16. One exception to this is Nina Baym's excellent work on nineteenth-century women

historians. Baym not only explores women's writing on classical and biblical history, but also references their interpretations of the Middle Ages, their treatment of various medieval women, and their understanding of the Reformation, showing how nineteenth-century women historians narrated Protestantism and women's progress going hand in hand. But Baym does not discuss how these women adapted and departed from prior religious historiography. Baym, "Onward Christian Women"; Nina Baym, "Women and the Republic: Emma Willard's Rhetoric of History," *American Quarterly* 43, no. 1 (1991): 1–23; Nina Baym, *American Women Writers and the Work of History, 1790–1860* (New Brunswick, NJ: Rutgers University Press, 1995). Another exception is chapter 8 of Elizabeth A. Clark, *Founding the Fathers: Early Church History and Protestant Professors in Nineteenth-Century America* (Philadelphia: University of Pennsylvania Press, 2011), which explores how Samuel Miller, Philip Schaff, and later history professors of the nineteenth century understood women's roles, marriage, and Christian asceticism.

13. An extensive literature followed Barbara Welter's argument that early national women were sequestered to a separate sphere. Barbara Welter, "The Cult of True Womanhood: 1820–1860," *American Quarterly* 18, no. 2 (1966): 151. Nancy Cott argued the domestic sphere gave women more social power and "formed a necessary stage in the process of shattering the hierarchy of sex." Nancy F. Cott, *The Bonds of Womanhood: "Woman's Sphere" in New England, 1780–1835* (New Haven, CT: Yale University Press, 1977), 197, 200. Linda Kerber, however, argued the ideal of "republican motherhood" justified a quite limited political role and prescribed a sentimental understanding of true womanhood. Linda K. Kerber, *Women of the Republic: Intellect and Ideology in Revolutionary America* (Chapel Hill: University of North Carolina Press, 1980), 12. Likewise, Mary Beth Norton argued women's work in the domestic sphere was connected to the public good and perceived as important. Mary Beth Norton, *Liberty's Daughters: The Revolutionary Experience of American Women, 1750–1800* (Ithaca, NY: Cornell University Press, 1980).

14. Baym argues that American women historians "drench[ed] the private sphere with newly recognized public significance . . . and also mov[ed] women out into the sphere already agreed on as public." Baym, *American Women Writers*, 1, 5. Margaret Nash argues that early national women enjoyed more educational opportunity than has been recognized. Margaret Nash, *Women's Education in the United States, 1780–1840* (New York: Palgrave Macmillan, 2007). Mary Kelley argues that female academies and seminaries moved into public life women who shaped opinion and civil society. See Mary Kelley, *Learning to Stand and Speak: Women, Education, and Public Life in America's Republic* (Chapel Hill: University of North Carolina Press, 2012). Lucia McMahon argues that educated women resisted separate sphere prescriptions but did not demand economic, social, or political equality. Lucia McMahon, *Mere Equals: The Paradox of Educated Women in the Early American Republic* (Ithaca, NY: Cornell University Press, 2012).

15. So argues Baym in Baym, *American Women Writers*, 5.

16. Even though these authors tended to stay firmly within the gendered conventions of the day, Kelley argues, they self-consciously contributed to public discourse and the

shape of society. Kelley, *Learning to Stand*, 193. The 1830s saw increasing numbers of women writing history, from the multivolume *Key to History* (1832) by Elizabeth Palmer Peabody to Anne Tuttle Bullard's *The Reformation: A True Tale of the Sixteenth Century* (1832). Several histories of the Reformation were produced by antebellum women, including three volumes from Hannah Farnham Sawyer Lee in the 1840s. See Baym, *American Women Writers*, 41–42, 55.

17. For the importance of history, see McMahon, *Mere Equals*, 25. For examples of recommending Christian history, see Mrs. Lincoln Phelps, *The Female Student: or, Lectures to Young Ladies on Female Education. For the Use of Mothers, Teachers, and Pupils* (New York: Leavitt, Lord & Company, 1836), 183, 189; "Editors' Table," 220, 269, 315.

18. As Baym argues, because history was a story of male dominance via physical force, "Women appearing rarely in history was actually a *positive* thing." Baym, *American Women Writers*, 214–15.

19. Mosheim mentioned Perpetua in passing. His translator, Archibald Maclaine, added references to several mothers, including Helena, Anthusa (mother of John Chrysostom), and Monica, in the footnotes. See Johannes Laurentius a Mosheim, *An Ecclesiastical History, Antient And Modern, From The Birth Of Christ, To The Beginning Of The Present Century* (London: A. Millar, 1765), I:191, 259, 279, 292, 304.

20. Edward Gibbon, *The History of the Decline and Fall of the Roman Empire* (London: Cowie and Co., 1825), I:558, II:429.

21. Joseph Milner, *The History of the Church of Christ* (York: G. Peacock, 1794), I:42.

22. Ibid., I:249–58, 331–36, II:324, 193, 288.

23. Rebecca Eaton, *An Abridgment of Milner's Church History, for the Use of Schools and Private Families* (Andover, MA: Flagg and Gould, 1817), iii, 45, 93, 100–101, 105–9, 169.

24. See Anne M. Boylan, *Sunday School: The Formation of an American Institution, 1790–1880* (New Haven, CT: Yale University Press, 1988), 116–17.

25. ASSU Committee of Publication, ed., *Letters on Ecclesiastical History* (Philadelphia: American Sunday-School Union, 1832), I:133.

26. For Rowson's publishing career, see Edward T. James et al., eds., *Notable American Women, 1607–1950: A Biographical Dictionary*, vol. III (Cambridge, MA: Belknap Press, 1971), 202–4. For her views on the importance of history, see Susanna Rowson, *A Present for Young Ladies* (Boston: John West & Co., 1811), 52–54.

27. Edward Gibbon, one of Rowson's favorites, made much of Hypatia's death, describing how she was "torn from her chariot, stripped naked, dragged to the church, and inhumanely butchered." Rowson followed Gibbon in narrating this gruesome death, but redacted the detail that the ancient philosopher had been killed by Christians. Rowson, *Present for Young Ladies*, 85–86. Celebrating Hypatia was not uncommon, as Mary Kelley notes: "Presented as the innocent victim of fanatical Christians, Hypatia came to symbolize the demise of classical antiquity for many eighteenth- and nineteenth-century Europeans and Americans." See Kelley, *Learning to Stand*, 199. See also Maria Dzielska, *Hypatia of Alexandria* (Cambridge, MA: Harvard University Press, 1996), 1–26. Other women historians, including Hale and Child,

also highlighted Hypatia as a martyr of religious persecution. See Hale, *Woman's Record*, 111–12; Lydia Maria Francis Child, *The Progress of Religious Ideas: Through Successive Ages* (New York: C. S. Francis & Company, 1855), 261–62.

28. See Rowson's poem "Rights of Woman," in Susanna Rowson, *Miscellaneous Poems* (Boston: Gilbert and Dean, 1804), 99. For Rowson's change on gender and politics, see Eve Kornfeld, "Women in Post-Revolutionary American Culture: Susanna Haswell Rowson's American Career," *Journal of American Culture* 6 (Winter 1983): 56–62; Rosemarie Zagarri, *Revolutionary Backlash: Women and Politics in the Early American Republic* (Philadelphia: University of Pennsylvania Press, 2007).

29. Baym, "Women and the Republic," 5–6. Among other popular universal histories were those written by Sarah Pierce (four volumes published 1811–18) and Elizabeth Peabody (1859).

30. See ibid., 5–6, 12.

31. As Nina Baym explains, this reflected the outlook of early republic historians: "History is a record of incessant warfare; warfare requires warriors; and only men can be warriors." Baym, *American Women Writers*, 6.

32. See Catherine Teets-Parzynski, "Child, Lydia Maria Francis (1802–1880)," *American National Biography Online*, February 2000, http://www.anb.org/articles/15/15-00127.html.

33. For Child's sources see Carolyn L. Karcher, *The First Woman in the Republic: A Cultural Biography of Lydia Maria Child* (Durham, NC: Duke University Press, 1994), 221.

34. Lydia Marie Francis Child, *The History of the Condition of Women* (Boston: J. Allen, 1835), 75–77.

35. Henry Card, *Literary Recreations* (London: W. Wilson, 1809), 86. Card was reprinted in "On the Condition and Character of Women in Different Countries and Ages," *American Review of History and Politics* 4, no. 2 (October 1812): 262–84.

36. For medieval views of women, see Child, *History*, 87–88, 116.

37. Ibid., 126. For gender in anti-Catholic literature, see Marie Anne Pagliarini, "The Pure American Woman and the Wicked Catholic Priest: An Analysis of Anti-Catholic Literature in Antebellum America," *Religion and American Culture* 9, no. 1 (1999): 97–128; Cassandra L. Yacovazzi, *Escaped Nuns: True Womanhood and the Campaign against Convents in Antebellum America* (Oxford: Oxford University Press, 2018); Jon Gjerde, *Catholicism and the Shaping of 19th Century America* (Cambridge: Cambridge University Press, 2012); Susan M. Griffin, *Anti-Catholicism and Nineteenth-Century Fiction* (Cambridge: Cambridge University Press, 2004).

38. Karcher, *The First Woman*, 14.

39. Child, *History*, 127, 208. She contrasted this not with Roman Catholicism, but rather with Islam, which "debases woman into a machine, and regards love as a merely sensual passion." Ibid., 120. Muslim women, she concluded, were essentially slaves. Ibid., 210.

40. Child's *History*, as Carolyn Karcher argues, stood "at the crossroads of Child's vocations as a purveyor of domestic advice and as a subversive political agitator." However, as Karcher points out, it was on the issue of slavery, not women's rights, that the book made its most explicit interventions. Karcher, *The First Woman*, 221,

224, 357, 610. This is not particularly surprising, given Child's consistent prioritization of abolition in her writing and activism. In the early 1840s, she served as editor for the *National Anti-Slavery Standard*. See Liz Watts, "Lydia Maria Child," *Journalism History* 35, no. 1 (Spring 2009): 12–22.

41. Sarah Josepha Buell Hale, "The History of the Condition of Women, in Various Ages and Nations. By Mrs. D. L. Child," *American Ladies' Magazine* 8 (October 1835): 588.

42. See Karcher, *The First Woman*, 225–26.

43. Elizabeth Cady Stanton et al., eds., *History of Woman Suffrage*, vol. I (New York: Fowler & Wells, 1881), 38.

44. Phelps, *The Female Student*, 191.

45. For Grimké's reliance on Child, see Gerda Lerner, *The Feminist Thought of Sarah Grimké* (Oxford: Oxford University Press, 1998), 25. For the rise of women's activism by the 1840s, see Anne Boylan, *The Origins of Women's Activism: New York and Boston, 1797–1840* (Chapel Hill: University of North Carolina Press, 2002).

46. Sarah Moore Grimké, *Letters on the Equality of the Sexes* (Boston: I. Knapp, 1838), 16, 37, 63, 86, 107, 119.

47. For Fuller, see Douglas, *Feminization of American Culture*, chap. 8.

48. Steele, ed., *The Essential Margaret Fuller*, 272–73.

49. See "Woman in the Nineteenth Century," *Southern Quarterly Review* 10, no. 19 (July 1846): 163. For appreciation of Mary in this time, see Elizabeth Hayes Alvarez, *The Valiant Woman: The Virgin Mary in Nineteenth-Century American Culture* (Chapel Hill: University of North Carolina Press, 2016).

50. In a sermon in 1849 on women's rights, Mott argued that "Ecclesiastical history" proved there were early female ministers. Lucretia Mott, *Complete Sermons and Speeches*, ed. Dana Green (New York: Edwin Mellen Press, 1980), 125, 147.

51. See Judith Wellman, *The Road to Seneca Falls: Elizabeth Cady Stanton and the First Woman's Rights Convention* (Champaign: University of Illinois Press, 2010). For the international context of American women's rights, see Bonnie S. Anderson, *Joyous Greetings: The First International Women's Movement, 1830–1860* (Oxford: Oxford University Press, 2000).

52. So argues Gerda Lerner in *The Feminist Thought*, 22–23.

53. Quoted in Elizabeth Cady Stanton, Susan Brownell Anthony, and Matilda Joslyn Gage, *History of Woman Suffrage*, 2nd ed. (Rochester, NY: Charles Mann, 1889), I:380.

54. For Monica's representation in the *Confessions*, see Gillian Clark, *Monica: An Ordinary Saint* (Oxford: Oxford University Press, 2015). See also several chapters in Judith Chelius Stark, ed., *Feminist Interpretations of Augustine* (University Park: Pennsylvania State University Press, 2007).

55. See Cotton Mather, *The Good Old Way* (Boston: B. Green, 1706); Cotton Mather, *Maternal Consolations* (Boston: T. Fleet, 1714); Increase Mather, *The Duty of Parents to Pray for Their Children* (Boston: Allen, 1719); Cotton Mather, *Ornaments for the Daughters of Zion* (Boston: Kneeland and Green, 1741).

56. See Whitefield's preface in Robert Cruttenden and George Whitefield, *The Experience of Mr. R. Cruttenden* (Boston: Kneeland and Green, 1744), v.

57. A selection of these titles show her attraction for antebellum Americans: "The Infidel Convinced by a Child," *New York Religious Chronicle* 3, no. 16 (April 16, 1825); "Blessing of Pious Parents," *Guardian and Monitor* 8, no. 1 (January 1, 1826); "Meditation on the Religious Education of Children," *Religious Monitor and Evangelical Repository* 12, no. 7 (December 1835); "Pious Mothers of the Early Church," *Zion's Herald and Wesleyan Journal* 18, no. 48 (December 1, 1847).

58. See Anderson, *Joyous Greetings*.

59. So argues Elizabeth Clark in *Founding the Fathers*, 174. Clark argues that Neander's book replacing Mosheim as the primary text in American seminaries brought about a new sympathy for the postapostolic church. See ibid., 176. For more on Neander's influence, see chapter 4.

60. August Neander, *History of the Planting and Training of the Christian Church by the Apostles*, trans. J. E. Ryland (Philadelphia: J. M. Campbell & Co., 1844), 217.

61. Schaff concludes that "Neander cherished her memory, and no doubt thought of her when he described the moulding influence of pious mothers upon the ancient fathers." Philip Schaff, *Saint Augustin, Melanchthon, Neander: Three Biographies* (London: James Nisbet, 1886), 132.

62. August Neander, *General History of the Christian Religion and Church*, 2nd American (Boston: Crocker & Brewster, 1849), II:226–27.

63. "Female Influence and Obligations—No. 226," American Tract Society Tracts Collection (Unprocessed Collection), 19th Century Collection, Drew University, Madison, NJ.

64. For example, see Baym's treatment of Hale's vision of Protestantism and women's advancement going together. Baym, "Onward Christian Women," 253. Baym makes a strong case for the ways in these women were authorized to speak through Protestant ideals of the written word. Baym, *American Women Writers*, 66. Susan Broomhall notes that women such as Clara Lucas Balfour and Harriet Beecher Stowe used their writings to show "that Christianity was a liberating force for women in the past and present." Susan Broomhall, "Religion," in *Companion to Women's Historical Writing*, ed. Mary Spongberg, Ann Curthoys, and Barbara Caine (London: Palgrave Macmillan, 2005), 460.

65. These women were St. Cecilia; Martha, sister of Mary; Petronilla; Flavia Domitilla; Felicitas; Potamlena; Adelaide; St. Agnes; Catharine of Alexandria; Helena, the mother of Constantine; Mary of Egypt; Monica; Genevieve; Bertha; Ebba, abbess of Coldingham; Hilda of Whitby; and Editha. Jesse Ames Spencer, ed., *The Women of Early Christianity: A Series of Portraits* (New York: D. Appleton, 1852), title page.

66. Ibid., 5–6.

67. Ibid., 134, 136–37.

68. Howe shows that the years 1820–1850 saw "the most rapid urbanization in American history," with an increase from five cities with populations over twenty-five thousand in 1820 to twenty-six cities in 1850. Daniel Walker Howe, *What Hath God Wrought: The Transformation of America, 1815-1848* (Oxford: Oxford University Press, 2007), 526. For more on urbanization, see Stuart M. Blumin, *The Emergence of the Middle Class: Social Experience in the American City, 1760-1900* (Cambridge: Cambridge

University Press, 1989); Sean Wilentz, *Chants Democratic: New York City and the Rise of the American Working Class, 1788–1850* (Oxford: Oxford University Press, 2004). See also Kyle B. Roberts, *Evangelical Gotham: Religion and the Making of New York City, 1783–1860* (Chicago: University of Chicago Press, 2016).

69. "The Absent Son," *New York Evangelist* 27, no. 23 (June 5, 1856), American Periodicals.

70. "The Mother's Cares," *German Reformed Messenger* 22, no. 28 (March 12, 1856); "The Mother's Cares," *New York Observer and Chronicle* 34, no. 23 (June 5, 1856), American Periodicals.

71. "The Christian Home: VI—Its Influence," *German Reformed Messenger* 22, no. 6 (October 8, 1856).

72. Joseph Parrish Thompson, *The Christian Graces: A Series of Lectures on 2 Peter I, 5–12* (New York: Sheldon & Company, 1859), 123–26; "Woman's Patience," *The Independent*, 11 (June 16, 1859): 6.

73. Jabez Burns, *Mothers of the Wise and Good* (London: Houston and Stoneman, 1846); William King Tweedie, *The Early Choice: A Book for Daughters* (Philadelphia: American Baptist Publication Society, 1855).

74. As Candy Gunther Brown shows, periodicals and books allowed women to participate in a community of readers that sought to overcome the isolation of the domestic sphere while at the same time infusing it with public significance. Candy Gunther Brown, *The Word in the World: Evangelical Writing, Publishing, and Reading in America, 1789–1880* (Chapel Hill: University of North Carolina Press, 2004), 184–85.

75. Sarah Stickney Ellis's *Mothers of Great Men* (London: Bentley, 1859). Ellis, as Daryl Ogden points out, "was by far the most popular author of the female advice books in the nineteenth-century Britain." Daryl Ogden, "Double Visions: Sarah Stickney Ellis, George Eliot and the Politics of Domesticity," *Women's Studies* 25, no. 6 (November 1, 1996): 585. See also Rohan Maitzen, "'This Feminine Preserve': Historical Biographies by Victorian Women," *Victorian Studies* 38, no. 3 (1995): 371–93; Miriam Elizabeth Burstein, "From Good Looks to Good Thoughts: Popular Women's History and the Invention of Modernity, ca. 1830–1870," *Modern Philology* 97, no. 1 (August 1999): 46–75.

76. Douglas, *Feminization of American Culture*, chap. 6.

77. Lydia Howard Sigourney, *Examples of Life and Death* (New York: C. Scribner, 1852), 26.

78. Child, *The Progress of Religious Ideas*, I:vii. Karcher argues that Child wrote to challenge Christian orthodoxy and undermine what she deemed an unhealthy Christian sexual asceticism. Karcher, *The First Woman*, 357.

79. Child believed that early Christianity was superstitious, severe, and opposed to worldly amusement or luxury. See Child, *Progress of Religious Ideas*, II:319, 321, 324, 351. "The outward benefits [Constantine] conferred on the Christian religion," Child concluded, "were perhaps balanced by the rapid degeneracy they induced." Ibid., III:15, 22–23. Even while many bishops enjoyed lives of luxury, Child noted that some were "real blessings to mankind" in building hospitals and caring for the poor, sick, and orphaned. Ibid., III:205–6.

80. Ibid., III:39–42, 51, 93, 261–62. At the end of the work, Child castigated theology "as one of the worst enemies of mankind." Its progress has been marked by "waste of life . . . disturbance of domestic and social happiness . . . perverted feelings . . . blighted hearts." She lamented that the efforts put into theology could have "been expended on science, agriculture, and the arts!" Ibid., III:451–52.

81. Ibid., III:171–72, 260–65. For Monica, see ibid., III:118ff.

82. Ibid., II:352–53. The practice of celibacy increased, Child argued, as "the oriental element became more and more obviously mingled with Christianity," an influence that she believed could be traced in part to the Christian adaptation of elements of Buddhist monasticism. While Child noted the achievements of some medieval monks and nuns, she criticized their celibacy as unnatural: "The more Christianity set itself up in opposition to nature, and demanded entire suppression of the instincts and affections, the more the separation widened between the worldly class and the religious." Ibid., 172, 256.

83. Ibid., II:414, 430–31.

84. Ibid., III:426, 430–31.

85. "Book Reviews," *Boston Recorder*, November 15, 1855, America's Historical Newspapers.

86. "Progress of Religious Ideas," *New York Evangelist*, December 6, 1855, America's Historical Newspapers.

87. "Literary Intelligence," *Christian Register* (Boston, MA), December 15, 1855, America's Historical Newspapers.

88. The review castigated Child for "putting out the flame of hope of immortality that now burns brightly on the altar of many a sorrowing heart, among her own sex. "Skepticism of Mrs. L. M. Child," *Star in the West* (Cincinnati, OH), December 29, 1855), America's Historical Newspapers.

89. This review reproduced in "New Books: Woman's Record," *Littell's Living Age* 36, no. 453 (January 21, 1853): 190.

90. "Woman's Record, or Sketches of All Distinguished Women," *North American Review* 76, no. 158 (January 1853): 260.

91. "Critical Notices," *Southern Quarterly Review* 7, no. 13 (January 1853): 233.

92. This historiography further complicates the private and public spheres dichotomy. Nina Baym has argued that women's history-writing filled "the private sphere with newly recognized public significance" while also "moving women out into the sphere already agreed on as public." Baym, *American Women Writers*, 5.

Chapter 6

1. James W. C. Pennington, *A Text Book of the Origin and History, of the Colored People* (Hartford, CT: L. Skinner, 1841), 6, 39.

2. For Pennington's work, see Stephen G. Hall, *A Faithful Account of the Race: African American Historical Writing in Nineteenth-Century America* (Chapel Hill: University

of North Carolina Press, 2009); John Ernest, *Liberation Historiography: African American Writers and the Challenge of History, 1794–1861* (Chapel Hill: University of North Carolina Press, 2004), 309ff.; Joel R. Iliff, "'Sustaining the Truth of the Bible': Black Evangelical Abolitionism and the Transatlantic Politics of Orthodoxy," *Journal of the Civil War Era* 11, no. 2 (2021): 164–93. For his life, see C. Johnson, "Pennington, James William Charles (1807–1870), Clergyman and Abolitionist," *American National Biography*, February 2000, https://doi.org/10.1093/anb/978019 8606697.article.0801167.

3. Pennington, *Text Book*, 7.

4. Ibid., 41.

5. Ibid., 43–44.

6. Several scholars have explored the southern use of history to defend slaveholding—particularly Eugene Genovese and Elizabeth Fox-Genovese, who show that some slaveholders argued that Christian acceptance of slavery continued in varying forms from the patristic period throughout the Middle Ages: Elizabeth Fox-Genovese and Eugene D. Genovese, *The Mind of the Master Class: History and Faith in the Southern Slaveholder's Worldview* (New York: Cambridge University Press, 2005), 306–7, 324. For the importance of history for southern thinkers, see Michael O'Brien, *Conjectures of Order: Intellectual Life and the American South, 1810–1860* (Chapel Hill: University of North Carolina Press, 2004). Larry Tise notes that some proslavery authors appealed to traditional Christian arguments regarding slavery but does not analyze this use of religious tradition: Larry E. Tise, *Proslavery: A History of the Defense of Slavery in America, 1701–1840* (Athens: University of Georgia Press, 1987), 118. Conversely, William Jason Wallace highlights the use of church history by northern evangelicals to portray both slaveholders and Catholics as un-American: William Jason Wallace, *Catholics, Slaveholders, and the Dilemma of American Evangelicalism, 1835–1860* (South Bend, IN: University of Notre Dame Press, 2010), chap. 2. Adam Tate examines the use of church tradition by Bishop England to defend slavery in principle, while also using the Catholic past to critique southern practices. See Adam Tate, *Catholics' Lost Cause: South Carolina Catholics and the American South, 1820–1861* (South Bend, IN: University of Notre Dame Press, 2018). However, none of these studies thoroughly explore pro- and antislavery uses of Christian tradition.

7. See Mark A. Noll, *America's God: From Jonathan Edwards to Abraham Lincoln* (New York: Oxford University Press, 2002); and Mark A. Noll, *The Civil War as a Theological Crisis* (Chapel Hill: University of North Carolina Press, 2006), chap. 3. Contra Noll, Fox-Genovese and Genovese argue that an antislavery argument from the Bible required departing from Protestant orthodoxy, not just the common-sense literal hermeneutic: Fox-Genovese and Genovese, *Mind of the Master Class*, 527.

8. E. Brooks Holifield, *Theology in America: Christian Thought from the Age of the Puritans to the Civil War* (New Haven, CT: Yale University Press, 2005), 496: Holifield concludes that the proslavery argument was defined by "biblical literalism and the Baconian habit of assembling proof-texts." George Rable follows Noll and Holifield, concluding that the debate remained dictated by biblical literalism: George C. Rable, *God's Almost Chosen Peoples: A Religious History of the American Civil War* (Chapel

Hill: University of North Carolina Press, 2010), 14. Molly Oshatz argues that Noll misses how a biblical argument against slavery "required an enormous departure not just from antebellum literal hermeneutics, but from the entire Protestant understanding of revelation": Molly Oshatz, *Slavery and Sin: The Fight against Slavery and the Rise of Liberal Protestantism* (New York: Oxford University Press, 2012), 10, 58. John Patrick Daly argues that straightforward biblical interpretation guided both southern and northern evangelical arguments: John Patrick Daly, *When Slavery Was Called Freedom: Evangelicalism, Proslavery, and the Causes of the Civil War* (Lexington: University Press of Kentucky, 2015), 31–56. Jordan T. Watkins shows how the growing sense of historical distance between the Bible and the nineteenth century contributed to an antislavery reading of the Christian scriptures. See Jordan T. Watkins, *Slavery and Sacred Texts: The Bible, the Constitution, and Historical Consciousness in Antebellum America* (Cambridge: Cambridge University Press, 2021).

9. Mosheim did not deal with the question of slavery at all, while Milner simply noted that by the fifth century Christian principles led to an improvement in the conditions of slavery: Joseph Milner, *The History of the Church of Christ* (Cambridge: J. Burges, 1795), II:560.

10. Edward Gibbon, *The History of the Decline and Fall of the Roman Empire* (London: Cowie, 1825), IV:478, note d; William Robertson, *History of the Reign of the Emperor Charles V* (London: Cadell and Davies, 1812), I:322.

11. For a survey of the historiography of the day on this question, see the prize-winning Cambridge thesis Churchill Babington, *The Influence of Christianity in Promoting the Abolition of Slavery in Europe* (Cambridge: Deighton, 1846), 40–41n. 1. Elizabeth Clark points out that prominent professors of church history opposed slavery but were not active in the abolition movement: Elizabeth A. Clark, *Founding the Fathers: Early Church History and Protestant Professors in Nineteenth-Century America* (Philadelphia: University of Pennsylvania Press, 2011), 292, 430 n. 55.

12. This underscores Manisha Sinha's argument that African Americans, both in their resistance and in their sophisticated arguments, represented the cutting edge of American abolitionism: Manisha Sinha, *The Slave's Cause: A History of Abolition* (New Haven, CT: Yale University Press, 2016), 2. For eighteenth-century Black Christianity, see Jon F. Sensbach, *Rebecca's Revival: Creating Black Christianity in the Atlantic World* (Cambridge, MA: Harvard University Press, 2005).

13. See John Saillant, *Black Puritan, Black Republican: The Life and Thought of Lemuel Haynes, 1753–1833* (New York: Oxford University Press, 2003), 18–19; Ernest, *Liberation Historiography*, 255. For the sources of Haynes's historical mindset, see Stephen G. Hall, *A Faithful Account of the Race: African American Historical Writing in Nineteenth-Century America* (Chapel Hill: University of North Carolina Press, 2009), 21–22.

14. See Thomas Clarkson, *The History of the Rise, Progress, and Accomplishment of the Abolition of the African Slave-Trade by the British Parliament* (London: Longman, Hurst, Rees, and Orme, 1808), I:88.

15. For this, see Richard S. Newman, *The Transformation of American Abolitionism: Fighting Slavery in the Early Republic* (Chapel Hill: University of North Carolina Press, 2002).

16. David Lee Child, *The Despotism of Freedom; or the Tyranny and Cruelty of American Republican Slave-Masters, Shown to be the Worst in the World . . .* (Boston: Boston Young Men's Anti-Slavery Association, 1833), 17.

17. Lydia Maria Child, *An Appeal in Favor of that Class of Americans Called Africans* (Boston: Allen and Ticknor, 1833), 56–57.

18. See Catherine Teets-Parzynski, "Child, Lydia Maria Francis," in *American National Biography,* https://doi.org/10.1093/anb/9780198606697.article.1500127. For Child's sources, see Carolyn L. Karcher, *The First Woman in the Republic: A Cultural Biography of Lydia Maria Child* (Durham, NC: Duke University Press, 1994), 221.

19. Douglas A. Sweeney, "Edwards, Bela Bates," in *American National Biography,* https://doi.org/10.1093/anb/9780198606697.article.0800426.

20. B. B. Edwards, "Roman Slavery in the Early Centuries of the Christian Era," *Biblical Repository and Quarterly Observer* 6, no. 20 (October 1835): 436; and B. B. Edwards, "Slavery in the Middle Ages," *Biblical Repository* 7, no. 21 (January 1836): 39.

21. Edwards, "Roman Slavery," 432–33, 434–35.

22. Edwards, "Slavery in the Middle Ages," 39, 44.

23. "Slavery in the Middle Ages," *Boston Recorder*, January 8, 1836; and "Slavery in the Middle Ages," *Connecticut Observer*, January 16, 1836.

24. Edwards was quoted in Albert Barnes, *An Inquiry into the Scriptural Views of Slavery* (Philadelphia: Perkins and Purves, 1846), 368, 371–72. For other uses of Edwards, see John G. Fee, *An Anti-Slavery Manual; Being an Examination, in Light of the Bible, and of Facts, into the Moral and Social Wrongs of American Slavery, with a Remedy for the Evil* (Maysville, KY: Herald, 1848), 124–25; Richard Fuller and Francis Wayland, *Domestic Slavery Considered as a Scriptural Institution . . .* (New York: L. Colby, 1845), 102; J. Blanchard and N. L. Rice, *A Debate on Slavery . . .* (Cincinnati: Wm. H. Moore, 1846), 22; and Charles Elliott, *The Bible and Slavery: In Which the Abrahamic and Mosaic Discipline is Considered in connection with the Most Ancient Forms of Slavery; And the Pauline Code on Slavery as Related to Roman Slavery and the Discipline of the Apostolic Churches* (Cincinnati: Poe and Hitchcock, 1863), 281; Alexander Campbell, "Weekly Herald and Philanthropist," *Millennial Harbinger*, 3rd ser., 2, no. 6 (June 1845): 269.

25. Robert Benjamin Lewis, *Light and Truth: From Ancient and Sacred History* (Portland, ME: D.C. Colesworthy, 1836), 5.

26. For details on Lewis's life and writing, see Marnie Hughes-Warrington, "Coloring Universal History: Robert Benjamin Lewis's 'Light and Truth' (1843) and William Wells Brown's 'The Black Man' (1863)," *Journal of World History* 20, no. 1 (2009): 107ff. Ernest argues that Lewis rewrote "the history of the community defined by white oppression without the defining terms of the white oppressors." Ernest, *Liberation Historiography*, 425–26.

27. Lewis, *Light and Truth*, 97–101. Hickman argues Cyprian was "something like a racial saint" who surfaced at important moments in the development of Black

intellectual life. See Jared Hickman, "The Recanonization of Saint Cyprian," in *Sainthood and Race: Marked Flesh, Holy Flesh*, ed. Molly H. Bassett and Vincent W. Lloyd (New York: Routledge, 2014), 75ff.

28. Lewis, *Light and Truth*, 107.

29. Ibid., 132.

30. Robert Benjamin Lewis, *Light and Truth; Collected from the Bible and Ancient and Modern History*, 2nd ed. (Boston: B. F. Roberts, 1844), 315–25.

31. For the varying kinds of proslavery arguments in the South, see Lacy K. Ford, *Deliver Us from Evil: The Slavery Question in the Old South* (New York: Oxford University Press, 2009).

32. The encyclical is given in John Forsyth, *Address to the People of Georgia* (n.p., 1840), 6–7.

33. Ibid.

34. Ibid.

35. *United States Catholic Miscellany*, March 14, 1840; *Pennsylvania Freeman*, March 5, 1840; and *Massachusetts Abolitionist*, March 19, 1840, p. 20. The encyclical was reproduced by the Quaker Benjamin Lunday in his *The Legion of Liberty! and Force of Truth, Containing the Thoughts, Words, and Deeds of Some Prominent Apostles, Champions and Martyrs* (New York: American Anti-Slavery Society, 1842), 5, 196–98. An 1858 Quaker publication also quoted Pope Gregory XVI: Anthony Benezet and John Wesley, *Views of American Slavery: Taken a Century Ago* (Philadelphia: Association of Friends for the Diffusion of Religious and Useful Knowledge, 1858), 125–26.

36. "Bull of Pope Gregory XVI., for the Abolition of the Negro Slave," *Liberator*, March 13, 1840, p. 42; and William Lloyd Garrison, *No Compromise with Slavery* (New York: American Anti-Slavery Society, 1854), 13.

37. *Speech of Mr. Slade, of Vermont, on the Right of Petition; The Power of Congress to Abolish Slavery and the Slave Trade in the District of Columbia; The Implied Faith of the North and the South to each other in Forming the Constitution; and the Principles, Purposes, and Prospects of Abolition* (Washington, DC: Gales and Seaton, 1840), 37.

38. By the late 1830s, the domestic slave trade was increasingly under attack from northern abolitionists. See Edward E. Baptist, *The Half Has Never Been Told: Slavery and the Making of American Capitalism* (New York: Basic Books, 2014).

39. Forsyth, *Address*, 3, 4.

40. For example, see "Pope Gregory's Bull," *Philanthropist* (Ohio), March 24, 1840.

41. Patrick W. Carey, "England, John," *American National Biography*, https://doi.org/10.1093/anb/9780198606697.article.0800441; R. Frank Saunders and George A. Rogers, "Bishop John England of Charleston: Catholic Spokesman and Southern Intellectual, 1820–1842," *Journal of the Early Republic* 13, no. 3 (1993): 301–22 . For England's republicanism, see Patrick W. Carey, *An Immigrant Bishop: John England's Adaptation of Irish Catholicism to American Republicanism* (Yonkers, NY: U.S. Catholic Historical Society, 1979). See also Jay P. Dolan, *In Search of an American Catholicism: A History of Religion and Culture in Tension* (New York: Oxford University Press, 2002), 22, 35–47. For the struggle Catholics faced to disarm

Protestant suspicions, see Jon Gjerde, *Catholicism and the Shaping of Nineteenth-Century America* (New York: Cambridge University Press, 2012). For southern Catholics and slavery, see Andrew H. M. Stern, *Southern Crucifix, Southern Cross: Catholic-Protestant Relations in the Old South* (Tuscaloosa: University of Alabama Press, 2012); Gracjan Kraszewski, *Catholic Confederates: Faith and Duty in the Civil War South* (Kent, OH: Kent State University Press, 2020); Leslie Woodcock Tentler, *American Catholics: A History* (New Haven, CT: Yale University Press, 2020).

42. For the ambiguity of the pope's letter, see John F. Quinn, "'Three Cheers for the Abolitionist Pope!': American Reaction to Gregory XVI's Condemnation of the Slave Trade, 1840–1860," *Catholic Historical Review* 90, no. 1 (2004): 67–93. See especially 71 n. 19.

43. Ibid., 74–75, 77.

44. For Bishop England's views on slavery, see Carey, "England, John."

45. For these numbers, see Walter Johnson, *Soul by Soul: Life inside the Antebellum Slave Market* (Cambridge, MA: Harvard University Press, 1999), 5, 17. Forsyth, *Address*, 7.

46. John England, *Letters of the Late Bishop England to the Hon. John Forsyth on the Subject of Domestic Slavery . . .* (Baltimore: John Murphy, 1844), 21.

47. Ibid., 23–24.

48. Ibid., 40, 44.

49. Ibid., 45, 47–49.

50. Ibid., 134–135.

51. Ibid., 136.

52. *Liberator*, November 17, 1843. See Quinn, "Three Cheers," 84–86.

53. England, *Letters*, v–vi.

54. Ibid., iv.

55. Quinn, "Three Cheers," 88.

56. "Review: Letters of the Late Bishop England," *National Anti-Slavery Standard*, March 28, 1844.

57. These reviews are quoted in Tate, *Catholics' Lost Cause*, 47.

58. Thus, in 1856 the Republican Party reprinted the papal letter in an effort to woo Catholic voters, while southern lawyers and politicians cited England's arguments about the early and medieval church. John Fletcher, whose *Studies on Slavery* opened this chapter, closely followed Bishop England's reasoning on spiritual freedom, and copied his patristic quotations. See Fletcher, *Studies on Slavery*, 266–67. John C. Hurd's legal treatise, *The Law of Freedom and Bondage in the United States*, vol. I (Boston: Little, Brown, and Co., 1858), also relied on Bishop England. Thomas Cobb cited Bishop England's study throughout his treatise: Thomas R. R. Cobb, *An Inquiry into the Law of Negro Slavery in the United States of America: To Which Is Prefixed, an Historical Sketch of Slavery* (Philadelphia: T. and J. W. Johnson, 1858), c, cix, 16, 115, 230. See also George S. Sawyer, *Southern Institutes; or, An Inquiry into the Origin and Early Prevalence of Slavery and the Slave-Trade . . .* (Philadelphia: J. B. Lippincott, 1858), 124.

59. As Sean Wilentz argues, slavery was the driving force behind the political fracturing of the two-party system by the mid-1850s: Sean Wilentz, *The Rise of American*

Democracy: Jefferson to Lincoln (New York: Norton, 2005). See also Elizabeth R. Varon, *Disunion! The Coming of the American Civil War, 1789-1859* (Chapel Hill: University of North Carolina Press, 2008).

60. The standard account is C. C. Goen, *Broken Churches, Broken Nation: Denominational Schisms and the Coming of the Civil War* (Macon, GA: Mercer University Press, 1985). See also Lucas Volkman, *Houses Divided: Evangelical Schisms and the Crisis of the Union in Missouri* (Oxford: Oxford University Press, 2018).

61. Robert D. Cross, "Wayland, Francis," *American National Biography*, https://doi.org/10.1093/anb/9780198606697.article.0801625.

62. Noll argues that "this exchange was one of the United States' last serious one-on-one debates" over slavery: Noll, *Civil War*, 36-37.

63. Fuller and Wayland, *Domestic Slavery*, 98-100, 101-2.

64. *The Homilies of S. John Chrysostom, Archbishop of Constantinople, on the First Epistle of St. Paul the Apostle to the Corinthians* (Oxford: John Henry Parker, 1839), 19.

65. Philip Schaff and Charles Hodge sided with Reformed exegesis over Chrysostom's interpretation. See Philip Schaff, *Slavery and the Bible: A Tract for the Times* (Chambersburg, PA: M. Kieffer, 1861), 25-26; and Charles Hodge, *An Exposition of the First Epistle to the Corinthians* (New York: Robert Carter and Brothers, 1860), 123-24.

66. See Chris L. de Wet, *Preaching Bondage: John Chrysostom and the Discourse of Slavery in Early Christianity* (Berkeley: University of California Press, 2015), 109.

67. See Babington, *Influence of Christianity*, 26-28.

68. Fuller and Wayland, *Domestic Slavery*, 140, 190-91. Rev. Ebenezer W. Warren (b. 1820), pastor of First Baptist of Macon, Georgia, quoted Chrysostom's commentary in a 1864 narrative. E. W. Warren, *Nellie Norton: or, Southern Slavery and the Bible* . . . (Macon, GA: Burke, Boykin, 1864), 169: "The early Fathers . . . believed this passage favored slavery."

69. Fuller and Wayland, *Domestic Slavery*, 219-20.

70. By the 1920s, Barnes's commentaries had sold over one million copies: T. H. Olbricht, "Barnes, Albert (1798-1870)," in *Dictionary of Major Biblical Interpreters*, ed. Donald K. McKim (Westmont, IL: InterVarsity Press, 2007).

71. Barnes, *Inquiry*, 367-72.

72. Frederick Douglass, "What to the Slave Is the Fourth of July?," in *Lift Every Voice: African American Oratory, 1787-1900*, ed. Philip S. Foner and Robert James Branham (Tuscaloosa: University of Alabama Press, 1998), 263.

73. Fee, *Anti-Slavery Manual*, 124-25.

74. William Graham, *The Contrast; or The Bible and Abolitionism: An Exegetical Argument* (Cincinnati: Daily Cincinnati Atlas Office, 1844), 33-35.

75. See Larry G. Willey, "John Rankin, Antislavery Prophet, and the Free Presbyterian Church," *American Presbyterians* 72, no. 3 (Fall 1994): 165-66.

76. Henry Bidleman Bascom, *Methodism and Slavery: With Other Matters in Controversy between the North and the South* . . . (Frankfort, KY: Hodges, Todd, and Pruett, 1845), 62, 65.

77. Charles Elliott, *Sinfulness of American Slavery* (Cincinnati: Swormstedt and Power, 1851), I:23, 306.

78. Charles Elliott, *History of the Great Secession from the Methodist Episcopal Church in the Year 1845* (Cincinnati: Swormstedt and Power, 1855), iv.

79. Elliott, *The Bible and Slavery*.

80. Campbell, "Weekly Herald and Philanthropist," 269.

81. Henry Martyn Baird, *The Life of the Rev. Robert Baird* (New York: A.D.F. Randolph, 1866), 32. As chapter 5 shows, in Miller's history courses Baird read a variety of church histories, particularly Mosheim's *Institutes*. Samuel Miller's papers show his reliance on and critical engagement with Mosheim's history. See Miller's notes on Mosheim's Ecclesiastical History, Box 5, Folders 1–8, The Samuel Miller Manuscript Collection, Princeton Theological Seminary Libraries, Special Collections.

82. "Members of the one invisible Church had, for so many ages showed much more zeal in maintaining and magnifying their divergence from one another, than eagerness in demonstrating their essential unity." This is his son's description of his views in Baird, *Life*, 228.

83. Robert Baird, *Religion in America: A Critical Abridgment with Introduction*, ed. Henry Warner Bowden (New York: Harper & Row, 1970), xi–xii.

84. Baird, *Life*, 203–4. Baird's work was widely acclaimed by early reviewers and continued to profoundly influence religious historiography through the twentieth century. See Baird, *Religion in America*, xiii. Brekus summarizes the tradition that built on Baird: "For more than one hundred years following the publication of Baird's book, historians of early American religion circled around the same themes: the formative influence of the Puritans, the close relationship between religion and nationalism, the advantages of the 'voluntary system,' and the dominance of the Protestant mainstream." Catherine A. Brekus, "Contested Words: History, America, Religion," *William and Mary Quarterly* 75, no. 1 (February 6, 2018): 4.

85. Baird, *Religion in America*, 299–303. As Henry Warner Bowden explains, Baird's belief in the superiority of Anglo-Saxon culture explains his dismissal of Native American rights and his views on slavery. See Bowden's preface in ibid., xxxvi–vii.

86. Ibid., 265, 269–70.

87. Baird believed missions undid the corruption of the past. He wrote of French missionaries that "the plain evangelist, and the colporteur with his tracts and religious books, were powerful engines to batter down the structure of superstition which ages of credulity and ignorance had erected." Ibid., 133.

Chapter 7

1. Robert L. Dabney, *A Defence of Virginia, And Through Her, of the South, in Recent and Pending Contests Against the Sectional Party* (New York: E. J. Hale and Son, 1867), 5–8.

2. For Dabney's life and thought, see Charles Reagan Wilson, "Robert Lewis Dabney: Religion and the Southern Holocaust," *Virginia Magazine of History and Biography* 89, no. 1 (January 1981): 79–89; Sean Michael Lucas, *Robert Lewis Dabney: A Southern Presbyterian Life* (Phillipsburg, NJ: P and R, 2005); John B. Boles, "Robert Lewis Dabney (1820–1898)," *Encyclopedia Virginia*, July 2020, https://www.encyclopediavirginia.org/Dabney_Robert_Lewis_1820-1898.

3. Dabney, *A Defence of Virginia*, 13.

4. Ibid., 186–87.

5. Ibid., 204.

6. So writes Paul Gutjahr, although he also points out that the antebellum years saw the Bible lose its place of "absolute dominance" in print culture. See Paul C. Gutjahr, *An American Bible: A History of the Good Book in the United States, 1777–1880* (Stanford, CA: Stanford University Press, 1999), 2–3.

7. For the place of the Bible during the Civil War, James P. Byrd, *A Holy Baptism of Fire and Blood: The Bible and the American Civil War* (Oxford: Oxford University Press, 2021).

8. The conventional scholarly account portrays the theological debate over slavery as biblicist. See Mark A. Noll, *America's God: From Jonathan Edwards to Abraham Lincoln* (New York: Oxford University Press, 2002); Mark A. Noll, *The Civil War as a Theological Crisis* (Chapel Hill: University of North Carolina Press, 2006), chap. 3; E. Brooks Holifield, *Theology in America: Christian Thought from the Age of the Puritans to the Civil War* (New Haven, CT: Yale University Press, 2005); George C. Rable, *God's Almost Chosen Peoples: A Religious History of the American Civil War* (Chapel Hill: University of North Carolina Press, 2010); Molly Oshatz, *Slavery and Sin: The Fight against Slavery and the Rise of Liberal Protestantism* (New York: Oxford University Press, 2012); John Patrick Daly, *When Slavery Was Called Freedom: Evangelicalism, Proslavery, and the Causes of the Civil War* (Lexington: University Press of Kentucky, 2015), 31–56.

9. Even as scholars modify or nuance Mark Noll's thesis about the theological controversy, they continue to overlook the role of Christian history in the debate. Arguments over Christian tradition do not appear in most works on religion and slavery, including Donald G. Mathews, *Slavery and Methodism: A Chapter in American Morality, 1780–1845* (Princeton, NJ: Princeton University Press, 1965); Richard J. Carwardine, *Evangelicals and Politics in Antebellum America* (Knoxville: University of Tennessee Press, 1993); John R. McKivigan and Mitchell Snay, eds., *Religion and the Antebellum Debate over Slavery* (Athens: University of Georgia Press, 1998); John R. McKivigan, ed., *Abolitionism and American Religion* (New York: Garland, 1999); David Brion Davis, *The Problem of Slavery in the Age of Revolution: 1770–1823* (New York: Oxford University Press, 1999); Beth Barton Schweiger and Donald G. Mathews, eds., *Religion in the American South: Protestants and Others in History and Culture* (Chapel Hill: University of North Carolina Press, 2005); Charles F. Irons, *The Origins of Proslavery Christianity: White and Black Evangelicals in Colonial and Antebellum Virginia* (Chapel Hill: University of North Carolina Press, 2009); Christopher Leslie Brown, *Moral Capital: Foundations of British Abolitionism* (Chapel Hill: University of

North Carolina Press, 2012); and Luke E. Harlow, *Religion, Race, and the Making of Confederate Kentucky, 1830–1880* (New York: Cambridge University Press, 2014).

10. Margaret Abruzzo notes that antislavery Quakers employed historical narratives about persecution, worldly power, and martyrdom: Margaret Abruzzo, *Polemical Pain: Slavery, Cruelty, and the Rise of Humanitarianism* (Baltimore: Johns Hopkins University Press, 2011), 37–38. Katherine Gerbner's excellent work traces the long history of Christianity and slaveholding, but does not address how nineteenth-century Protestants interacted with this tradition: Katharine Gerbner, *Christian Slavery: Conversion and Race in the Protestant Atlantic World* (Philadelphia: University of Pennsylvania Press, 2018), 14–30. One other exception is a study of antislavery uses of martyrology: Heike Jablonski, *John Foxe in America: Discourses of Martyrdom in the Eighteenth- and Nineteenth-Century United States* (Paderborn: Ferdinand Schöningh, 2017).

11. See Bruce Dain, *A Hideous Monster of the Mind: American Race Theory in the Early Republic* (Cambridge, MA: Harvard University Press, 2002); and Eugene D. Genovese and Elizabeth Fox-Genovese, *Fatal Self-Deception: Slaveholding Paternalism in the Old South* (New York: Cambridge University Press, 2011).

12. John Fletcher, *Studies on Slavery* (Natchez, MS: Jackson Warner, 1852), iv.

13. Ibid., 256, 259.

14. Ibid., 276–77, 422.

15. See Davis, *Problem of Slavery*, 123.

16. Henry Highland Garnet, *The Past and the Present Condition, and the Destiny, of the Colored Race* (Troy, NY: Kneeland, 1848), 11–13, 28.

17. Samuel Ringgold Ward, *Autobiography of a Fugitive Negro* (London: John Snow, 1855), 87–88.

18. For example, in his defense of enacting church discipline on slaveholders, the Presbyterian John Fee argued that the history of Christianity proved that Africans were not inferior to Europeans: John G. Fee, *An Anti-Slavery Manual; Being an Examination, in Light of the Bible, and of Facts, into the Moral and Social Wrongs of American Slavery, with a Remedy for the Evil* (Maysville, KY: The Herald Office, 1848), 211–12.

19. John H. Giltner, "Moses Stuart: 1780–1852," *Church History* 25, no. 3 (September 1956): 265.

20. M. Stuart, *Conscience and the Constitution* . . . (Boston: Crocker and Brewster, 1850), 54, 103, 112–13. Stuart's moderation was unpopular in some circles. Rufus Wheelwright Clark, a Congregationalist minister in Portsmouth, New Hampshire, wrote a review of Stuart's work castigating it and calling for immediate abolition. Clark cited B. B. Edwards, Clement, Cyprian, Paulinus, Ambrose, and more to show "the practical effects of the principles of the Gospel upon slavery, among the early Christians." An antislavery patron then offered to pay for three thousand copies of Clark's review to be published and circulated for free. Rufus Wheelwright Clark, *A Review of the Rev. Moses Stuart's Pamphlet on Slavery* (Boston: C.C.P. Moody, 1850), 2, 64–65.

21. John Codman Hurd, *The Law of Freedom and Bondage in the United States* (Boston: Little, Brown, 1858), I:156–57, 159–60, 164.

22. Edward Coit Rogers [O. S. Freeman, pseud.], *Letters on Slavery, Addressed to the Pro-Slavery Men of America* . . . (Boston: Bela Marsh, 1855), 28–33; cf. Fletcher, *Studies on Slavery*, 277.

23. Rogers, *Letters on Slavery*, 42–46.

24. Historians of the Civil War generally concur that the question of slavery's expansion into the West was what precipitated the secession crisis. See, for example, James M. McPherson, *Battle Cry of Freedom: The Civil War Era* (New York: Oxford University Press, 1988); Michael A. Morrison, *Slavery and the American West: The Eclipse of Manifest Destiny and the Coming of the Civil War* (Chapel Hill: University of North Carolina Press, 1997); and Orville Vernon Burton, *The Age of Lincoln* (New York: Hill and Wang, 2007).

25. Philip Schaff, *History of the Apostolic Church; With a General Introduction to Church History*, trans. Edward D. Yeomans (New York: C. Scribner, 1854), 460.

26. [Philip Schaff], "The Influence of the Early Church on the Institution of Slavery," *Mercersburg Review* 10 (October 1858): 616; and Philip Schaff, *Slavery and the Bible: A Tract for the Times* (Chambersburg, PA: M. Kieffer, 1861), 30–31.

27. L. Maria Child, *The Progress of Religious Ideas, Through Successive Ages* (New York: C. S. Francis, 1855), III:183–89, 280–84. For her antislavery activism, see Carolyn L. Karcher, *The First Woman in the Republic: A Cultural Biography of Lydia Maria Child* (Durham, NC: Duke University Press, 1994).

28. Nathan Lord, *A Letter of Inquiry to Ministers of the Gospel of All Denominations, on Slavery* (Boston: Fetridge, 1854), 3.

29. For Lord's transformation, see "A History of Opposition," *Dartmouth Review*, October 2016, http://dartreview.com/a-history-of-opposition/.

30. Lord, *A Letter of Inquiry*, 13–14.

31. See Robert Tracy McKenzie, *Lincolnites and Rebels: A Divided Town in the American Civil War* (New York: Oxford University Press, 2006), 38–39. Interestingly, during the Civil War, Brownlow changed sides again and called for emancipation.

32. See William Gannaway Brownlow, *A Sermon on Slavery: A Vindication of the Methodist Church, South: Her Position Stated* (Knoxville, TN: Kinsloe and Rice, 1857), 21. See also [William Gannaway] Brownlow and [Abram] Pryne, *Ought American Slavery to Be Perpetuated? A Debate between Rev. W. G. Brownlow and Rev. A. Pryne* (Philadelphia: J.B. Lippincott and Co., 1858), 85.

33. *Letter of an Adopted Catholic, addressed to the President of the Kentucky Democratic Association* (Washington, DC: s.n., 1856), 7. Thanks to David Roach for bringing this source to my attention.

34. The article complained that "leaders of the Roman Catholics of this country have generally adopted the policy of the late Bishop England . . . in limiting the application of [Gregory's letter] to the slavery and slave traffic of Africa . . . and have practically regarded American slavery as a thing which even the Pope must not venture to pass judgment upon." Quoted in Quinn, "Three Cheers," 89.

35. *The Pope's Bull and the words of Daniel O'Connell* (New York: Joseph H. Ladd, 1856).

36. Albert Barnes, *The Church and Slavery* (Philadelphia: Parry and McMillan, 1857), 44, 26.

37. See Fox-Genovese and Genovese, *Mind of the Master Class*, 80.

38. For Fitzhugh's thought, see Michael O'Brien, *Conjectures of Order: Intellectual Life and the American South, 1810–1860* (Chapel Hill: University of North Carolina Press, 2004), 251–52; and Thomas E. Schneider, "George Fitzhugh: The Turn to History," in *Lincoln's Defense of Politics: The Public Man and His Opponents in the Crisis over Slavery* (Columbia: University of Missouri Press, 2006), 54–72.

39. George Fitzhugh, *Cannibals All! or, Slaves Without Masters* (Richmond: A. Morris, 1857), 158.

40. For examples, see Wallace, *Catholics, Slaveholders, and the Dilemma of American Evangelicalism*, 139.

41. Fitzhugh, *Cannibals All!*, 194, 196–99.

42. In 1864, Presbyterian minister William A. Hall argued that the South was ultimately fighting against the Reformation's emphasis on personal conscience. See Wallace, *Catholics, Slaveholders*, 102.

43. One discussion of slavery in the South Carolina assembly cited Bishop England's interpretation of Catholic tradition: *Report of the Minority of the Special Committee of Seven, to whom was Referred so much of Gov. Adams' Message, No. 1, as Relates to Slavery and the Slave Trade* (Columbia, SC: Steam Power Press Carolina Times, 1857), 8.

44. So argues Alfred L. Brophy, *University, Court, and Slave: Pro-slavery Thought in Southern Colleges and Courts and the Coming of Civil War* (New York: Oxford University Press, 2016), 227.

45. Thomas R. R. Cobb, *An Inquiry into the Law of Negro Slavery in the United States of America. To Which Is Prefixed, an Historical Sketch of Slavery* (Philadelphia: T. & J.W. Johnson, 1858), cvi–cix.

46. See Brophy, *University, Court, and Slave*, 251–53.

47. George S. Sawyer, *Southern Institutes; or, An Inquiry into the Origin and Early Prevalence of Slavery and the Slave-Trade* (Philadelphia: J.B. Lippincott, 1858), 122–24, 147.

48. See John Ernest, *Liberation Historiography: African American Writers and the Challenge of History, 1794–1861* (Chapel Hill: University of North Carolina Press, 2004), 309; and J. W. C. Pennington, "A Review of Slavery and the Slave-Trade," *Anglo-African Magazine* 1, no. 5 (May 1859): 156.

49. For example, see Adam Gurowski, *Slavery in History* (New York: A. B. Burdick, 1860), 165–66.

50. Ebenezer Boyden, *The Epidemic of the Nineteenth Century* (Richmond: Chas. H. Wynne, 1860), 14, 16–18.

51. See Leonard Marsh [A Vermonter, pseud.], preface to *Review of a Letter from the Right Rev. John H. Hopkins, D.D. LL.D., Bishop of Vermont, on the Bible View of Slavery* (Burlington, VT: Free Press Print, 1861).

52. For Hopkins's developing views on Christianity and slavery, see Ronald Levy, "Bishop Hopkins and the Dilemma of Slavery," *Pennsylvania Magazine of History and Biography* 91, no. 1 (January 1967): 56–71.

53. Marsh, *Review of a Letter*, 4–5.

54. See Thomas Atkins, *American Slavery: Reply to the Letter of Bishop Hopkins of Vermont* (New York: W. G. Green et al., 1861).

55. T. W. MacMahon, *Cause and Contrast: An Essay on the American Crisis* (Richmond: West and Johnston, 1862), ix–x, 4, 21, 25.

56. David T. Gleeson, *The Green and the Gray: The Irish in the Confederate States of America* (Chapel Hill: University of North Carolina Press, 2013), 115–117.

57. Joseph P. Thompson, *Christianity and Emancipation; or, The Teachings and the Influence of the Bible Against Slavery* (New York: Anson D. F. Randolph, 1863), 14, 41, 51–52. Thompson traced antislavery sentiments throughout the Middle Ages and quoted from a number of fathers, councils, and popes: Ibid., 53–56, 58–59.

58. See Wallace, *Catholics, Slaveholders*, 2.

59. Daniel R. Goodwin, *Southern Slavery in Its Present Aspects: Containing a Reply to a Late Work of the Bishop of Vermont on Slavery* (Philadelphia: J. B. Lippincott, 1864), 7.

60. One article noted that Henry VIII was more enlightened than Bishop Hopkins: "Slavery in England," *National Anti-Slavery Standard*, August 27, 1864. For the polygamy satire, see "A Bishop Basted," *Harper's Weekly*, December 5, 1863, 770; and "A Bishop Basted," *National Anti-Slavery Standard*, June 11, 1864. For a list of other responses, see Levy, "Bishop Hopkins," 56–57.

61. George Stroud, *The Views of Judge Woodward and Bishop Hopkins on Negro Slavery at the South, Illustrated from the Journal of a Residence on a Georgian Plantation* (Philadelphia: s.n., 1863).

62. Goodwin, *Southern Slavery*, 16–17. For Northern support of slavery, see Jennifer L. Weber, *Copperheads: The Rise and Fall of Lincoln's Opponents in the North* (New York: Oxford University Press, 2008).

63. See the title page of *Bible View of Slavery* (London: Saunders, Otley, & Co., 1863).

64. John Henry Hopkins, *A Scriptural, Ecclesiastical, and Historical View of Slavery, from the Days of the Patriarch Abraham, to the Nineteenth Century* . . . (New York: W. I. Pooley, 1864), 211, 100–102, 115–16.

65. See "*A Scriptural, Ecclesiastical, and Historical View of Slavery, from the Days of the Patriarch Abraham, to the Nineteenth Century* . . . by John Henry Hopkins," *North American Review* 99, no. 205 (October 1864): 619–20.

66. M. A. de Wolfe Howe, *A Reply to the Letter of Bishop Hopkins* (Philadelphia: King and Baird, 1864), 18.

67. Goodwin, *Southern Slavery*, 70–73, 123–29, 142, 144–46, 149–51.

68. In this sense, uses of tradition and history mirror what Molly Oshatz argues about biblical exegesis—namely, that antislavery activists focused on the "spirit" of the text, while proslavery authors insisted on the "letter": Oshatz, *Slavery and Sin*, 59–60.

69. John Henry Hopkins III, "John Henry Hopkins, First Bishop of Vermont," *Historical Magazine of the Protestant Episcopal Church* 6, no. 2 (June 1937): 201.

70. For the role of religion in this eliding of slavery for the sake of national unity, see Edward J. Blum, *Reforging the White Republic: Race, Religion, and American Nationalism, 1865–1898* (Baton Rouge: Louisiana State University Press, 2007).

71. Scholarship by David Blight and Leslie Schwalm has shown how quickly during Reconstruction slavery was lost in white American memory. In the crucial years of postbellum reunification, the importance of slavery for bringing about the Civil War was immediately downplayed. David W. Blight, *Race and Reunion: The Civil War in American Memory* (Cambridge, MA: The Belknap Press of Harvard University Press, 2001); Leslie A. Schwalm, *Emancipation's Diaspora: Race and Reconstruction in the Upper Midwest* (Chapel Hill: University of North Carolina Press, 2009).

72. Robert L. Dabney, *Ecclesiastical Relation of Negroes: Speech of Robert L. Dabney, in the Synod of Virginia, Nov. 9, 1867, Against the Ecclesiastical Equality of Negro Preachers in Our Church, and Their Right to Rule Over White Christians* (Richmond, VA: Boys & Girls Monthly, 1868).

73. Dabney, *A Defence of Virginia*, 204.

74. Noll, *Civil War as a Theological Crisis*, 8.

Epilogue

1. For examples of these, see "'Biblical Womanhood': A Year of Living by the Book," *National Public Radio*, September 25, 2011, https://www.npr.org/2011/09/25/140761 994/biblical-womanhood-a-year-of-living-by-the-book; Tim Challies, "Why Social Justice Is Not Biblical Justice," *Challies.com*, October 9, 2020, https://www.chall ies.com/book-reviews/why-social-justice-is-not-biblical-justice/; Albert Mohler, "Twelve Principles for a Biblical Worldview on Economics," *Institute for Faith, Work & Economics*, May 31, 2019, https://tifwe.org/twelve-principles-for-a-biblical-worldv iew-on-economics/.

2. William Craig Brownlee, *Popery, an Enemy to Civil and Religious Liberty; and Dangerous to Our Republic* (New York: Bowne & Wisner, 1836), 106.

3. See Rodney Stark, *Bearing False Witness: Debunking Centuries of Anti-Catholic History* (Conshohocken, PA: Templeton Foundation Press, 2016), 117–18.

4. Archival records show that after the first several decades, which saw as many as eighteen hundred executions, the execution rate plummeted to less than 2 percent, or fewer than three deaths per year. Henry Kamen, *The Spanish Inquisition: A Historical Revision* (New Haven, CT: Yale University Press, 1997), 203.

5. As medievalist Kate Wiles explains, this term grew popular in the mid-nineteenth century and its imperialist "belief in the dawn of a modern age." Kate Wiles, "Back to the Dark Ages," *History Today*, May 5, 2016, https://www.historytoday.com/ back-dark-ages.

6. Against the grain of prior Protestant historiography, theologians and historians show a remarkable degree of continuity between the pre- and post-Constantinian church, and so highlight the limitations and flaws of a sharp-decline narrative. See

Peter J. Leithart, *Defending Constantine: The Twilight of an Empire and the Dawn of Christendom* (Downers Grove, IL: InterVarsity Press, 2010); Edward L. Smither, *Rethinking Constantine: History, Theology, and Legacy* (Eugene, OR: Wipf and Stock, 2014). For a recent account that stretches "early Christianity" both beyond Constantine's reign and beyond the bounds of the Roman Empire, see Robert Louis Wilken, *The First Thousand Years: A Global History of Christianity* (New Haven, CT: Yale University Press, 2013).

7. As Robert Louis Wilken argues, "Hellenization" conveys more about nineteenth-century Protestant assumptions than it does about the actual development of the Christian Platonic tradition. See Robert Louis Wilken, *The Spirit of Early Christian Thought: Seeking the Face of God* (New Haven, CT: Yale University Press, 2003), xvi.

Bibliography

Manuscript Collections

America's Historical Newspapers. Readex.com. Accessed March 25, 2019. https://info web.newsbank.com/apps/readex/?p=EANX.

"Class Lecture Notes and Account Book, 1810." AR87, Box 1, Folder 2. Luther Rice Collection, Southern Baptist Historical Library and Archives, Nashville, TN.

"Female Influence and Obligations—No. 226." American Tract Society Tracts Collection (Unprocessed Collection). 19th Century Collection, Drew University, Madison, New Jersey.

Gillett, Charles R. "Notes by Gillett, C.R." 1877, UTS1: Philip Schaff Papers, 1838–1896, Series 3, Box 1, Folder 10. The Burke Library at Union Theological Seminary, Columbia University in the City of New York.

Howell, Robert Boyte Crawford. "The true relations between religion and civil government." July 4, 1845. AR595, Box 2, Volume 3. Robert Boyte Crawford Howell Collection, Southern Baptist Historical Library and Archives, Nashville, TN.

Jefferson, Thomas. *Catalog of books for the University of Virginia Library, 1825*, Accession #38-747. Special Collections, University of Virginia Library, Charlottesville, VA.

Jefferson, Thomas. The Papers of Thomas Jefferson Digital Edition. Edited by James P. McClure and J. Jefferson Looney. Charlottesville: University of Virginia Press, 2008. https://rotunda.upress.virginia.edu/founders/default.xqy?keys=TSJN-print& mode=TOC.

Madison, James. The Papers of James Madison Digital Edition. Edited by J. C. A. Stagg. Charlottesville: University of Virginia Press, Rotunda, 2010. https://rotunda.upress. virginia.edu/founders/default.xqy?keys=JSMN-print&mode=TOC.

McFarland, Francis. Francis McFarland Papers. RG 459, Box 3, Folder 5. Presbyterian Historical Society, Philadelphia, PA.

Perrine, Matthew. "Catalogue of Books for a Young Minister on Different Subjects." The Matthew LaRue Perrine Manuscript Collection, Special Collections, Princeton Theological Seminary Library, Princeton, NJ.

The Samuel Miller Manuscript Collection, Special Collections, Princeton Theological Seminary Library, Princeton, NJ.

Primary Sources

No Author Given

"The Absent Son." *New York Evangelist* 27, no. 23 (June 5, 1856): 26.

The American Almanac and Repository of Useful Knowledge for the Year. Vol. 32. Series 4, no. 2. Boston: Gray and Bowen, 1861.

"Article V. The History of England." *American Monthly Review* 3, no. 1 (September 1795): 29–43.

"A Bishop Basted." *Harper's Weekly* 7, no. 362 (December 5, 1863): 770.

"A Bishop Basted." *National Anti-Slavery Standard* 25, no. 5 (June 11, 1864): 1.

"Blessing of Pious Parents." *Guardian and Monitor* 8, no. 1 (January 1, 1826): 31.

"Brief Survey of Ecclesiastical History, in A Series of Letters." *Massachusetts Missionary Magazine* 5, no. 2 (July 1807): 47–56.

Catalogue of Books in the Library of Yale College. New Haven, CT: S. Converse, 1823.

Catalogue of the Library Belonging to the Theological Institution in Andover. Andover, MA: Flagg and Gould, 1819.

A Catalogue of the Library of Brown University. Andover, MA: Allen, Morrill and Wardwell, 1843.

Christian Disciple and Theological Review 4, no. 22 (1822): 307–9.

"The Christian Home: VI—Its Influence." *German Reformed Messenger* 22, no. 6 (October 8, 1856): 1.

"Critical Notices." *Southern Quarterly Review* 7, no. 13 (January 1853): 233.

"Ecclesiastical History." *Christian Review* 1, no. 3 (1836): 428.

"Editors' Table." *Godey's Magazine and Lady's Book* 34 (1847).

Eggemoggin Baptist Church. "History." Accessed October 12, 2018. http://ebctest.dow neastit.com/history/.

Founders Online. "82. A Bill for Establishing Religious Freedom, 18 June 1779." *National Archives.* Version of January 18, 2019.

"The Importance of American Freedom to Christianity." *Christian Review* 1, no. 2 (June 1836): 193–214.

"The Infidel Convinced by a Child." *New York Religious Chronicle* 3, no. 16 (April 16, 1825): 61–62.

Journals of the General Conference of the Methodist Episcopal Church. New York: Carlton & Porter, 1856.

Journal of the Proceedings of the Bishops, Clergy, and Laity, of the Protestant Episcopal Church. New York: T. & J. Swords, 1804.

The Legion of Liberty! New York: American Anti-Slavery Society, 1842.

Letter of an Adopted Catholic, addressed to the President of the Kentucky Democratic Association. Washington, DC.: s.n., 1856.

The Liberator, no. 11 (March 13, 1840): 42.

The Life of Samuel Miller. Philadelphia: Claxton, Remsen and Haffelfinger, 1869.

"The Life of Samuel Miller." *Biblical Repertory and Princeton Review* 42, no. 1 (January 1870): 33–49.

"Literary Notice." *New England Galaxy and Masonic Magazine* 1, no. 49 (September 18, 1818): 2.

"Meditation on the Religious Education of Children." *Religious Monitor and Evangelical Repository* 12, no. 7 (December 1835): 199.

"Milner's Church History." *Episcopal Recorder* 13, no. 44 (1836): 175.

Minutes of the Redstone Baptist Association, Held at Washington, Washington County, PA. Accessed October 12, 2018. http://www.sidneyrigdon.com/Reds1819.htm#1822-01.

"The Mother's Cares." *German Reformed Messenger* 22, no. 28 (March 12, 1856): 4272.

"The Mother's Cares." *New York Observer and Chronicle* 34, no. 23 (June 5, 1856): 1.

"New Books: Woman's Record." *Littell's Living Age* 36, no. 453 (January 21, 1853): 190.

"On some uses of ecclesiastical history." *Evangelical and Literary Magazine* 11, no. 3 (1823): 113.

"On the Condition and Character of Women in Different Countries and Ages." *American Review of History and Politics* 4, no. 2 (October 1812): 262–84.

"Parallel between Hume, Robertson and Gibbon." *Monthly Magazine, and American Review* 1, no. 2 (May 1799): 90–95.

Phelps, Lincoln. *The Female Student: or, Lectures to Young Ladies on Female Education. For the Use of Mothers, Teachers, and Pupils.* New York: Leavitt, Lord & Company, 1836.

"Pious Mothers of the Early Church." *Zion's Herald and Wesleyan Journal* 18, no. 48 (December 1, 1847): 192.

The Pope's Bull and the Words of Daniel O'Connell. New York: Joseph H. Ladd, 1856.

A Refutation of Some of the Misrepresentations and Aspersions, of the Society of Friends, in Mosheim's Ecclesiastical History. Charleston, MA: S. Etheridge, 1812.

Report of the Minority of the Special Committee of Seven. Columbia, SC: Carolina Times, 1857.

"Review: A Scriptural, Ecclesiastical, and Historical View of Slavery." *North American Review* 99, no. 205 (1864): 619–20.

"Review: Institutes of Ecclesiastical History, Ancient and Modern." *Christian Examiner* 54, no. 24 (1833): 273–84.

"Review: Letters of the Late Bishop England." *National Anti-Slavery Standard* 4, no. 43 (March 28, 1844): 170.

"Schaff's Church History." *Bibliotheca Sacra* 16, no. 62 (April 1859): 454–56.

The Semi-Centennial of Philip Schaff. New York: n.p., 1893.

"Slavery in England." *National Anti-Slavery Standard* 25, no. 16 (August 27, 1864): 1.

Speech of Mr. Slade, of Vermont, on the Right of Petition: The Power of Congress to Abolish Slavery and the Slave Trade in the District of Columbia. Washington, DC: Gales and Seaton, 1840.

Thirty-Third Annual Catalogue of the Mount Holyoke Female Seminary. Northampton, MA: Bridgman & Childs, 1870.

Twenty-Second Annual Catalogue of the Mount Holyoke Female Seminary. Northampton, MA: Bridgman & Childs, 1859.

Views of American Slavery: Taken a Century Ago. Philadelphia: Association of Friends for the Diffusion of Religious and Useful Knowledge, 1858.

"Woman in the Nineteenth Century." *Southern Quarterly Review* 10, no. 19 (July 1846): 148–73.

"Woman's Patience." *The Independent* 11 (June 16, 1859): 6.

"Woman's Record, or Sketches of All Distinguished Women." *North American Review* 76, no. 158 (January 1853): 260–62.

Author Given

Adams, Hannah. *An Alphabetical Compendium of the Various Sects.* Boston: Manning & Loring, 1801.

Alexander, J. A. "Art. VI.—What Is Church History?" *Biblical Repertory and Princeton Review* 19, no. 1 (January 1847): 91–113.

American Sunday School Union. *First Report.* Philadelphia: ASSU, 1824.

American Sunday School Union. *Fourth Report.* Philadelphia: ASSU, 1828.

American Sunday School Union. *Ninth Report.* Philadelphia: ASSU, 1833.

ASSU Committee of Publication, ed. *Letters on Ecclesiastical History*. Philadelphia: American Sunday School Union, 1832.

Atkins, Thomas. *American Slavery: Reply to the Letter of Bishop Hopkins of Vermont*. New York: W. G. Green, 1861.

Austin, Samuel. *A View of the Economy of the Church of God, as It Existed Primitively*. Worcester, MA: Thomas & Sturtevant, 1807.

Babington, Churchill. *The Influence of Christianity in Promoting the Abolition of Slavery in Europe*. Cambridge: Deighton, 1846.

Backus, Isaac. *An Appeal to the Public for Religious Liberty, against the Oppressions of the Present Day*. Boston: John Boyle, 1773.

Baird, Henry Martyn. *The Life of the Rev. Robert Baird*. New York: A.D.F. Randolph, 1866.

Baird, Robert. *The Life of Ramon Monsalvatge, a Converted Spanish Monk, of the Order of the Capuchins*. New York: J.F. Trow & Co., 1845.

Baird, Robert. *Religion in America: A Critical Abridgment with Introduction*. Edited by Henry Warner Bowden. New York: Harper & Row, 1970.

Baird, Robert. *Religion in the United States of America*. 1st British Edition. Edinburgh: Blackie and Son, 1844.

Baldwin, Thomas. *The Baptism of Believers Only*. Boston: Manning & Loring, 1806.

Baldwin, Thomas. *A Series of Letters*. Boston: Manning & Loring, 1810.

Barnes, Albert. *An Inquiry into the Scriptural Views of Slavery*. Philadelphia: Perkins & Purves, 1846.

Barnes, Albert. *The Church and Slavery*. Philadelphia: Parry & McMillan, 1857.

Barton, David. *Original Intent: The Courts, the Constitution, and Religion*. Aledo, TX: Wallbuilder Press, 2013.

Bascom, Henry Bidleman. *Methodism and Slavery: With Other Matters in Controversy between the North and the South*. Frankfort, KY: Hodges, Todd & Pruett, 1845.

Beecher, Lyman. *A Plea for the West*. 2nd ed. Cincinnati: Truman & Smith, 1836.

Benedict, David. *A General History of the Baptist Denomination in America: And Other Parts of the World*. Boston: Lincoln & Edmands, 1813.

Blanchard, Jonathan, and N. L. Rice. *A Debate on Slavery*. Cincinnati: W.H. Moore & Company, 1846.

Bowden, John. *The Apostolic Origin of Episcopacy Asserted: In a Series of Letters, Addressed to the Rev. Dr. Miller*. Vol. II. New York: T.& J. Swords, 1808.

Bowden, John. *Observations, by a Protestant, on a Profession of Catholic Faith*. New York: Clayton & Kingsland, 1816.

Bowden, John. *A Series of Letters, Addressed to the Rev. Dr. Miller*. New York: T. & J. Swords, 1811.

Boyden, Ebenezer. *The Epidemic of the Nineteenth Century*. Richmond, VA: C. H. Wynne, 1860.

Broadus, John Albert. *Memoir of James Petigru Boyce, D.D., LL.D.: Late President of the Southern Baptist Theological Seminary*. New York: A. C. Armstrong and Son, 1893.

Brown, Clark. *The Covenant of God's Mercy*. Keene, NH: John Prentiss, 1814.

Brownlee, William Craig. *A Careful and Free Inquiry Into the True Nature and Tendency of the Religious Principles of the Society of Friends, Commonly Called Quakers*. Philadelphia: J. Mortimer, 1824.

Brownlee, William Craig. *Popery, an Enemy to Civil and Religious Liberty; and Dangerous to Our Republic*. New York: Bowne & Wisner, 1836.

Brownlow, William Gannaway. *A Sermon on Slavery: A Vindication of the Methodist Church, South: Her Position Stated*. Knoxville, TN: Kinsloe & Rice, 1857.

Brownlow, William Gannaway, and Abram Pryne. *Ought American Slavery to Be Perpetuated? A Debate between Rev. W.G. Brownlow and Rev. A. Pryne*. Philadelphia: J.B. Lippincott & Co., 1858.

Burns, Jabez. *Mothers of the Wise and Good*. London: Houston and Stoneman, 1846.

Campbell, Alexander, ed. *The Christian Baptist*. Cincinnati: D.S. Burnet, 1835.

Campbell, Alexander. *A Debate on Christian Baptism: Between the Rev. W. L. MacCalla, a Presbyterian Teacher, and Alexander Campbell*. Buffaloe, VA: Campbell & Sala, 1824.

Campbell, Alexander, ed. *The Millennial Harbinger*. Vol. II. Bethany, VA: W.K. Pendleton, 1731.

Campbell, Alexander. "Notes of Apostacy." *Millennial Harbinger* 1, no. 1 (January 1837): 15–19.

Campbell, Alexander. *Strictures on Three Letters Respecting the Debate at Mount Pleasant*. Pittsburgh, PA: Eichbaum and Johnston, 1822.

Campbell, Alexander. "Weekly Herald and Philanthropist." *Millennial Harbinger* 2, no. 6 (June 1845): 266–71.

Campbell, Alexander, and John Baptist Purcell. *A Debate on the Roman Catholic Religion*. Cincinnati: J.A. James, 1837.

Campbell, John P. *A Sermon, Preached in Stoner-Mouth Meeting House*. Lexington, KY: Thomas Smith, 1811.

Campbell, Thomas. *Declaration and Address of the Christian Association of Washington*. Centennial Edition. Pittsburgh, PA: Christian Association of Washington, 1908.

Card, Henry. *Literary Recreations*. London: W. Wilson, 1809.

Chadwick, Jabez. *Four Sermons, on the Mode and Subjects of Christian Baptism*. Utica, NY: Seward and Williams, 1811.

Chapin, Stephen. *A Series of Letters on the Mode and Subjects of Baptism*. Boston: Lincoln & Edmands, 1819.

Chase, Heman Lincoln. *A Tribute of Affection to the Memory of Professor Irah Chase*. Boston: G.C. Rand & Avery, 1865.

Child, David Lee. *The Despotism of Freedom; or the Tyranny and Cruelty of American Republican Slave-Masters, Shown to be the Worst in the World*. Boston: Boston Young Men's Anti-Slavery Association, 1833.

Child, Lydia Marie Francis. *An Appeal in Favor of that Class of Americans Called Africans*. Boston: Allen and Ticknor, 1833.

Child, Lydia Marie Francis. *The History of the Condition of Women*. Boston: J. Allen, 1835.

Child, Lydia Marie Francis. *The Progress of Religious Ideas: Through Successive Ages*. New York: C. S. Francis & Company, 1855.

Clark, Rufus Wheelwright. *A Review of the Rev. Moses Stuart's Pamphlet on Slavery*. Boston: C.C.P. Moody, 1850.

Clarkson, Thomas. *The History of the Rise, Progress, and Accomplishment of the Abolition of the African Slave-Trade by the British Parliament*. Vol. I. London: Longman, 1808.

Cobb, Thomas R. R. *An Inquiry into the Law of Negro Slavery in the United States of America. To Which Is Prefixed, an Historical Sketch of Slavery*. Philadelphia: T. & J.W. Johnson, 1858.

Cruttenden, Robert, and George Whitefield. *The Experience of Mr. R. Cruttenden*. Boston: Kneeland and Green, 1744.

Dabney, Robert Lewis. *A Defence of Virginia and through Her, of the South.* New York: E.J. Hale, 1867.

Dabney, Robert Lewis. *Ecclesiastical Relation of Negroes: Speech of Robert L. Dabney, in the Synod of Virginia, Nov. 9, 1867, Against the Ecclesiastical Equality of Negro Preachers in Our Church, and Their Right to Rule Over White Christians.* Richmond, VA: Boys & Girls Monthly, 1868.

Dalcho, Frederick. *Practical Considerations Founded on the Scriptures: Relative to the Slave Population of South-Carolina.* Charleston, SC: A.E. Miller, 1823.

Douglass, Frederick. "What to the Slave Is the Fourth of July?" In *Lift Every Voice: African American Oratory, 1787–1900*, edited by Philip S. Foner and Robert J. Branham, 246–67. Tuscaloosa: University of Alabama Press, 1998.

Dow, Lorenzo. *History of Cosmopolite: Or the Four Volumes of Lorenzo Dow's Journal.* 4th ed. Washington, OH: Joshua Martin, 1848.

Drinker, John. *A Vindication of the Religious Society Called Quakers: Addressed to the Editors of the American Edition of Mosheim's Ecclesiastical History.* Mount Holly, NJ: S. C. Ustick, 1800.

Eaton, George W. *Claims of Civil and Ecclesiastical History as Indispensable Branches of Ministerial Education.* Utica, NY: Bennett, Backus, & Hawley, 1841.

Eaton, Rebecca. *An Abridgment of Milner's Church History, for the Use of Schools and Private Families.* Andover, MA: Flagg and Gould, 1817.

Edwards, Bela Bates. "Roman Slavery in the Early Centuries of the Christian Era." *Biblical Repository* 6, no. 20 (October 1835): 411–36.

Edwards, Bela Bates. "Slavery in the Middle Ages." *Biblical Repository* 7, no. 21 (January 1836): 33–45.

Elliott, Charles. *The Bible and Slavery: In Which the Abrahamic and Mosaic Discipline is Considered in connection with the Most Ancient Forms of Slavery; And the Pauline Code on Slavery as Related to Roman Slavery and the Discipline of the Apostolic Churches.* Cincinnati: Poe & Hitchcock, 1863.

Elliott, Charles. *History of the Great Secession from the Methodist Episcopal Church in the Year 1845.* Cincinnati: Swormstedt and Power, 1855.

Elliott, Charles. *Sinfulness of American Slavery.* Cincinnati: Swormstedt and Power, 1851.

Emerson, Ralph Waldo, Margaret Fuller, and George Ripley, eds. "Review: Institutes of Ecclesiastical History, Ancient and Modern." *The Dial: A Magazine for Literature, Philosophy, and Religion* 2, no. 4 (April 1842): 531–35.

England, John. *Letters of the Late Bishop England to the Hon. John Forsyth on the Subject of Domestic Slavery.* Baltimore: J. Murphy, 1844.

Fee, John G. *An Anti-Slavery Manual; Being an Examination, in Light of the Bible, and of Facts, into the Moral and Social Wrongs of American Slavery, with a Remedy for the Evil.* Maysville, KY: The Herald Office, 1848.

Field, Joseph. *Strictures on Seven Sermons.* Northampton, MA: T. M. Pomroy, 1806.

Findley, William. *Observations on "The Two Sons of Oil": Containing a Vindication of the American Constitutions, and Defending the Blessings of Religious Liberty and Toleration.* Pittsburgh, PA: Patterson & Hopkins, 1812.

Finney, Charles G. *Lectures on Revivals of Religion.* New York: Leavitt, Lord & Co., 1835.

Fitzhugh, George. *Cannibals All! or, Slaves Without Masters.* Richmond, VA: A. Morris, 1857.

Fletcher, John. *Studies on Slavery.* Natchez, MS: Jackson Warner, 1852.

Forsyth, John. *Address to the People of Georgia.* N.p., 1840.

Fuller, Margaret. *The Essential Margaret Fuller.* Edited by Jeffrey Steele. New Brunswick, NJ: Rutgers University Press, 1992.

Fuller, Richard, and Francis Wayland. *Domestic Slavery Considered as a Scriptural Institution.* New York: L. Colby, 1845.

Garnet, Henry Highland. *The Past and the Present Condition, and the Destiny, of the Colored Race.* Troy, NY: Kneeland, 1848.

Garrison, William Lloyd. *No Compromise with Slavery.* New York: American Anti-Slavery Society, 1854.

Gibbon, Edward. *The History of the Decline and Fall of the Roman Empire.* London: W. Strahan and T. Cadell, 1776.

Gibbon, Edward. *The History of the Decline and Fall of the Roman Empire.* Vol. IV. London: Cowie and Co., 1825.

Gisborne, Thomas. *A Familiar Survey of the Christian Religion: And of History.* 2nd ed. London: A. Strahan, 1799.

Goodwin, Daniel R. *Southern Slavery in Its Present Aspects: Containing a Reply to a Late Work of the Bishop of Vermont on Slavery.* Philadelphia: J. B. Lippincott, 1864.

Graham, James. *Reasons for Renouncing Infant Baptism.* Charleston, SC: J. Hoff, 1810.

Graham, William. *The Contrast; or The Bible and Abolitionism: An Exegetical Argument.* Cincinnati: Daily Cincinnati Atlas Office, 1844.

Gregory, George. *An History of the Christian Church, from the Earliest Periods to the Present Time.* Vol. I. London: G. Kearsley, 1790.

Grimké, Sarah Moore. *Letters on the Equality of the Sexes.* Boston: I. Knapp, 1838. https://founders.archives.gov/documents/Jefferson/01-02-02-0132-0004-0082.

Grimké, Thomas Smith. *Reflections on the Character and Objects of All Science and Literature: And on the Relative Excellence and Value of Religious and Secular Education, and of Sacred and Classical Literature.* New Haven, CT: Hezekiah Howe, 1831.

Guirey, William. *The History of Episcopacy.* Raleigh, NC: Joseph Gales, 1799.

Gurowski, Adam G. *Slavery in History.* New York: A.B. Burdick, 1860.

Hale, Sarah Josepha Buell. "The History of the Condition of Women, in Various Ages and Nations. By Mrs. D. L. Child." *American Ladies' Magazine* 8 (October 1835): 588–91.

Hale, Sarah Josepha Buell. *Woman's Record, or, Sketches of All Distinguished Women: From the Creation to A.D. 1854.* New York: Harper, 1855.

Hobart, John Henry. *A Collection of the Essays on the Subject of Episcopacy, Which Originally Appeared in the Albany Centinel.* New York: T. & J. Swords, 1806.

Hodge, Charles. *An Exposition of the First Epistle to the Corinthians.* New York: Carter, 1860.

Hodge, Charles. "History of the Apostolic Church." *Biblical Repertory and Princeton Review* 26, no. 1 (January 1854): 148–92.

Hodge, Charles and Lyman Hotchkiss Atwater, eds. "Review: Institutes of Ecclesiastical History, Ancient and Modern." *Biblical Repertory and Princeton Review* 41, no. 4 (October 1869): 632.

Hopkins, John Henry. *A Scriptural, Ecclesiastical, and Historical View of Slavery, from the Days of the Patriarch Abraham, to the Nineteenth Century.* New York: W. I. Pooley & Co., 1864.

Hopkins, Samuel. *The Works of Samuel Hopkins.* Edited by Sewall Harding. Boston: Doctrinal Tract and Book Society, 1852.

Hotchkin, James Harvey. *A History of the Purchase and Settlement of Western New York, and of the Rise, Progress, and Present State of the Presbyterian Church in That Section.* New York: M. W. Dodd, 1848.

Howe, Mark. *A Reply to the Letter of Bishop Hopkins.* Philadelphia: King & Baird, 1864.

Hume, David. *The History of England, from the Invasion of Julius Caesar to the Revolution in 1688.* London: A. Millar, 1762.

Hume, David. "Of Superstition and Enthusiasm." In *Essays, Moral, Political and Literary.* Basil: J.J. Tourneisen, 1793.

Hurd, John Codman. *The Law of Freedom and Bondage in the United States.* Vol. I. Boston: Little, Brown, and Co., 1858.

Janeway, Jacob J. *Antidote to the Poison of Popery in the Writings and Conduct of Professors Nevin & Schaff.* New Brunswick, NJ: J. Terhune, 1856.

Jefferson, Thomas. *Notes on the State of Virginia.* Edited by William Peden. Chapel Hill: University of North Carolina Press, 1954.

John Chrysostom, Saint. *The Homilies of S. John Chrysostom, Archbishop of Constantinople, on the First Epistle of St. Paul the Apostle to the Corinthians.* Oxford: John Henry Parker, 1839.

Jones, David. *Peter Edwards's Candid Reasons Examined, and Answered.* Philadelphia: Dennis Heartt, 1811.

Kerr, David R. *Church History—What It Is—How It Should Be Studied—And for What Ends.* Pittsburgh, PA: W.S. Haven, 1855.

Knowles, James Davis. *Importance of Theological Institutions.* Boston: Lincoln & Edmands, 1832.

Lasher, George William. *George W. Eaton, D.D., LL.D: A Memorial.* Hamilton, NY: Colgate University, 1913.

Leland, John. *The Writings of the Late Elder John Leland: Including Some Events in His Life.* Edited by L. F. Greene. New York: G.W. Wood, 1845.

Lewis, Robert Benjamin. *Light and Truth; Collected from the Bible and Ancient and Modern History.* Portland, ME: D.C. Colesworthy, 1836.

Lewis, Robert Benjamin. *Light and Truth; Collected from the Bible and Ancient and Modern History.* 2nd ed. Boston: B. F. Roberts, 1844.

Loomis, Hubbel. *Defence of Letters on Christian Baptism.* Hartford, CT: Peter B. Gleason, 1819.

Lord, Nathan. *A Letter of Inquiry to Ministers of the Gospel of All Denominations, on Slavery.* Boston: Fetridge, 1854.

MacMahon, T. W. *Cause and Contrast: An Essay on the American Crisis.* Richmond, VA: West & Johnston, 1862.

Maitland, S. R. *A Letter to the Rev. H. J. Rose with Strictures on Milner's Church History.* London: J. G. & F. Rivington, 1834.

Marrant, John. *A Sermon Preached on the 24th Day of June 1789.* Boston: Thomas and John Fleet, 1789.

Marsh, John. *An Epitome of General Ecclesiastical History.* 4th ed. New York: W. E. Dean, 1834.

Marsh, Leonard. *Review of a Letter from the Right Rev. John H. Hopkins.* Burlington, VT: Free Press Print, 1861.

Mather, Cotton. *The Good Old Way.* Boston: B. Green, 1706.

Mather, Cotton. *Maternal Consolations.* Boston: T. Fleet, 1714.

Mather, Cotton. *Ornaments for the Daughters of Zion.* Boston: Kneeland and Green, 1741.

Mather, Increase. *The Duty of Parents to Pray for Their Children.* Boston: Allen, 1719.

Maxcy, Jonathan. *A Course of Historical & Miscellaneous Reading, Drawn up for the Use of the Students of the South-Carolina College.* Columbia, SC: Telescope Office, 1816.

McDowell, Stephen K. *Building Godly Nations*. Charlottesville, VA: Providence Foundation, 2004.

Merrill, Daniel. *Letters Occasioned by Rev. Samuel Worcester's Two Discourses*. Boston: Manning & Loring, 1807.

Merrill, Daniel. *A Miniature History of the Baptists*. New Haven, CT: J. Barber, 1815.

Merrill, Daniel. *The Mode and Subjects of Baptism Examined, in Seven Sermons. To Which Is Added, A Brief History of the Baptists*. Salem, MA: Joshua Cushing, 1804.

Merrill, Daniel. *Twelve Letters, Addressed to Rev. Samuel Austin*. Boston: Manning & Loring, 1806.

Miller, Samuel. *A Brief Retrospect of the Eighteenth Century*. Vol. II. New York: T. and J. Swords, 1803.

Miller, Samuel. *An Essay on the Warrant, Nature, and Duties of the Office of the Ruling Elder, in the Presbyterian Church*. Philadelphia: Presbyterian Board of Publication, 1832.

Miller, Samuel, ed. *A History of Popery: Including Its Origin, Progress, Doctrines, Practice, Institutions, and Fruits, to the Commencement of the Nineteenth Century*. New York: J.B. Haven, 1834.

Miller, Samuel. *The Importance of Mature Preparatory Study for the Ministry*. Princeton, NJ: Princeton Press, 1829.

Miller, Samuel. *Letters Concerning the Constitution and Order of the Christian Ministry: As Deduced from Scripture and Primitive Usage*. New York: Hopkins and Seymour, 1807.

Millett, Joshua. *A History of the Baptists in Maine*. Portland, ME: C. Day, 1845.

Milner, Joseph. *The History of the Church of Christ, Volume the First. Containing the First Three Centuries*. York: G. Peacock, 1794.

Milner, Joseph. *The History of the Church of Christ, Volume the Second. Containing the Fourth and Fifth Centuries*. Cambridge: J. Burges, 1795.

Milner, Joseph. *The History of the Church of Christ, Volume the Third. Containing the Sixth, Seventh, Eighth, Ninth, Tenth, Eleventh, and Twelfth, Centuries*. Cambridge: J. Burges, 1797.

Milner, Joseph. *The History of the Church of Christ, Volume the Fourth, Part I. Containing the Remainder of the Thirteenth Century; Also the Fourteenth, Fifteenth, and Part of the Sixteenth, Centuries*. Edited by Isaac Milner. Cambridge: University Press, 1803.

Morse, Samuel Finley Breese. *Foreign Conspiracy Against the Liberties of the United States*. New York: Leavitt, Lord & Co., 1835.

Mosheim, Johannes Laurentius a. *An Ecclesiastical History, Antient And Modern, From The Birth Of Christ, To The Beginning Of The Present Century*. London: A. Millar, 1765.

Mosheim, Johann Lorenz. *Institutes of Ecclesiastical History, Ancient and Modern*. Translated by James Murdock. New Haven, CT: A.H. Maltby, 1832.

Mott, Lucretia. *Complete Sermons and Speeches*. Edited by Dana Green. New York: Edwin Mellen Press, 1980.

Neander, August. *General History of the Christian Religion and Church*. 2nd American Edition. Vol. II. Boston: Crocker & Brewster, 1849.

Neander, August. *History of the Planting and Training of the Christian Church by the Apostles*. Translated by J. E. Ryland. Philadelphia: J. M. Campbell & Co., 1844.

Ogilvie, James G. *A Sermon, Delivered in the Baptist Meeting House*. Hudson, NY: William L. Stone, 1816.

O'Kelly, James. *The Author's Apology for Protesting against the Methodist Episcopal Government*. Hillsborough, NC: Dennis Heartt, 1829.

Oson, Jacob. *A Search for Truth; or, an Inquiry for the Origin of the African Nation.* New York: Christopher Rush, 1817.

Peden, William. *1828 Catalogue of the Library of the University of Virginia.* Charlottesville: Printed for the Alderman Library of the University of Virginia, 1945.

Pennington, James W. C. "A Review of Slavery and the Slave-Trade." *Anglo-African Magazine* 1, no. 5 (May 1859): 123–26.

Pennington, James W. C. *A Text Book of the Origin and History, of the Colored People.* Hartford, CT: L. Skinner, 1841.

Presbytery of Springfield. *An Apology for Renouncing the Jurisdiction of the Synod of Kentucky.* Lexington, KY: John Weaver, 1804.

Priestley, Joseph. *A General History of the Christian Church, from the Fall of the Western Empire to the Present Time.* Northumberland, PA: A. Kennedy, 1802.

Priestley, Joseph. *An History of the Corruptions of Christianity.* Birmingham: Piercy & Jones, 1782.

Prime, Nathaniel Scudder. *A Familiar Illustration of Christian Baptism.* Salem, NY: Dodd & Stevenson, 1818.

Richardson, Nathaniel S. "The Rev. James Murdock." *Church Review* 9, no. 4 (January 1857): 501–20.

Robertson, William. *History of the Reign of the Emperor Charles V.* Vol. I. London: Cadell and Davies, 1812.

Robertson, William. "View of the State of Society in the Middle Ages." In *The History of the Reign of the Emperor Charles V.*, vol. I. London: W. and W. Strahan, 1769.

Rogers, Edward Coit. *Letters on Slavery, Addressed to the Pro-Slavery Men of America.* Boston: B. Marsh, 1855.

Rousseau, Jean-Jacques. *The Social Contract & Discourses.* Translated by George D. H. Cole. London: J.M. Dent & Sons, 1913.

Rowson, Susanna. *An Abridgment of Universal Geography: Together with Sketches of History, Designed for the Use of Schools and Academies in the United States.* Boston: John West & Co., 1806.

Rowson, Susanna. *Biblical Dialogues Between a Father and His Family.* Vol. II. Boston: Richardson and Lord, 1822.

Rowson, Susanna. *Miscellaneous Poems.* Boston: Gilbert and Dean, 1804.

Rowson, Susanna. *A Present for Young Ladies.* Boston: John West & Co., 1811.

Ruter, Martin. *A Concise History of the Christian Church.* Pittsburgh, PA: B. Waugh and T. Mason, 1834.

Ruter, Martin. *A Concise History of the Christian Church, from Its First Establishment to the Nineteenth Century.* Edited by Charles K. True. New York: Carlton & Lanahan, 1865.

Sawyer, George S. *Southern Institutes; or, An Inquiry into the Origin and Early Prevalence of Slavery and the Slave-Trade.* Philadelphia: J.B. Lippincott, 1858.

Schaff, Philip. *The Development of the Church: "The Principle of Protestantism" and Other Historical Writings of Philip Schaff.* Edited by David R. Bains and Theodore Louis Trost. Eugene, OR: Wipf and Stock, 2017.

Schaff, Philip. *History of the Apostolic Church.* New York: C. Scribner, 1854.

Schaff, Philip. *History of the Christian Church.* 2nd ed. Edinburgh: T&T Clark, 1883.

Schaff, Philip. "The Influence of the Early Church on the Institution of Slavery." *Mercersburg Review* 10 (1858): 614–20.

Schaff, Philip. *The Principle of Protestantism as Related to the Present State of the Church.* Translated by John Williamson Nevin. Chambersburg, PA: Publication Office of the German Reformed Church, 1845.

Schaff, Philip. *Saint Augustin, Melanchthon, Neander: Three Biographies.* London: James Nisbet, 1886.

Schaff, Philip. *Slavery and the Bible: A Tract for the Times.* Chambersburg, PA: M. Kieffer & Co., 1861.

Schaff, Philip. *What is Church History? A Vindication of the Idea of Historical Development.* Philadelphia: J.B. Lippincott, 1846.

Sherman, David. *History of the Wesleyan Academy, in Wilbraham, Mass. 1817–1890.* Boston: McDonald & Gill, 1893.

Sigourney, Lydia Howard. *Examples of Life and Death.* New York: C. Scribner, 1852.

Smith, Elias. "History." *Christian's Magazine, Reviewer, and Religious Intelligencer* 1, no. 2 (January 2, 1805): 39–48.

Smith, Ernest A. *Allegheny—a Century of Education.* Meadville, PA: Allegheny College History Co., 1916.

Smith, Henry Boynton. "Schaff's Church History." *American Theological Review* 1, no. 2 (May 1859): 318–26.

Smith, Henry Boynton. *Henry Boynton Smith: His Life and Work.* Edited by Elizabeth L. Smith. New York: A. C. Armstrong & Son, 1881.

Spencer, Jesse Ames, ed. *The Women of Early Christianity: A Series of Portraits.* New York: D. Appleton, 1852.

Stanton, Elizabeth Cady, et al., eds. *History of Woman Suffrage.* Vol. I. New York: Fowler & Wells, 1881.

Stanton, Elizabeth Cady, et al., eds. *History of Woman Suffrage.* Vol. I. 2nd ed. Rochester, NY: Charles Mann, 1889.

Stroud, George. *The Views of Judge Woodward and Bishop Hopkins on Negro Slavery At the South.* Philadelphia: n.p., 1863.

Stuart, Moses. *Conscience and the Constitution.* Boston: Crocker & Brewster, 1850.

Thompson, Joseph Parrish. *The Christian Graces: A Series of Lectures on 2 Peter I, 5–12.* New York: Sheldon & Company, 1859.

Thompson, Joseph Parrish. *Christianity and Emancipation: or, The Teachings and the Influence of the Bible Against Slavery.* New York: A.D.F. Randolph, 1863.

Tweedie, William King. *The Early Choice: A Book for Daughters.* Philadelphia: American Baptist Publication Society, 1855.

Tytler, Alexander Fraser. *Elements of General History, Ancient & Modern.* 3rd ed. Edinburgh: Creech, 1805.

Walker, John. *Elements of Geography and of Natural and Civil History.* 3rd ed. Dublin: T. M. Bates, 1797.

Ward, Samuel Ringgold. *Autobiography of a Fugitive Negro.* London: John Snow, 1855.

Warren, E. W. *Nellie Norton: or, Southern Slavery and the Bible.* Macon, GA: Burke, Boykin & Co., 1864.

Wetmore, Izrahiah. *A Sermon Preached before the General Assembly.* New London, CT: n.p., 1773.

White, William. *Christian Baptism: Exhibiting Various Proofs.* Burlington, NJ: S.C. Ustick, 1808.

White, William. "An Essay, Noticing Some Errors in the Ecclesiastical History of Dr. Lawrence Mosheim." *Christian Journal, and Literary Register* 2, no. 8 (April 2, 1818): 120–22.

Willard, Emma. *A System of Universal History, in Perspective.* Hartford, CT: F. J. Huntington, 1835.

Williams, Roger. *The Bloudy Tenent of Persecution for Cause of Conscience.* Edited by Richard Groves. Macon, GA: Mercer University Press, 2001.

Williams, Roger. *The Bloody Tenent yet more Bloody.* London: Giles Calvert, 1652.

Witherell, George. *A Sermon, on the Subjects and Mode of Baptism.* Plattsburgh, NY: A.C. Flagg, 1817.

Woods, Leonard. *History of the Andover Theological Seminary.* Boston: J. R. Osgood, 1885.

Worcester, Samuel. *Serious and Candid Letters to the Rev. Thomas Baldwin.* Salem, MA: Haven Pool, 1807.

Worcester, Samuel. *Two Discourses, on God's Gracious Covenant.* Salem, MA: Haven Pool, 1805.

Youngs, Benjamin S. *The Testimony of Christ's Second Appearing.* Lebanon, OH: John M'Clean, 1808.

Secondary Sources

Abruzzo, Margaret. *Polemical Pain: Slavery, Cruelty, and the Rise of Humanitarianism.* Baltimore: Johns Hopkins University Press, 2011.

Albaugh, Gaylord P. *History and Annotated Bibliography of American Religious Periodicals and Newspapers Established from 1730 through 1830.* Worcester, MA: American Antiquarian Society, 1994.

Allen, Crawford Leonard, and Richard T. Hughes. *Discovering Our Roots: The Ancestry of Churches of Christ.* Abilene, TX: Abilene Christian University Press, 1988.

Alvarez, Elizabeth Hayes. *The Valiant Woman: The Virgin Mary in Nineteenth-Century American Culture.* Chapel Hill: University of North Carolina Press, 2016.

Anderson, Bonnie S. *Joyous Greetings: The First International Women's Movement, 1830–1860.* Oxford: Oxford University Press, 2000.

Anderson, Matthew Lee. "Will the Trump Presidency Lead to Renewed Dialogue between Catholics and Evangelicals?" *America Magazine,* October 19, 2018. https://www.americamagazine.org/politics-society/2018/10/19/will-trump-presidency-lead-renewed-dialogue-between-catholics-and.

Appleby, Joyce Oldham. *Inheriting the Revolution: The First Generation of Americans.* Cambridge, MA: Harvard University Press, 2009.

Asbury, Francis. *The Journal and Letters of Francis Asbury.* Edited by Elmer T. Clark. Nashville, TN: Abingdon Press, 1958.

Assmann, Jan. *Moses the Egyptian: The Memory of Egypt in Western Monotheism.* Cambridge, MA: Harvard University Press, 1997.

Aubert, Annette G. "Henry Boynton Smith and Church History in Nineteenth-Century America." *Church History* 85, no. 2 (June 2016): 302–27.

Bains, David R., and Theodore Louis Trost. "Philip Schaff: The Flow of Church History and the Development of Protestantism." *Theology Today* 71, no. 4 (January 1, 2015): 416–28.

Baptist, Edward E. *The Half Has Never Been Told: Slavery and the Making of American Capitalism.* New York: Basic Books, 2014.

Barnes, H. E. *A History of Historical Writing*. New York: Dover Publications, 1963.

Barnes, W. W. *The Southern Baptist Convention, 1845–1953*. Nashville, TN: Broadman and Holman, 1954.

Barnett, S. J. "Where Was Your Church before Luther? Claims for the Antiquity of Protestantism Examined." *Church History* 68 (1999): 14–41.

Barr, Beth Allison. *The Pastoral Care of Women in Late Medieval England*. Suffolk, UK: Boydell Press, 2008.

Baym, Nina. *American Women Writers and the Work of History, 1790–1860*. New Brunswick, NJ: Rutgers University Press, 1995.

Baym, Nina. "Onward Christian Women: Sarah J. Hale's History of the World." *New England Quarterly* 63, no. 2 (1990): 249–70.

Baym, Nina. "Women and the Republic: Emma Willard's Rhetoric of History." *American Quarterly* 43, no. 1 (1991): 1–23.

Bebbington, David. *Evangelicalism in Modern Britain: A History from the 1730s to the 1980s*. London: Routledge, 1993.

Beckwith, Francis J. *Return to Rome: Confessions of an Evangelical Catholic*. Grand Rapids, MI: Brazos Press, 2008.

Bell, James B. *A War of Religion: Dissenters, Anglicans, and the American Revolution*. New York: Palgrave Macmillan, 2008.

Bendroth, Margaret Lamberts. *A School of the Church: Andover Newton across Two Centuries*. Grand Rapids, MI: Eerdmans, 2008.

Bennett, Joshua. "August Neander and the Religion of History in the Nineteenth-Century 'Priesthood of Letters.'" *Historical Journal* 63, no. 3 (2020): 633–59.

Bercovitch, Sacvan. *The American Jeremiad*. 2nd ed. Madison: University of Wisconsin Press, 2012.

Berkin, Carol. "Adams, Hannah (1755–1831), Historian of Religions and Writer." In *American National Biography Online*. February 2000. https://doi.org/10.1093/anb/9780198606697.article.1400008.

Berlin, Ira. *Many Thousands Gone: The First Two Centuries of Slavery in North America*. Cambridge, MA: Harvard University Press, 1998.

Black, John Bennett. *The Art of History: A Study of Four Great Historians of the Eighteenth Century*. New York: Russell & Russell, 1965.

Blight, David W. *Race and Reunion: The Civil War in American Memory*. Cambridge, MA: Belknap Press of Harvard University Press, 2001.

Bloch, Ruth H. *Visionary Republic: Millennial Themes in American Thought, 1756–1800*. Cambridge: Cambridge University Press, 1988.

Blum, Edward J. *Reforging the White Republic: Race, Religion, and American Nationalism, 1865–1898*. Baton Rouge: Louisiana State University Press, 2007.

Blumin, Stuart M. *The Emergence of the Middle Class: Social Experience in the American City, 1760–1900*. Cambridge: Cambridge University Press, 1989.

Boles, John B. *The Great Revival: Beginnings of the Bible Belt*. Lexington: University Press of Kentucky, 1996.

Boles, John B. "Robert Lewis Dabney (1820–1898)." *Encyclopedia Virginia*, July 2020, https://www.encyclopediavirginia.org/Dabney_Robert_Lewis_1820-1898.

Bowden, Henry Warner. *Church History in the Age of Science: Historiographical Patterns in the United States, 1876–1918*. Carbondale: Southern Illinois University Press, 1991.

Bowers, J. D. *Joseph Priestley and English Unitarianism in America*. University Park: Penn State University Press, 2010.

Bowman, Matthew, and Samuel Brown. "Reverend Buck's Theological Dictionary and the Struggle to Define American Evangelicalism, 1802–1851." *Journal of the Early Republic* 29, no. 3 (2009): 441–73.

Boylan, Anne M. *The Origins of Women's Activism: New York and Boston, 1797–1840.* Chapel Hill: University of North Carolina Press, 2002.

Boylan, Anne M. *Sunday School: The Formation of an American Institution, 1790–1880.* New Haven, CT: Yale University Press, 1988.

Bradburn, Douglas. *The Citizenship Revolution: Politics and the Creation of the American Union, 1774–1804.* Charlottesville: University of Virginia Press, 2009.

Bradley, James E. *Church History: An Introduction to Research, Reference Works, and Methods.* Grand Rapids, MI: Eerdmans, 1995.

Bratt, James D., ed. *Antirevivalism in Antebellum America: A Collection of Religious Voices.* New Brunswick, NJ: Rutgers University Press, 2006.

Breisach, Ernst. *Historiography: Ancient, Medieval, and Modern.* Chicago: University of Chicago Press, 1994.

Brekus, Catherine A. "Contested Words: History, America, Religion." *William and Mary Quarterly* 75, no. 1 (February 6, 2018): 3–36.

Brekus, Catherine A. *Strangers and Pilgrims: Female Preaching in America, 1740–1845.* Chapel Hill: University of North Carolina Press, 1999.

Broomhall, Susan. "Religion." In *Companion to Women's Historical Writing,* edited by Mary Spongberg, Ann Curthoys, and Barbara Caine, 455–65. London: Palgrave Macmillan, 2005.

Brophy, Alfred L. *University, Court, and Slave: Pro-Slavery Thought in Southern Colleges and Courts and the Coming of Civil War.* Oxford: Oxford University Press, 2016.

Brown, Candy Gunther. *The Word in the World: Evangelical Writing, Publishing, and Reading in America, 1789–1880.* Chapel Hill: University of North Carolina Press, 2004.

Brown, Christopher Leslie. *Moral Capital: Foundations of British Abolitionism.* Chapel Hill: University of North Carolina Press, 2012.

Buckley, Thomas E. *Church and State in Revolutionary Virginia, 1776–1787.* Charlottesville: University Press of Virginia, 1977.

Buehrens, John A. *Universalists and Unitarians in America: A People's History.* Boston: Skinner House Books, 2011.

Burin, Eric. *Slavery and the Peculiar Solution: A History of the American Colonization Society.* Gainesville: University Press of Florida. 2005.

Burkett, Randall K. "The Reverend Harry Croswell and Black Episcopalians in New Haven, 1820–1860." *North Star* 7, no. 1 (Fall 2003): 1–20.

Burstein, Miriam Elizabeth. "From Good Looks to Good Thoughts: Popular Women's History and the Invention of Modernity, ca. 1830–1870." *Modern Philology* 97, no. 1 (August 1999): 46–75.

Burton, Orville Vernon. *The Age of Lincoln.* New York: Hill and Wang, 2007.

Butler, Diana. *Standing against the Whirlwind: Evangelical Episcopalians in Nineteenth-Century America.* Oxford: Oxford University Press, 1995.

Byrd, James P. *A Holy Baptism of Fire and Blood: The Bible and the American Civil War.* Oxford: Oxford University Press, 2021.

Caldwell, Robert W. *Theologies of the American Revivalists: From Whitefield to Finney.* Westmont, IL: InterVarsity Press, 2017.

Calhoun, Daniel H. "Eyes for the Jacksonian World: William C. Woodbridge and Emma Willard." *Journal of the Early Republic* 4, no. 1 (1984): 1–26.

Cameron, Euan. *Interpreting Christian History*. New York: Wiley, 2008.

Cameron, Euan. *Waldenses: Rejections of Holy Church in Medieval Europe*. Hoboken, NJ: Wiley, 2001.

Cameron, James K. "Maclaine, Archibald (1722–1804)." In *Oxford Dictionary of National Biography*. Oxford University Press, 2004. http://www.oxforddnb.com/view/article/17636.

Carey, Patrick W. "England, John (1786–1842), the First Catholic Bishop of Charleston, South Carolina." In *American National Biography Online*. February 2000. https://doi.org/10.1093/anb/9780198606697.article.0800441.

Carey, Patrick W. *An Immigrant Bishop: John England's Adaptation of Irish Catholicism to American Republicanism*. Yonkers, NY: The Society, 1979.

Carwardine, Richard. *Evangelicals and Politics in Antebellum America*. Knoxville: University of Tennessee Press, 1993.

Clanton, J. Caleb. *The Philosophy of Religion of Alexander Campbell*. Knoxville: University of Tennessee Press, 2013.

Clark, Elizabeth A. *Founding the Fathers: Early Church History and Protestant Professors in Nineteenth-Century America*. Philadelphia: University of Pennsylvania Press, 2011.

Clark, Gillian. *Monica: An Ordinary Saint*. Oxford: Oxford University Press, 2015.

Clark, J. C. D. *The Language of Liberty, 1660–1832: Political Discourse and Social Dynamics in the Anglo-American World*. Cambridge: Cambridge University Press, 1994.

Clark, Robert D. *The Life of Matthew Simpson of the Methodist Episcopal Church*. New York: Macmillan, 1956.

Cobb, Sanford Hoadley. *The Rise of Religious Liberty in America: A History*. New York: Macmillan, 1902.

Colbourn, H. Trevor. *The Lamp of Experience: Whig History and the Intellectual Origins of the American Revolution*. Chapel Hill: University of North Carolina Press, 1965.

Coleman, Dawn. "The Antebellum American Sermon as Lived Religion." In *A New History of the Sermon: The Nineteenth Century*, edited by Robert H. Ellison, 521–54. Boston: Brill, 2010.

Coleman, Dawn. *Preaching and the Rise of the American Novel*. Columbus: Ohio State University Press, 2013.

Conkin, Paul K. *American Originals: Homemade Varieties of Christianity*. Chapel Hill: University of North Carolina Press, 2000.

Conkin, Paul K. *Cane Ridge: America's Pentecost*. Madison: University of Wisconsin Press, 1990.

Conrad, Susan Phinney. *Perish the Thought: Intellectual Women in Romantic America, 1830–1860*. Oxford: Oxford University Press, 1976.

Conroy-Krutz, Emily. "No Acknowledged Standard: The Female Seminary Curriculum of the Early Nineteenth Century." In *Inequity in Education: A Historical Perspective*, edited by Debra Meyers and Burke Miller, 55–68. New York: Rowman & Littlefield, 2009.

Cott, Nancy F. *The Bonds of Womanhood: "Woman's Sphere" in New England, 1780–1835*. New Haven, CT: Yale University Press, 1977.

Cross, Robert D. "Wayland, Francis (1796–1865), Moral Philosopher and University President." In *American National Biography*. February 2000. https://doi.org/10.1093/anb/9780198606697.article.0801625.

Crow, Matthew. *Thomas Jefferson, Legal History, and the Art of Recollection*. Cambridge: Cambridge University Press, 2017.

Curry, Thomas J. *Farewell to Christendom: The Future of Church and State in America.* Oxford: Oxford University Press, 2001.

Curry, Thomas J. *The First Freedoms: Church and State in America to the Passage of the First Amendment.* Oxford: Oxford University Press, 1987.

Dain, Bruce. *A Hideous Monster of the Mind: American Race Theory in the Early Republic.* Cambridge, MA: Harvard University Press, 2002.

Daly, John Patrick. *When Slavery Was Called Freedom: Evangelicalism, Proslavery, and the Causes of the Civil War.* Lexington: University Press of Kentucky, 2015.

Davis, David Brion. *The Problem of Slavery in the Age of Emancipation.* New York: Alfred A. Knopf, 2014.

Davis, David Brion. *The Problem of Slavery in the Age of Revolution, 1770–1823.* Oxford: Oxford University Press, 1999.

Davis, Richard Beale. *A Colonial Southern Bookshelf: Reading in the Eighteenth Century.* Athens: University of Georgia Press, 1979.

Dawley, Powel M. *The Story of the General Theological Seminary: A Sesquicentennial History, 1817–1967.* Oxford: Oxford University Press, 1969.

Dickens, A. G., John Tonkin, and Kenneth Powell. *The Reformation in Historical Thought.* Cambridge, MA: Harvard University Press, 1985.

Diner, Hasia. *Erin's Daughters in America: Irish Immigrant Women in the Nineteenth Century.* Baltimore: Johns Hopkins University Press, 1983.

Dolan, Jay P. *In Search of an American Catholicism: A History of Religion and Culture in Tension.* Oxford: Oxford University Press, 2002.

Douglas, Ann. *The Feminization of American Culture.* London: Macmillan, 1977.

Duffy, Eamon. *The Stripping of the Altars: Traditional Religion in England, C.1400–c.1580.* New Haven, CT: Yale University Press, 2005.

Dzielska, Maria. *Hypatia of Alexandria.* Cambridge, MA: Harvard University Press, 1996.

Ellison, Robert H., ed. *A New History of the Sermon: The Nineteenth Century.* Boston: Brill, 2010.

Emery, Robert. "Church and State in the Early Republic: The Covenanters' Radical Critique." *Journal of Law and Religion* 25, no. 2 (2009): 487–501.

Ernest, John. *Liberation Historiography: African American Writers and the Challenge of History, 1794–1861.* Chapel Hill: University of North Carolina Press, 2004.

Esbeck, Carl H. "Dissent and Disestablishment: The Church-State Settlement in the Early American Republic." *Brigham Young University Law Review,* no. 4 (2004): 1386–589.

Esbeck, Carl H., and Jonathan J. Den Hartog, eds. *Disestablishment and Religious Dissent: Church-State Relations in the New American States, 1776–1833.* Columbia: University of Missouri Press, 2019.

Farrelly, Maura Jane. *Anti-Catholicism in America, 1620–1860.* Cambridge: Cambridge University Press, 2017.

Fea, John. *The Bible Cause: A History of the American Bible Society.* Oxford: Oxford University Press, 2016.

Fearnley-Sander, Mary. "Philosophical History and the Scottish Reformation: William Robertson and the Knoxian Tradition." *Historical Journal* 33, no. 2 (1990): 323–38.

Field, Peter S. *The Crisis of the Standing Order: Clerical Intellectuals and Cultural Authority in Massachusetts, 1780–1833.* Amherst: University of Massachusetts Press, 1998.

Finke, Roger, and Rodney Stark. *The Churching of America, 1776–1990: Winners and Losers in Our Religious Economy.* New Brunswick, NJ: Rutgers University Press, 1992.

Finn, Bernard S. "Morse, Samuel Finley Breese (1791–1872)." In *American National Biography Online*. February 2000. http://www.anb.org/articles/13/13-01183.html.

Ford, Lacy K. *Deliver Us from Evil: The Slavery Question in the Old South*. New York: Oxford University Press, 2009.

Foster, Douglas A. *A Life of Alexander Campbell*. Grand Rapids, MI: Eerdmans, 2020.

Foster, Douglas A. "Stone-Campbell History over Three Centuries: A Survey and Analysis." In *The Encyclopedia of the Stone-Campbell Movement*, edited by Douglas A. Foster, xxi–xxxv. Grand Rapids, MI: Eerdmans, 2004.

Foster, S. P. *Melancholy Duty: The Hume-Gibbon Attack on Christianity*. Dordrecht: Springer Science & Business Media, 1997.

Fox-Genovese, Elizabeth, and Eugene D. Genovese. *Fatal Self-Deception: Slaveholding Paternalism in the Old South*. Cambridge: Cambridge University Press, 2011.

Fox-Genovese, Elizabeth, and Eugene D. Genovese. *The Mind of the Master Class: History and Faith in the Southern Slaveholders' Worldview*. Cambridge: Cambridge University Press, 2005.

Franchot, Jenny. *Roads to Rome: The Antebellum Protestant Encounter with Catholicism*. Berkeley: University of California Press, 1994.

Frontani, Michael R. "Alternative Press." In *Encyclopedia of American Journalism*, edited by Stephen L. Vaughn, 13–17. New York: Routledge, 2008.

Garrett, James Leo, Jr. *Baptist Theology: A Four-Century Study*. Macon, GA: Mercer University Press, 2009.

Gaustad, Edwin Scott. *Neither King nor Prelate: Religion and the New Nation, 1776–1826*. Grand Rapids, MI: Eerdmans, 1993.

Geiger, Roger L. *The History of American Higher Education: Learning and Culture from the Founding to World War II*. Princeton, NJ: Princeton University Press, 2014.

George, Timothy, and Thomas G. Guarino. *Evangelicals and Catholics Together at Twenty: Vital Statements on Contested Topics*. Grand Rapids, MI: Brazos Press, 2015.

Gerbner, Katharine. *Christian Slavery: Conversion and Race in the Protestant Atlantic World*. Philadelphia: University of Pennsylvania Press, 2018.

Gilmore, Peter E. "Rebels and Revivals: Ulster Immigrants, Western Pennsylvania Presbyterianism and the Formation of Scotch-Irish Identity, 1780–1830." PhD diss., Carnegie Mellon University, 2009.

Giltner, John H. "Moses Stuart: 1780–1852." *Church History* 25, no. 3 (1956): 265.

Gjerde, Jon. *Catholicism and the Shaping of 19th Century America*. Cambridge: Cambridge University Press, 2012.

Gleeson, David T. *The Green and the Gray: The Irish in the Confederate States of America*. Chapel Hill: University of North Carolina Press, 2013.

Goen, C. C. *Broken Churches, Broken Nation: Denominational Schisms and the Coming of the American Civil War*. Macon, GA: Mercer University Press, 1985.

Gorman, James L. *Among the Early Evangelicals: The Transatlantic Origins of the Stone-Campbell Movement*. Abilene, TX: Abilene Christian University Press, 2017.

Graebner, Norman A. "Christianity and Democracy: Tocqueville's Views of Religion in America." *Journal of Religion* 56, no. 3 (1976): 263–73.

Grasso, Christopher. *A Speaking Aristocracy: Transforming Public Discourse in Eighteenth-Century Connecticut*. Chapel Hill: University of North Carolina Press, 2012.

Greene, Jack P. *The Intellectual Construction of America: Exceptionalism and Identity from 1492 to 1800*. Chapel Hill: University of North Carolina Press, 1993.

Grenda, Christopher S. "Faith, Reason, and Enlightenment: The Cultural Sources of Toleration in Early America." In *The First Prejudice: Religious Tolerance and Intolerance in Early America*, edited by Chris Beneke and Christopher S. Grenda, 23–52. Philadelphia: University of Pennsylvania Press, 2011.

Griffin, Susan M. *Anti-Catholicism and Nineteenth-Century Fiction*. Cambridge: Cambridge University Press, 2004.

Grigg, Susan. "Willard, Emma Hart (1787–1870), Educator and Historian." In *American National Biography Online*. February 2000. https://doi.org/10.1093/anb/9780198606 697.article.0900806.

Gross, John. *The Beginnings of American Methodism*. Nashville, TN: Abingdon Press, 1961.

Guggisberg, Hans R. "Religious Freedom and the History of the Christian World in Roger Williams' Thought." Early American Literature 12, no. 1 (1977): 36–48.

Gutacker, Paul. "Joseph Milner and His Editors: Eighteenth- and Nineteenth-Century Evangelicals and the Christian Past." *Journal of Ecclesiastical History* 69, no. 1 (January 2018): 86–104.

Gutacker, Paul. "Recovering the Ancient Roots of Evangelical Protestantism." Review of *In Search of Ancient Roots: The Christian Past and the Evangelical Identity Crisis* by Kenneth Stewart, *Fides et Historia* 50, no. 2 (Summer–Fall 2018): 144–50.

Guthman, Joshua. *Strangers Below: Primitive Baptists and American Culture*. Chapel Hill: University of North Carolina Press, 2015.

Gutjahr, Paul C. *An American Bible: A History of the Good Book in the United States, 1777–1880*. Stanford, CA: Stanford University Press, 1999.

Guyatt, Nicholas. *Providence and the Invention of the United States, 1607–1876*. Cambridge: Cambridge University Press, 2007.

Hall, Mark David. "Madison's Memorial and Remonstrance, Jefferson's Statute for Religious Liberty, and the Creation of the First Amendment." *American Political Thought* 3, no. 1 (2014): 32–63.

Hall, Stephen G. *A Faithful Account of the Race: African American Historical Writing in Nineteenth-Century America*. Chapel Hill: University of North Carolina Press, 2009.

Hall, Stephen G. "'A Search for Truth': Jacob Oson and the Beginnings of African American Historiography." *William and Mary Quarterly* 64, no. 1 (2007): 139–48.

Hamburger, Philip. *Separation of Church and State*. Cambridge, MA: Harvard University Press, 2002.

Harlow, Luke E. *Religion, Race, and the Making of Confederate Kentucky, 1830–1880*. Cambridge: Cambridge University Press, 2014.

Haselby, Sam. *The Origins of American Religious Nationalism*. Oxford: Oxford University Press, 2015.

Hatch, Nathan O. *The Democratization of American Christianity*. New Haven, CT: Yale University Press, 1989.

Haveman, Heather A. *Magazines and the Making of America: Modernization, Community, and Print Culture, 1741–1860*. Princeton, NJ: Princeton University Press, 2015.

Haynes, Charles C. *Religion in American History: What to Teach and How*. Alexandria, VA: Association for Supervision and Curriculum Development, 1990.

Henderson, Rodger C. "Findley, William (1742–1821), Member of the U.S. House of Representatives." In *American National Biography Online*. February 2000. http://www.anb.org/articles/03/03-00170.html.

Hickman, Jared. "The Recanonization of Saint Cyprian." In *Sainthood and Race: Marked Flesh, Holy Flesh*, edited by Molly H. Bassett and Vincent W. Lloyd, 66–81. New York: Routledge, 2014.

Hing, Bill Ong. *Defining America through Immigration Policy*. Philadelphia: Temple University Press, 2004.

Hinks, Peter P. *To Awaken My Afflicted Brethren: David Walker and the Problem of Antebellum Slave Resistance*. University Park: Pennsylvania State University Press, 1997.

Hoffman, Ronald, and Peter J. Albert, eds. *Women in the Age of the American Revolution*. Charlottesville: University Press of Virginia, 1989.

Holifield, E. Brooks. *Theology in America: Christian Thought from the Age of the Puritans to the Civil War*. New Haven, CT: Yale University Press, 2003.

Holloway, Gary, and Douglas A. Foster. *Renewing the World: A Concise Global History of the Stone-Campbell Movement*. Abilene, TX: Abilene Christian University Press, 2015.

Hopkins, John Henry, III. "John Henry Hopkins, First Bishop of Vermont." *Historical Magazine of the Protestant Episcopal Church* 6, no. 2 (June 1937): 187–206.

Horsman, Reginald. *Race and Manifest Destiny*. Cambridge, MA: Harvard University Press, 1986.

Horton, James Oliver, and Lois E. Horton. *In Hope of Liberty: Culture, Community, and Protest among Northern Free Blacks, 1700–1860*. Oxford: Oxford University Press, 1997.

Howard, Thomas A. *Protestant Theology and the Making of the Modern German University*. Oxford: Oxford University Press, 2006.

Howard, Thomas A. *Remembering the Reformation: An Inquiry into the Meanings of Protestantism*. Oxford: Oxford University Press, 2016.

Howe, Daniel Walker. *What Hath God Wrought: The Transformation of America, 1815–1848*. Oxford: Oxford University Press, 2007.

Hughes, Richard T., ed. *The American Quest for the Primitive Church*. Urbana: University of Illinois Press, 1988.

Hughes, Richard T. "Historical Models of Restoration." In *The Encyclopedia of the Stone-Campbell Movement*, edited by Douglas A. Foster, 635–38. Grand Rapids, MI: Eerdmans, 2004.

Hughes, Richard T. *Reviving the Ancient Faith: The Story of Churches of Christ in America*. 2nd ed. Abilene, TX: Abilene Christian University Press, 2008.

Hughes, Richard T., and Crawford Leonard Allen. *Illusions of Innocence: Protestant Primitivism in America, 1630–1875*. Chicago: University of Chicago Press, 1988.

Hughes, Richard T., and R. L. Roberts. *The Churches of Christ*. Westport, CT: Greenwood Publishing Group, 2001.

Hughes-Warrington, Marnie. "Coloring Universal History: Robert Benjamin Lewis's 'Light and Truth' (1843) and William Wells Brown's 'The Black Man' (1863)." *Journal of World History* 20, no. 1 (2009): 99–130.

Hunt, William C. "Part II: Separate Denominations: History, Description, and Statistics." In *Bureau of the Census Special Reports: Religious Bodies*. Washington, DC: U.S. Government Printing Office, 1910.

Hussey, M. Edmund. "Fenwick, Edward Dominic (1768–1832), First Bishop of Cincinnati and Founder of the Order of Dominican Friars in the United States." In *American National Biography Online*. February 2000. https://doi.org/10.1093/anb/9780198606 697.article.0800464.

Iliff, Joel R. "'Sustaining the Truth of the Bible': Black Evangelical Abolitionism and the Transatlantic Politics of Orthodoxy." *Journal of the Civil War Era* 11, no. 2 (2021): 164–93.

Irons, Charles F. *The Origins of Proslavery Christianity: White and Black Evangelicals in Colonial and Antebellum Virginia*. Chapel Hill: University of North Carolina Press, 2009.

Jablonski, Heike. *John Foxe in America: Discourses of Martyrdom in the Eighteenth- and Nineteenth-Century United States.* Paderborn: Ferdinand Schöningh, 2017.

Jacobs, Donald M., ed. *Antebellum Black Newspapers.* Westport, CT: Greenwood Press, 1976.

James, Edward T., et al., eds. *Notable American Women, 1607–1950: a Biographical Dictionary.* Vol. III. Cambridge, MA: Belknap Press of Harvard University Press, 1971.

Johnson, C. "Pennington, James William Charles (1807–1870), Clergyman and Abolitionist." *American National Biography.* February 2000. https://doi.org/10.1093/anb/9780198606697.article.0801167.

Johnson, Walter. *Soul by Soul: Life inside the Antebellum Slave Market.* Cambridge, MA: Harvard University Press, 1999.

Kalantzis, George, and Andrew Tooley. *Evangelicals and the Early Church: Recovery, Reform, Renewal.* Eugene, OR: Wipf and Stock, 2011.

Kamen, Henry. *The Spanish Inquisition: A Historical Revision.* New Haven, CT: Yale University Press, 1997.

Kamrath, Mark. *The Historicism of Charles Brockden Brown: Radical History and the Early Republic.* Kent, OH: Kent State University Press, 2010.

Karcher, Carolyn L. *The First Woman in the Republic: A Cultural Biography of Lydia Maria Child.* Durham, NC: Duke University Press, 1994.

Kelley, Mary. *Learning to Stand and Speak: Women, Education, and Public Life in America's Republic.* Chapel Hill: University of North Carolina Press, 2012.

Kennedy, Alison. "Historical Perspectives in the Mind of Joseph Priestley." In *Joseph Priestley, Scientist, Philosopher, and Theologian,* edited by Isabel Rivers and David L. Wykes, 172–202. Oxford: Oxford University Press, 2008.

Kerber, Linda K. *Women of the Republic: Intellect and Ideology in Revolutionary America.* Chapel Hill: University of North Carolina Press, 1980.

Kidd, Thomas S. *God of Liberty: A Religious History of the American Revolution.* New York: Basic Books, 2012.

Kidd, Thomas S. *The Protestant Interest: New England after Puritanism.* New Haven, CT: Yale University Press, 2004.

Kidd, Thomas S., and Barry Hankins. *Baptists in America: A History.* New York: Oxford University Press, 2015.

Klassen, John. "Hus, the Hussites and Bohemia." In *The New Cambridge Medieval History,* edited by Christopher Allmand, 367–91. Cambridge: Cambridge University Press, 1998.

Knobel, Dale T. *Paddy and the Republic: Ethnicity and Nationality in Antebellum America.* Middletown, CT: Wesleyan University Press, 1986.

Kornfeld, Eve. "Women in Post-Revolutionary American Culture: Susanna Haswell Rowson's American Career." *Journal of American Culture* 6 (Winter 1983): 56–62.

Kraszewski, Gracjan. *Catholic Confederates: Faith and Duty in the Civil War South.* Kent, OH: Kent State University Press, 2020.

Krieger, Leonard. "The Heavenly City of the Eighteenth-Century Historians." *Church History* 47, no. 3 (2009): 279–97.

Leal, K. Elise. "'All Our Children May Be Taught of God': Sunday Schools and the Roles of Childhood and Youth in Creating Evangelical Benevolence." *Church History* 87, no. 4 (December 2018): 1056–90.

Leithart, Peter J. *Defending Constantine: The Twilight of an Empire and the Dawn of Christendom.* Downers Grove, IL: InterVarsity Press, 2010.

Lerner, Gerda. *The Feminist Thought of Sarah Grimké*. Oxford: Oxford University Press, 1998.

Levy, Ronald. "Bishop Hopkins and the Dilemma of Slavery." *Pennsylvania Magazine of History and Biography* 91, no. 1 (1967): 56–71.

Liftin, Bryan M. *Getting to Know the Church Fathers: An Evangelical Introduction*. Grand Rapids, MI: Baker Academic, 2016.

Lippy, Charles H. "Worcester, Noah (1758–1837), Clergyman and Founder of the Massachusetts Peace Society." In *American National Biography Online*. February 2000. http://www.anb.org/articles/08/08-01704.html.

Litwack, Leon F. *North of Slavery: The Negro in the Free States, 1790–1860*. Chicago: University of Chicago Press, 1961.

Lucas, Sean Michael. *Robert Lewis Dabney: A Southern Presbyterian Life*. Phillipsburg, NJ: P & R Pub., 2005.

Lunger, Harold. *The Political Ethics of Alexander Campbell*. Eugene, OR: Wipf and Stock, 2012.

Lutz, Alma. *Emma Willard: Daughter of Democracy*. Boston: Houghton Mifflin, 1929.

Lyon, Mary. "The Character of Young Ladies." In *American Educational Thought: Essays from 1640–1940*, edited by Andrew J. Milson et al., 105–14. Charlotte, NC: Information Age Publishing, 2010.

Madigan, Kevin. *Medieval Christianity: A New History*. New Haven, CT: Yale University Press, 2015.

Maffly-Kipp, Laurie F. *Setting Down the Sacred Past: African-American Race Histories*. Cambridge, MA: Harvard University Press, 2010.

Maitzen, Rohan. "'This Feminine Preserve': Historical Biographies by Victorian Women." *Victorian Studies* 38, no. 3 (1995): 371–93.

Malamud, Margaret. "Black Minerva: Antiquity in Antebellum African American History." In *African Athena: New Agendas*, edited by Daniel Orrells, Gurminder K. Bhambra, and Tessa Roynon, 71–89. Oxford: Oxford University Press, 2011.

Marty, Martin E. "The American Religious History Canon." *Social Research* 53, no. 3 (Fall 1986): 513–28.

Marty, Martin E. *Righteous Empire: The Protestant Experience in America*. New York: Dial Press, 1970.

Mason, Lockert B. "Separation and Reunion of the Episcopal Church 1861–1865: The Role of Bishop Thomas Atkinson." *Anglican and Episcopal History* 59, no. 3 (September 1990): 345–65.

Massa, Mark Stephen. *Anti-Catholicism in America: The Last Acceptable Prejudice*. New York: Crossroad Publishers, 2003.

Mathews, Donald G. *Slavery and Methodism: A Chapter in American Morality, 1780–1845*. Princeton, NJ: Princeton University Press, 1965.

May, Henry F. *The Enlightenment in America*. Oxford: Oxford University Press, 1978.

McBeth, H. Leon. *The Baptist Heritage*. Nashville, TN: B & H Publishing Group, 1987.

Mcclelland, Clarence P. "The Education of Females in Early Illinois." *Journal of the Illinois State Historical Society* 36, no. 4 (December 1943): 378–407.

McCoy, Michael R. "O'Kelly, James (1735?–16 October 1826), Methodist Preacher and Schismatic." In *American National Biography Online*. February 2000. http://www.anb.org/articles/01/01-00678.html.

McDonald, Forrest. *Novus Ordo Seclorum: The Intellectual Origins of the Constitution*. Lawrence: University Press of Kansas, 1985.

McKenzie, Robert. *Lincolnites and Rebels: A Divided Town in the American Civil War.* Oxford: Oxford University Press, 2006.

McKivigan, John R. *Abolitionism and American Religion.* New York: Taylor & Francis, 1999.

McKivigan, John R., and Mitchell Snay, eds. *Religion and the Antebellum Debate over Slavery.* Athens: University of Georgia Press, 1998.

McLachlan, John. "Joseph Priestley and the Study of History." *Transactions of the Unitarian Historical Society* 19, no. 4 (April 1990): 252–63.

McMahon, Lucia. "'Memorials of Exemplary Women Are Peculiarly Interesting': Female Biography in Early National America." *Legacy: A Journal of American Women Writers* 31, no. 1 (June 4, 2014): 52–57.

McMahon, Lucia. *Mere Equals: The Paradox of Educated Women in the Early American Republic.* Ithaca, NY: Cornell University Press, 2012.

McPherson, James M. *Battle Cry of Freedom: The Civil War Era.* Oxford: Oxford University Press, 1988.

Meijering, E. P. "Mosheim on the Difference between Christianity and Platonism: A Contribution to the Discussion about Methodology." *Vigiliae Christianae* 31, no. 1 (March 1977): 68–73.

Meijering, E. P. "Mosheim on the Philosophy of the Church Fathers." In *Nederlands Archief Voor Kerkgeschiednis* 56, 367–83. Leiden: Brill, 1976.

Messer, Peter C. *Stories of Independence: Identity, Ideology, and History in Eighteenth-Century America.* DeKalb: Northern Illinois University Press, 2005.

Meyerson, Michael I. *Endowed by Our Creator: The Birth of Religious Freedom in America.* New Haven, CT: Yale University Press, 2012.

Miller, Floyd J. "'The Father of Black Nationalism': Another Contender." *Civil War History* 17, no. 4 (December 1971): 310–19.

Miller, Glenn T. *Piety and Intellect: The Aims and Purposes of Antebellum Theological Education.* Atlanta, GA: Scholars Press, 1990.

Moore, Joseph S. *Founding Sins: How a Group of Antislavery Radicals Fought to Put Christ into the Constitution.* Oxford: Oxford University Press, 2016.

Morgan, Marie Caskey. "Beecher, Lyman (1775–1863)." In *American National Biography Online.* February 2000. http://www.anb.org/articles/08/08-00113.html.

Morris, Edward. "Ary Scheffer and His English Circle." *Oud Holland* 99, no. 4 (1985): 294–323.

Morrison, Michael A. *Slavery and the American West: The Eclipse of Manifest Destiny and the Coming of the Civil War.* Chapel Hill: University of North Carolina Press, 1997.

Mott, Frank Luther. *A History of American Magazines: 1741–1850.* Cambridge, MA: Harvard University Press, 1930.

Murphy, Andrew R. *Conscience and Community: Revisiting Toleration and Religious Dissent in Early Modern England and America.* University Park: Pennsylvania State University Press, 2001.

Nash, Gary B. *Forging Freedom: The Formation of Philadelphia's Black Community, 1720–1840.* Cambridge, MA: Harvard University Press, 1988.

Nash, Margaret. *Women's Education in the United States, 1780–1840.* New York: Palgrave Macmillan, 2007.

Newman, Richard S. *The Transformation of American Abolitionism: Fighting Slavery in the Early Republic.* Chapel Hill: University of North Carolina Press, 2002.

Noll, Mark A. *America's God: From Jonathan Edwards to Abraham Lincoln.* Oxford: Oxford University Press, 2002.

Noll, Mark A. *The Civil War as a Theological Crisis*. Chapel Hill: University of North Carolina Press, 2006.

Noll, Mark A. *Princeton and the Republic, 1768–1822: The Search for a Christian Enlightenment in the Era of Samuel Stanhope Smith*. Princeton, NJ: Princeton University Press, 1989.

Noll, Mark A., and Carolyn Nystrom. *Is the Reformation Over? An Evangelical Assessment of Contemporary Roman Catholicism*. Grand Rapids, MI: Baker Academic, 2005.

Nord, David Paul. *Faith in Reading: Religious Publishing and the Birth of Mass Media in America*. Oxford: Oxford University Press, 2004.

Norton, Mary Beth. *Liberty's Daughters: The Revolutionary Experience of American Women, 1750–1800*. Ithaca, NY: Cornell University Press, 1980.

O'Brien, Karen. "English Enlightenment Histories, 1750–c.1815." In *The Oxford History of Historical Writing*, edited by Axel Schneider, vol. III., 518–35. Oxford: Oxford University Press, 2011.

O'Brien, Karen. *Narratives of Enlightenment: Cosmopolitan History from Voltaire to Gibbon*. Cambridge: Cambridge University Press, 1997.

O'Brien, Michael. *Conjectures of Order: Intellectual Life and the American South, 1810–1860*. Chapel Hill: University of North Carolina Press, 2004.

Ogden, Daryl. "Double Visions: Sarah Stickney Ellis, George Eliot and the Politics of Domesticity." *Women's Studies* 25, no. 6 (November 1, 1996): 585–602.

Okker, Patricia. *Our Sister Editors: Sarah J. Hale and the Tradition of Nineteenth-Century American Women Editors*. Athens: University of Georgia Press, 1995.

Olbricht, T. H. "Barnes, Albert (1798–1870)." In *Dictionary of Major Biblical Interpreters*, edited by Donald K. McKim, 147–50. Westmont, IL: InterVarsity Press, 2007.

O'Malley, John W., SJ. *The Jesuits: A History from Ignatius to the Present*. Lanham, MD: Rowman & Littlefield, 2014.

Onuf, Peter S. "American Exceptionalism and National Identity." *American Political Thought* 1, no. 1 (May 1, 2012): 77–100.

Oshatz, Molly. *Slavery and Sin: The Fight against Slavery and the Rise of Liberal Protestantism*. Oxford: Oxford University Press, 2012.

Pagliarini, Marie Anne. "The Pure American Woman and the Wicked Catholic Priest: An Analysis of Anti-Catholic Literature in Antebellum America." *Religion and American Culture* 9, no. 1 (1999): 97–128.

Parker, Patricia L. "Rowson, Susanna Haswell (1762–1824), Writer and Educator." In *American National Biography Online*. February 2000. https://doi.org/10.1093/anb/9780198606697.article.1601419.

Parkinson, Robert G. "Enemies of the People: The Revolutionary War and Race in the New American Nation." PhD diss., University of Virginia, 2005.

Perry, Seth. *Bible Culture and Authority in the Early United States*. Princeton, NJ: Princeton University Press, 2018.

Phillipson, Nicholas T. *David Hume: The Philosopher as Historian*. New Haven, CT: Yale University Press, 2012.

Pocock, J. G. A. *The Machiavellian Moment: Florentine Political Thought and the Atlantic Republican Tradition*. Princeton, NJ: Princeton University Press, 1974.

Polgar, Paul J. "'To Raise Them to an Equal Participation': Early National Abolitionism, Gradual Emancipation, and the Promise of African American Citizenship." *Journal of the Early Republic* 31, no. 2 (April 21, 2011): 229–58. https://doi.org/10.1353/jer.2011.0023.

Pollard, Arthur. "Milner, Joseph." In *The Blackwell Dictionary of Evangelical Biography, 1730–1860*, edited by Donald Lewis, 776. Oxford: Oxford University Press, 1995.

Printy, Michael. "The Reformation of the Enlightenment: German Histories in the Eighteenth Century." In *Politics and Reformations: Histories and Reformations: Essays in Honor of Thomas A. Brady, Jr*, edited by Christopher Ocker et al., 135–53. Boston: Brill, 2007.

Quinn, John F. "'Three Cheers for the Abolitionist Pope!': American Reaction to Gregory XVI's Condemnation of the Slave Trade, 1840–1860." *Catholic Historical Review* 90, no. 1 (2004): 67–93.

Rable, George C. *God's Almost Chosen Peoples: A Religious History of the American Civil War*. Chapel Hill: University of North Carolina Press, 2010.

Ragosta, John A. *Wellspring of Liberty: How Virginia's Religious Dissenters Helped Win the American Revolution and Secured Religious Liberty*. Oxford: Oxford University Press, 2010.

Rasor, Paul, and Richard E. Bond, eds. *From Jamestown to Jefferson: The Evolution of Religious Freedom in Virginia*. Charlottesville: University of Virginia Press, 2011.

Riordan, Liam. *Many Identities, One Nation: The Revolution and Its Legacy in the Mid-Atlantic*. Philadelphia: University of Pennsylvania Press, 2007.

Roberts, Kyle B. *Evangelical Gotham: Religion and the Making of New York City, 1783–1860*. Chicago: University of Chicago Press, 2016.

Rogers, James A. *Richard Furman: Life and Legacy*. Macon, GA: Mercer University Press, 2001.

Rothman, Adam. *Slave Country: American Expansion and the Origins of the Deep South*. Cambridge, MA: Harvard University Press, 2005.

Roy, Jody M. "Nineteenth-Century American Anti-Catholicism and the Catholic Response." PhD diss., Indiana University, 1997.

Russell, Jeffrey Burton. *Dissent and Reform in the Early Middle Ages*. Eugene, OR: Wipf and Stock, 2005.

Rust, Marion. *Prodigal Daughters: Susanna Rowson's Early American Women*. Chapel Hill: University of North Carolina Press, 2008.

Saillant, John. *Black Puritan, Black Republican: The Life and Thought of Lemuel Haynes, 1753–1833*. Oxford: Oxford University Press, 2003.

Sanders, L. C. "Gregory, George (1754–1808), Church of England Clergyman and Writer." In *Oxford Dictionary of National Biography*. Oxford University Press, 2004. https://doi.org/10.1093/ref:odnb/11463.

Sandoz, Ellis, ed. *Political Sermons of the American Founding Era: 1730–1805*. 2nd ed. Vol. II. Indianapolis, IN: Liberty Fund, 1998.

Saunders, R. Frank, and George A. Rogers. "Bishop John England of Charleston: Catholic Spokesman and Southern Intellectual, 1820–1842." *Journal of the Early Republic* 13, no. 3 (1993): 301–22.

Scarberry, Mark S. "John Leland and James Madison: Religious Influence on the Ratification of the Constitution and on the Proposal of the Bill of Rights." *Penn State Law Review* 113, no. 3 (2009): 733–800.

Schlereth, Eric R. *An Age of Infidels: The Politics of Religious Controversy in the Early United States*. Philadelphia: University of Pennsylvania Press, 2013.

Schmidt, Darren W. "Reviving the Past: Eighteenth-Century Evangelical Interpretations of Church History." PhD diss., University of St Andrews, 2009.

Schneider, Thomas E. "George Fitzhugh: The Turn of History." In *Lincoln's Defense of Politics: The Public Man and His Opponents in the Crisis over Slavery*, 54–72. Columbia, MO: University of Missouri Press, 2006.

Schofield, Robert E. *The Enlightened Joseph Priestley: A Study of His Life and Work from 1773 to 1804*. University Park: Penn State University Press, 2009.

Schofield, Robert E. "Priestley, Joseph (1733–1804), Theologian and Natural Philosopher." In *Oxford Dictionary of National Biography*. Oxford University Press, 2004; online ed., 2013. https://doi.org/10.1093/ref:odnb/22788.

Schulten, Susan. "Emma Willard and the Graphic Foundations of American History." *Journal of Historical Geography* 33, no. 3 (July 2007): 542–64.

Schwalm, Leslie A. *Emancipation's Diaspora: Race and Reconstruction in the Upper Midwest*. Chapel Hill: University of North Carolina Press, 2009.

Schweiger, Beth Barton. *A Literate South: Reading before Emancipation*. New Haven: Yale University Press, 2019.

Schweiger, Beth Barton, and Donald G. Mathews, eds. *Religion in the American South: Protestants and Others in History and Culture*. Chapel Hill: University of North Carolina Press, 2005.

Scott, Anne Firor. "What, Then, Is the American: This New Woman?" *Journal of American History* 65, no. 3 (1978): 679–703.

Sensbach, Jon F. *Rebecca's Revival: Creating Black Christianity in the Atlantic World*. Cambridge, MA: Harvard University Press, 2005.

Shaffer, Arthur H. *The Politics of History: Writing the History of the American Revolution, 1783–1815*. New Brunswick, NJ: Transaction Publishers, 2011.

Shalev, Eran. *American Zion: The Old Testament as a Political Text from the Revolution to the Civil War*. New Haven, CT: Yale University Press, 2013.

Shalev, Eran. *Rome Reborn on Western Shores: Historical Imagination and the Creation of the American Republic*. Charlottesville: University of Virginia Press, 2009.

Sher, Richard B. *The Enlightenment & the Book: Scottish Authors & Their Publishers in Eighteenth-Century Britain, Ireland, & America*. Chicago: University of Chicago Press, 2006.

Shriver, George H. *Philip Schaff: Christian Scholar and Ecumenical Prophet*. Macon, GA: Mercer, 1987.

Shriver, George H. "Philip Schaff as a Teacher of Church History." *Journal of Presbyterian History* 47 (March 1969): 74–92.

Sidbury, James. *Becoming African in America: Race and Nation in the Early Black Atlantic*. Oxford: Oxford University Press, 2007.

Sinha, Manisha. *The Slave's Cause: A History of Abolition*. New Haven, CT: Yale University Press, 2016.

Smith, Leonard. *The Unitarians: A Short History*. Cumbria: Lensden Publishing, 2006.

Smither, Edward L. *Rethinking Constantine: History, Theology, and Legacy*. Eugene, OR: Wipf and Stock, 2014.

Spangler, Jewel L. *Virginians Reborn: Anglican Monopoly, Evangelical Dissent, and the Rise of the Baptists in the Late Eighteenth Century*. Charlottesville: University of Virginia Press, 2008.

Spencer, Mark G. "Campbell, Robert (1769–1800)." In *The Bloomsbury Encyclopedia of the American Enlightenment*. New York: Bloomsbury Publishing, 2015.

Spencer, Mark G. *David Hume and Eighteenth-Century America*. Suffolk, UK: Boydell and Brewer, 2005.

Spencer, Mark G. "Hume and Madison on Faction." *William and Mary Quarterly* 59, no. 4 (2002): 869–96.

Spitz, Lewis. "Johann Lorenz Mosheim's Philosophy of History." *Concordia Theological Monthly* 20, no. 5 (May 1949): 321–39.

Stark, Judith Chelius, ed. *Feminist Interpretations of Augustine*. University Park: Pennsylvania State University Press, 2007.

Stark, Rodney. *Bearing False Witness: Debunking Centuries of Anti-Catholic History*. Conshohocken, PA: Templeton Foundation Press, 2016.

Stein, Stephen J. *The Shaker Experience in America: A History of the United Society of Believers*. New Haven, CT: Yale University Press, 1994.

Stern, Andrew H. M. *Southern Crucifix, Southern Cross: Catholic-Protestant Relations in the Old South*. Tuscaloosa: University of Alabama Press, 2012.

Stewart, Kenneth J. *In Search of Ancient Roots: The Christian Past and the Evangelical Identity Crisis*. Downers Grove, IL: InterVarsity Press Academic, 2017.

Stookey, Stephen. "Baptists and Landmarkism and the Turn toward Provincialism: 1851." In *Turning Points in Baptist History*, edited by Michael Edward Williams and Walter B. Shurden, 178–93. Macon, GA: Mercer University Press, 2008.

Sweeney, Douglas A. "Edwards, Bela Bates (1802–1852), Editor and Clergyman." In *American National Biography Online*. February 2000. https://doi.org/10.1093/anb/9780198606697.article.0800426.

Tate, Adam. *Catholics' Lost Cause: South Carolina Catholics and the American South, 1820–1861*. South Bend, IN: University of Notre Dame Press, 2018.

Teets-Parzynski, Catherine. "Child, Lydia Maria Francis (1802–1880)." In *American National Biography Online*. February 2000. http://www.anb.org/articles/15/15-00127.html.

Tennent, William, and Newton B. Jones. "Writings of the Reverend William Tennent, 1740–1777 (Continued)." *South Carolina Historical Magazine* 61, no. 4 (1960): 189–209.

Tentler, Leslie Woodcock. *American Catholics: A History*. New Haven, CT: Yale University Press, 2020.

Thompson, J. Earl. "Church History Comes to Andover: The Persecution of James Murdock." *Andover Newton Quarterly* 15, no. 4 (March 1975): 213–27.

Tise, Larry. *Proslavery: A History of the Defense of Slavery in America, 1701–1840*. Athens: University of Georgia Press, 1987.

Tracy, David. "African American Thought: The Discovery of Fragments." In *Black Faith and Public Talk: Critical Essays on James H. Cone's Black Theology and Black Power*, edited by Dwight N. Hopkins, 29–40. Waco, TX: Baylor University Press, 1999.

Trevor-Roper, Hugh. *History and the Enlightenment*. New Haven, CT: Yale University Press, 2010.

Tucker, William E., and Lester G. McAllister. *Journey in Faith: A History of the Christian Church*. Atlanta, GA: Chalice Press, 1975.

Turner, James. *Religion Enters the Academy: The Origins of the Scholarly Study of Religion in America*. Athens: University of Georgia Press, 2011.

Tweed, Thomas A. "An American Pioneer in the Study of Religion: Hannah Adams (1755–1831) and Her Dictionary of All Religions." *Journal of the American Academy of Religion* 60, no. 3 (1992): 437–64.

Van Cleve, George William. *A Slaveholders' Union: Slavery, Politics, and the Constitution in the Early American Republic*. Chicago: University of Chicago Press, 2010.

Van Tassel, David D. *Recording America's Past: An Interpretation of the Development of Historical Studies in America, 1607–1884.* Chicago: University of Chicago Press, 1960.

Varon, Elizabeth R. *Disunion! The Coming of the American Civil War, 1789–1859.* Chapel Hill: University of North Carolina Press, 2008.

Volkman, Lucas. *Houses Divided: Evangelical Schisms and the Crisis of the Union in Missouri.* Oxford: Oxford University Press, 2018.

Waldstreicher, David. *In the Midst of Perpetual Fetes: The Making of American Nationalism, 1776–1820.* Chapel Hill: University of North Carolina Press, 1997.

Wallace, William Jason. *Catholics, Slaveholders, and the Dilemma of American Evangelicalism, 1835–1860.* South Bend, IN: University of Notre Dame Press, 2010.

Walsh, John. "Joseph Milner's Evangelical Church History." *Journal of Ecclesiastical History* 10 (1959): 174–87.

Walters, W. D. "Emma Willard's Geographies." *Pennsylvania Geographer* 37, no. 1 (1999): 118–38.

Warren, Joyce W. "Hale, Sarah Josepha Buell (1788–1879), Magazine Editor." In *American National Biography Online.* February 2000. http://www.anb.org/articles/16/16-00686.html.

Watkins, Jordan T. *Slavery and Sacred Texts: The Bible, the Constitution, and Historical Consciousness in Antebellum America.* Cambridge: Cambridge University Press, 2021.

Watts, Liz. "Lydia Maria Child." *Journalism History* 35, no. 1 (Spring 2009): 12–22.

Weber, Jennifer L. *Copperheads: The Rise and Fall of Lincoln's Opponents in the North.* Oxford: Oxford University Press, 2008.

Wedgeworth, Steven. "'The Two Sons of Oil' and the Limits of American Religious Dissent." *Journal of Law and Religion* 27, no. 1 (2011): 141–61.

Weimer, Adrian Chastain. *Martyrs' Mirror: Persecution and Holiness in Early New England.* Oxford: Oxford University Press, 2011.

Wellman, Judith. *The Road to Seneca Falls: Elizabeth Cady Stanton and the First Woman's Rights Convention.* Champaign: University of Illinois Press, 2010.

Welter, Barbara. "The Cult of True Womanhood: 1820–1860." *American Quarterly* 18, no. 2 (1966): 151–74.

Wenger, Tisa. *Religious Freedom: The Contested History of an American Ideal.* Chapel Hill: University of North Carolina Press, 2017.

Wentz, Richard E. "Nevin, John Williamson (1803–1886), Religious Thinker and Educator." In *American National Biography Online.* February 2000. https://doi.org/10.1093/anb/9780198606697.article.0801082.

Wet, Chris L. de. *Preaching Bondage: John Chrysostom and the Discourse of Slavery in Early Christianity.* Berkeley: University of California Press, 2015.

Whitford, David M. *The Curse of Ham in the Early Modern Era: The Bible and the Justifications for Slavery.* New York: Routledge, 2017.

Wigger, John H. *Taking Heaven by Storm: Methodism and the Rise of Popular Christianity in America.* Oxford: Oxford University Press, 1998.

Wilentz, Sean. *Chants Democratic: New York City and the Rise of the American Working Class, 1788–1850.* Oxford: Oxford University Press, 2004.

Wilentz, Sean. *The Rise of American Democracy: Jefferson to Lincoln.* New York: Norton, 2005.

Wiles, Kate. "Back to the Dark Ages." *History Today,* May 5, 2016. https://www.historyto day.com/back-dark-ages.

Wilken, Robert Louis. *The First Thousand Years: A Global History of Christianity*. New Haven, CT: Yale University Press, 2013.

Wilken, Robert Louis. *Liberty in the Things of God: The Christian Origins of Religious Freedom*. New Haven, CT: Yale University Press, 2019.

Wilken, Robert Louis. *The Spirit of Early Christian Thought: Seeking the Face of God*. New Haven, CT: Yale University Press, 2003.

Willey, Larry G. "John Rankin, Antislavery Prophet, and the Free Presbyterian Church." *American Presbyterians* 72, no. 3 (1994): 157–71.

Williams, D. Newell, Douglas A. Foster, and Paul M. Blowers, eds. *The Stone-Campbell Movement: A Global History*. Atlanta, GA: Chalice Press, 2013.

Wilsey, John D. *American Exceptionalism and Civil Religion: Reassessing the History of an Idea*. Downers Grove, IL: InterVarsity Press, 2015.

Wilson, Charles Reagan. "Robert Lewis Dabney: Religion and the Southern Holocaust." *Virginia Magazine of History and Biography* 89, no. 1 (1981): 79–89.

Winch, Julie. *A Gentleman of Color: The Life of James Forten*. Oxford: Oxford University Press, 2003.

Winterer, Caroline. *The Culture of Classicism: Ancient Greece and Rome in American Intellectual Life, 1780–1910*. Baltimore: Johns Hopkins University Press, 2002.

Winterer, Caroline. *The Mirror of Antiquity: American Women and the Classical Tradition, 1750–1900*. Ithaca, NY: Cornell University Press, 2009.

Witte, John, Jr. "'A Most Mild and Equitable Establishment of Religion': John Adams and the Massachusetts Experiment." In *Religion and the New Republic: Faith in the Founding of America*, edited by James H. Hutson, 1–31. New York: Rowman & Littlefield, 2000.

Witte, John, and Joel A. Nichols. *Religion and the American Constitutional Experiment*. 4th ed. Oxford: Oxford University Press, 2016.

Wolffe, John. "Anti-Catholicism and Evangelical Identity in Britain and the United States, 1830–1860." In *Evangelicalism: Comparative Studies of Popular Protestantism in North America, the British Isles, and beyond 1700–1900*, edited by Mark A. Noll, David Bebbington, and George A. Rawlyk, 179–97. Oxford: Oxford University Press, 1994.

Wood, Arthur Skevington. *Thomas Haweis, 1734–1820*. London: S.P.C.K., 1957.

Wood, Gordon S. *Empire of Liberty: A History of the Early Republic, 1789–1815*. Oxford University Press, 2009.

Woodson, Byron W. *A President in the Family: Thomas Jefferson, Sally Hemings, and Thomas Woodson*. Santa Barbara, CA: Praeger, 2001.

Wrather, Eva Jean. *Alexander Campbell: Adventurer in Freedom: A Literary Biography*. Edited by D. Duane Cummins. Fort Worth, TX: TCU Press, 2005.

Wright, Conrad. *The Beginnings of Unitarianism in America*. Boston: Starr King Press, 1955.

Wright, Conrad. *The Unitarian Controversy: Essays on American Unitarian History*. Boston: Skinner House Books, 1994.

Yacovazzi, Cassandra L. *Escaped Nuns: True Womanhood and the Campaign against Convents in Antebellum America*. Oxford: Oxford University Press, 2018.

Zagarri, Rosemarie. *Revolutionary Backlash: Women and Politics in the Early American Republic*. Philadelphia: University of Pennsylvania Press, 2007.

Index

For the benefit of digital users, indexed terms that span two pages (e.g., 52–53) may, on occasion, appear on only one of those pages.